Palgrave Gothic

Series Editor
Clive Bloom
Middlesex University
London, UK

This series of Gothic books is the first to treat the genre in its many inter-related, global and 'extended' cultural aspects to show how the taste for the medieval and the sublime gave rise to a perverse taste for terror and horror and how that taste became not only international (with a huge fan base in places such as South Korea and Japan) but also the sensibility of the modern age, changing our attitudes to such diverse areas as the nature of the artist, the meaning of drug abuse and the concept of the self. The series is accessible but scholarly, with referencing kept to a minimum and theory contextualised where possible. All the books are readable by an intelligent student or a knowledgeable general reader interested in the subject.

Editorial Advisory Board

Dr. Ian Conrich, University of South Australia
Barry Forshaw, author/journalist, UK
Prof. Gregg Kucich, University of Notre Dame, USA
Prof. Gina Wisker, University of Brighton, UK
Dr. Catherine Wynne, University of Hull, UK
Dr. Alison Peirse, University of Yorkshire, UK
Dr. Sorcha Ní Fhlainn, Manchester Metropolitan University, UK
Prof. William Hughes, Bath Spa University, UK

More information about this series at
http://www.palgrave.com/gp/series/14698

Melissa Edmundson

Women's Colonial Gothic Writing, 1850–1930

Haunted Empire

Melissa Edmundson
Clemson University
Clemson, SC, USA

Palgrave Gothic
ISBN 978-3-319-76916-5   ISBN 978-3-319-76917-2 (eBook)
https://doi.org/10.1007/978-3-319-76917-2

Library of Congress Control Number: 2018936597

© The Editor(s) (if applicable) and The Author(s) 2018
This work is subject to copyright. All rights are solely and exclusively licensed by the Publisher, whether the whole or part of the material is concerned, specifically the rights of translation, reprinting, reuse of illustrations, recitation, broadcasting, reproduction on microfilms or in any other physical way, and transmission or information storage and retrieval, electronic adaptation, computer software, or by similar or dissimilar methodology now known or hereafter developed.
The use of general descriptive names, registered names, trademarks, service marks, etc. in this publication does not imply, even in the absence of a specific statement, that such names are exempt from the relevant protective laws and regulations and therefore free for general use.
The publisher, the authors and the editors are safe to assume that the advice and information in this book are believed to be true and accurate at the date of publication. Neither the publisher nor the authors or the editors give a warranty, express or implied, with respect to the material contained herein or for any errors or omissions that may have been made. The publisher remains neutral with regard to jurisdictional claims in published maps and institutional affiliations.

Cover credit: Group of men and women, unidentified, in bush setting (ca. 1880–ca. 1890). From a glass negative by John William Lindt. Image courtesy of State Library of Victoria, Melbourne, Australia

Printed on acid-free paper

This Palgrave Macmillan imprint is published by the registered company Springer International Publishing AG part of Springer Nature
The registered company address is: Gewerbestrasse 11, 6330 Cham, Switzerland

Dedicated to my grandparents

Acknowledgements

Several libraries provided research assistance and access to unpublished manuscripts. The University of Calgary Library supplied a copy of Penny Petrone's unpublished doctoral thesis. The staff of the Manuscripts Department, Wilson Library, University of North Carolina at Chapel Hill, patiently assisted with my search through the A. P. Watt archive. I am also grateful to the State Library of Victoria for granting permission to reproduce the cover image.

I would like to express my appreciation to the editorial staff at Palgrave Macmillan. Lina Aboujieb, Ellie Freedman, and Karina Jakupsdottir were all instrumental in shepherding the manuscript through the various stages of production from initial submission to final publication.

I would also like to thank Wendy Bower Catalano for her careful work compiling the index.

Claire Charlotte McKechnie graciously provided a copy of her unpublished doctoral thesis, as well as a copy of her article from *Nineteenth-Century Prose*.

A version of Chapter 5 appeared in the Summer 2015 special issue of *Supernatural Studies* dedicated to the Victorian Supernatural. My thanks to Janine Hatter, editor of the issue, for her helpful comments and suggestions. A portion of Chapter 7 appeared in *The Male Empire under the Female Gaze: The British Raj and the Memsahib* (2013), edited by Susmita Roye and Rajeshwar Mittapalli. My thanks to Susmita Roye for her useful suggestions for this chapter, as well as to Cambria Press for permission to reprint this portion.

I am grateful to my parents and grandparents for a lifetime of love and support. Jeff Makala provided valuable research assistance and feedback on early drafts of each chapter. He knows more than anyone should about haunted bungalows. As always, Dalton, Murray, and Maggie helped keep things in perspective and reminded me of the importance of companionship, fresh air, and squeaky toys.

Contents

1 Introduction: Reclaiming Women's Colonial Gothic Writing ... 1

2 Susanna Moodie, Colonial Exiles, and the Frontier Canadian Gothic ... 23

3 Gothic Romance and Retribution in the Short Fiction of Isabella Valancy Crawford ... 45

4 Generations of the Female Vampire: Colonial Gothic Hybridity in Florence Marryat's *The Blood of the Vampire* ... 73

5 Mary Kingsley and the Ghosts of West Africa ... 95

6 The African Stories of Margery Lawrence ... 115

7 Colonial Gothic Framework: Haunted Houses in the Anglo-Indian Ghost Stories of Bithia Mary Croker ... 139

8 Animal Gothic in Alice Perrin's *East of Suez* ... 157

9   The Past Will Not Stay Buried: Female Bodies
    and Colonial Crime in the Australian Ghost Stories
    of Mary Fortune   177

10 Fear and Death in the Outback: Barbara Baynton's
    Bush Studies   197

11 Katherine Mansfield and the Troubled Homes
    of Colonial New Zealand   217

12 Conclusion: "Cicatrice of an Old Wound"   239

Index   245

CHAPTER 1

Introduction: Reclaiming Women's Colonial Gothic Writing

Women's Colonial Gothic Writing, 1850–1930: Haunted Empire is the first extended critical study of Colonial Gothic writing by nineteenth- and early twentieth-century women who lived within the borders of the British Empire during its height. This book expands on recent critical interest in women's involvement with the Gothic to examine how these writers appropriated the genre—and its emphasis on fear, racial otherness, isolation, identity, enforced silence, and sexual deviancy—in order to explore these anxieties in the farthest reaches of the British Empire. When read in light of the Colonial Gothic, the histories and social structures of these individual colonies are transformed into wide-reaching critiques of power structures and the impact colonialism had on both the British colonizers and local populations. As many of these women were truly cosmopolitan—frequently moving back and forth from Great Britain to the various locations of empire—their writing gives us a unique view of the colonial experience. The varied subject matter in their fiction reflects a broad range of colonial experience: from imperialism in Africa and the dehumanizing effects of the ivory trade, to the destructive aftereffects of slavery in Jamaica, and the violent consequences of imperial rule in India. Grisly death and violent crime are frequently present in these works, as are more personal stories of the harsh realities of settler life in Canada, Australia, and New Zealand. Women's Colonial Gothic thereby insists on bringing to light the darker, hidden motives and untold stories that complicate the contemporary narratives which foregrounded the ideology of

© The Author(s) 2018
M. Edmundson, *Women's Colonial Gothic Writing, 1850–1930*,
Palgrave Gothic, https://doi.org/10.1007/978-3-319-76917-2_1

British expansion as a noble quest that would improve the lives of colonized and colonizer alike.

In her study of women's contemporary Gothic, Gina Wisker has noted, "Gothic is everywhere. Through its relentless questioning, it exposes dis-ease and discomfort, sometimes only to reinforce the complacencies it disrupts, but more thrillingly, very often leaving writers and readers more aware and less comfortable" (2016, p. 1). This statement pertains to many aspects of the Gothic, as it takes various forms, infiltrates a variety of genres, moves across time, and travels across the world. It is this notion of a Gothic which travels geographically across nations and cultures that is of particular interest in this book. In *A Geography of Victorian Gothic Fiction* (1999), Robert Mighall expands Gothic literature past its psychological origins, calling these origins a sort of "centripetal pull" that robs supernatural texts from what he calls "historical and 'geographical' considerations" (p. xi). *Women's Colonial Gothic Writing* reclaims these "historical and 'geographical' considerations," moving the Gothic beyond the borders of Great Britain and what has, until very recently, been a Eurocentric critical approach to the genre. This project also seeks to expand our notion of Colonial Gothic writing in terms of gender. By intentionally choosing lesser-known women writers and women whose works are typically not read as Gothic, this book attempts to enrich and complicate the existing parameters of the Colonial Gothic beyond the traditional male-authored imperial literature of nineteenth- and twentieth-century Britain. While this new study acknowledges the importance of previous (post)colonial readings of contemporary canonical works such as *Jane Eyre* (1847), *The Moonstone* (1868), *Dracula* (1897), and *Heart of Darkness* (1902), this book also seeks to expand our current understandings of imperial literature by focusing on women's responses to empire as an important bridge between imperial Gothic texts of the nineteenth and twentieth centuries and postcolonial Gothic literature of the later twentieth and twenty-first centuries. When read as a kind of middle ground between these two strains of the Gothic, women's Colonial Gothic writing becomes a kind of blending that James Procter and Angela Smith, in their discussion of Dickens and Kipling, describe as "a critique of the empire from within" that ultimately "unsettle[s] grand narratives" (2007, pp. 97, 103).

This book is organized around women writers who had some connection to the British Commonwealth during the height of the

British Empire, including colonies, former colonies, and settler/invader nations. The respective birthplaces of these true citizens of empire contribute to a broad range of colonial voices. Some writers, such as Margery Lawrence, Florence Marryat, and Mary Kingsley, were born in England but traveled frequently and set their writing in imperial regions. A native of England, Susanna Moodie immigrated to Canada with her husband and daughter out of financial necessity. Born in New Zealand, Katherine Mansfield later moved to England and then to France. Other writers can also be considered transnational. Alice Perrin, the daughter of a British Army officer, was born and spent half her life in India before moving to England. The life of Perrin's contemporary, Bithia Mary Croker, followed much the same pattern. The Irish-born Croker moved with her husband to India, lived there for many years, and then retired to England. Mary Fortune was born in Ireland, spent many years in Canada, and then emigrated to Australia. Other writers spent almost their entire lives in the colonies. Isabella Valancy Crawford was born in Dublin and moved to Canada as a child. Barbara Baynton was born in Australia and, after a few years living in England, returned to her native land to live out her final years.

Though each writer discussed in the following chapters could be the subject of a book in her own right, when read together, the works of these women gain even greater significance. In addition to themes of fear and anxiety, there is a recurring examination of colonial women's experience that remains largely absent from male-authored Colonial Gothic works. Through an analysis of these texts, I argue that women's Colonial Gothic writing tends to be more critical of imperialism—and thereby more subversive—because it brings to the surface a troubled past of struggle and hardship that tends to be overlooked, or that official histories would keep buried. In these narratives of silencing and otherizing, these women simultaneously call attention to and challenge cross-cultural experiences of oppression. And while the themes of fear, anxiety, isolation, and threatening landscapes within the British Empire are subjects that travel across the authors' works, these themes, each told through a woman's perspective, emerge in unique ways when set in the different colonial regions that comprise the scope of this book: Canada, the Caribbean, Africa, India, Australia, and New Zealand.

Women's Gothic and the Colonial/Postcolonial Tradition

Beginning with Ellen Moers's use of the term "Female Gothic" in *Literary Women* (1976), scholars have been increasingly drawn to the social aspects of women's Gothic writing. Diana Wallace and Andrew Smith provide an overview of these debates in *The Female Gothic: New Directions* (2009), as they call attention to the form's engagement with cultural issues which make it "a broad and fluid category" that continues to be of "major literary and cultural importance" (pp. 10–11). I have likewise suggested that examining the ghost story from a "social supernatural" perspective provides new avenues for appreciating such literature that emphasizes themes of sexuality, economics, class, and imperialism (Edmundson Makala 2013, pp. 7, 17–18). The ghosts that arise because of these concerns reveal contemporary anxieties and women's intellectual involvement with social and historical issues.

In addition to their employment of social themes, women's Gothic shows a more developed sympathy for the complexities of human relationships than is typically found in male-authored narratives. According to Lynette Carpenter and Wendy K. Kolmar, ghost stories written by women "explore different areas of concern, and express their responses differently" (1991, p. 10). Gothic fiction written by men often concerns a masculine desire to (re)claim dominance over a supernatural force, while characters imagined by women tend to be more accepting of the supernatural and unexplained. Yet, even as women authors were more likely to be at peace with their fictional ghosts, they also demanded more from them in terms of cultural critique. Their ghosts exist not only to entertain, but also to make readers uncomfortable as they question the social, political, and natural world around them. These spectres reflect troubled relationships, nebulous identity, poverty, and personal loss. Even more importantly, the Gothic and supernatural elements that appear in women's writing almost always have a reason for being there. Instead of "investigat[ing] 'horror' for its own sake," an interest that Rosemary Jackson notes is often present in Gothic stories by men, women use the ghost story "in order to extend our sense of the human, the real, beyond the blinkered limits of male science, language, and rationalism" (1989, p. xviii). Women thus connect the experience of fear and anxiety with a greater social message and lesson that the protagonist must learn through her/his experience with Gothic unsettlement.

The narrative framework that underpins the supernatural tale lends itself well to the exploration of social messages because it is, at its heart, a *story* of human experience. As Nickianne Moody suggests, "the conventions of the ghost story provide a rhetoric for presenting personal experience." In these stories, "telling and listening become imperative" and "the reader must engage with a chain of consequence" (1996, p. 87).

It is perhaps not surprising then that much of the writing discussed in this book takes the form of the short story. Clare Hanson has noted the subversive qualities of the form, claiming that the "short story is a vehicle for different *kinds* of knowledge, knowledge which may be in some way at odds with the 'story' of dominant culture." For Hanson, the defining qualities of the short story, "disjunction, inconclusiveness, obliquity," represent "its ideological marginality." This marginality, in turn, allows the story "to express something suppressed/repressed in mainstream literature" (Hanson 1989, p. 6). Likewise, Ellen Burton Harrington sees similar disrupting tendencies in the short story. She claims that the downplaying of plot and the lack of resolution in these stories "undermines a simple linear narrative of culture and progress by demonstrating the underlying complexity of apparently simple relationships" (Harrington 2008, p. 8). Though neither Hanson nor Harrington explicitly include colonial writing in these appraisals, their ideas point to the ways in which women's Colonial Gothic stories similarly subvert mainstream narratives of imperial progress and expansion, as they frequently create stories that refuse narrative closure and that leave characters with a lingering sense of danger and uncertainty by the narrative's end. This sense of disunity works beyond the narrative to function as a critique of a greater uncertainty that underlies the colonial enterprise.

Women's Gothic situates itself within a larger tradition of utilizing fantasy/horror as a means of conveying broader, real world socio-cultural messages. As Rosemary Jackson has made clear, the fantasy genre "is produced within, and determined by, its social context. Though it might struggle against the limits of this context, often being articulated upon that very struggle, it cannot be understood in isolation from it" (Jackson 1981, p. 3). This idea melds very well with the preoccupations of colonial and postcolonial writing. In the seminal *Rule of Darkness* (1988), Patrick Brantlinger posits that the imperial Gothic in the late Victorian period arose out of deep-seated colonial anxieties about the expansion of the British Empire, and these ideas have more recently transformed into extended studies of postcolonial narratives.

Yet, attempts to define the postcolonial Gothic, much like the Gothic itself, continue to prove challenging for scholars. As Shelley Kulperger warns in her study of postcolonial Gothic by contemporary Canadian women writers, "Any attempt to define a genre such as the 'postcolonial Gothic' needs to be aware of the inadequacy of its capacity to capture a myriad of literary practices, narratives, and voices" (2009, p. 97). Because it is intimately tied to history, the postcolonial functions well within a Gothic setting, a setting that is equally tied to the past. William Hughes and Andrew Smith claim that "the Gothic is, and has always been, *post*-colonial" and becomes the point where "disruption accelerates into change, where the colonial encounter—or the encounter which may be read or interpreted through the colonial filter—proves a catalyst to corrupt, to confuse or to redefine the boundaries of power, knowledge and ownership" (2003, p. 1). In other words, many nineteenth- and twentieth-century Colonial Gothic texts—and, I would argue, particularly ones written by women—were progressive critiques of power structures. Simon Hay likewise discusses how the modern British ghost story represents a troubled connection with the past and "holds to a model of history as traumatically rather than nostalgically available to us" (2011, p. 15). As Hay remarks, "The social relationships that the ghost story addresses, as it tries to imagine solutions for the social crises these relations increasingly find themselves confronting throughout modernity, are insistently imperial ones" (ibid., p. 11). He observes that "the social totality that structures the world of the ghost stories, the truth underlying the mere experiences of the lives of characters and readers—this social reality has included from the genre's beginnings absolutely the hard facts of empire" (ibid., p. 11). As with Hay's discussion of the importance of the ghost, Jennifer Lawn, in her study of New Zealand Gothic, has argued, "The figure of the ghost [...] aligns with models of collective history that emphasise mediating processes of transference and transformation." These spectres thus "open avenues to new modes of knowledge" (Lawn 2006, p. 152).

Gerry Turcotte, discussing the similarities between Canadian and Australian Gothic fiction, likewise notes that the "instability, curiosity and sense of disjunction which was exported to the colonies [...] was supplemented by a further sense of spiritual and physical alienation in the so-called barren lands" (2009, p. 17). Indeed, a key idea here is the profound sense of dislocation that accompanies Gothic set in a colonial world. Andrew Hock-soon Ng identifies loss and transgression as two fundamental characteristics of postcolonial Gothic. For Ng, this sense of loss haunts its text, as a "lingering presence [...] which refuses to dissolve" (2007, p. 18). Alison Rudd likewise expands on the Gothic preoccupations discussed by Turcotte and Ng, including "fragmented histories," memory, and forgetting as vital concepts within the postcolonial Gothic. These writings "expose the fault-lines in colonial ideologies and political and economic systems" (Rudd 2010, p. 3).

The inherent marginalization of colonial writing lends itself well to fictional explorations by other socially peripheral groups, or what Smith and Hughes call the "culturally dispossessed" (2003, p. 1). Anne McClintock has explored the relationship between colonization and gender in terms similar to Jackson's discussion of the social context of fantasy, concluding that "the dynamics of colonial power are fundamentally, though not solely, the dynamics of gender" (1995, p. 364). Within a Gothic context, Carol Margaret Davison continues this discussion of gender and empire: "In this narrative dynamic of revelation, indictment and purification, the empire Gothic's closest generic relative is perhaps the Female Gothic which, on the basis of established gender ideology, advances, to varying degrees, a critique of enlightened paternalism" (2003, p. 138). This "critique," of course, has been a prominent theme within the Female Gothic from the early nineteenth century onwards. Commenting on this tradition in women's Gothic, Jennifer Uglow suggests, "Women bring to their writing the qualities of their particular experience, their history of living on the margins" (1990, p. ix).

For Hughes and Smith, Gothic depictions of empire are "frequently conducted at a personal level" (2003, p. 2). To fully appreciate this tendency, they advocate looking beyond "the slavery conscious narratives of the Romantic era" and "the immigration- and degeneration-obsessed novels" of the late Victorian period (ibid., p. 3). By moving away from the traditional imperial Gothic texts written by Kipling, Haggard, and Conrad, we can begin to recognize "the experience of writers writing out of colonised countries, and those who attempt to rationalise the confused and competing power structures and identities that may follow the departure of the absolutist-colonialist" (ibid., p. 3). Many colonial adventure tales follow the same formulaic pattern, which again gives readers a limited appreciation of more complex colonial issues. In their discussion of the imperial short story, Emma Liggins, Andrew Maunder, and Ruth Robbins describe these plots as "tend[ing] to deal with adventurous men coping with violent situations: monsters or villainous 'savages,' or 'non-white' masculinities more generally." They continue by saying that "these events are invariably described in the same terms: 'them' and 'us.' Women, when they appear, tend to feature in one of two guises: innocent victim or *femme fatale*" (Liggins et al. 2011, p. 91). Similarly, Rebecca Stott has claimed that much of imperial writing is "a man-made discourse, expressing male fantasies, fears, anxieties. It is a discourse that emphasizes the importance of male camaraderie and which implicitly warns of the debilitating effects of women" (Stott 1989, p. 70). Women writers provide an alternative perspective that expands the constricting tendencies of "traditional" or canonical colonial narratives. As a group, British and Commonwealth women were "in between" in many respects. They were part of the colonizing power structure but, as the "second sex," were also denied direct access to those power structures that created imperial policy. Women's perspectives regarding empire thus repeatedly complicate the official/canonical narratives. By writing about the colonial experience, particularly from a Gothic slant, women could write their own fears and anxieties back into the imperial narrative. Whether written within the borders of England proper or from the margins of empire, their narratives call into question the imperial mission and its promises of land, riches, and opportunity. Instead of bringing the Gothic home to England in tales of reverse colonization, these women turned the reading public's attention outward to the far reaches of empire. And while male Gothic writers frequently focus on the threat posed by the racial Other, women's writing is less concerned with describing the threat of foreign invasion within Britain or dominating indigenous populations in foreign lands. Instead, women are more critical of the white/European presence in colonial regions. Their fiction is more concerned with the weaknesses and flaws inherent within the colonial system (and within the colonizer) and how colonizers themselves ultimately experience suffering and loss, rather than prosperity, while residing in the colonial space. As Roger Luckhurst has suggested, women's ghosts become "signals of atrocities, marking sites of an *untold* violence, a traumatic past whose traces remain to attest to the fact of a lack of testimony [or] memorializing narrative" (1996, p. 247). With this idea in mind, Colonial Gothic writing by women combines the personal with regional concerns and notions of national identity, and thus gives us a unique view into the colonial experience during the height of the British Empire. This female point-of-view is, at times, more troubling because it is grounded in real world fears and hardships, but it is also often a more sympathetic rendering of the negative consequences of imperialism, a warning about the dehumanizing aspects of empire that are brought about not by contact with the colonial Other, but instead self-induced by the colonizer's own desperate, traumatic experiences while residing in colonial regions.

Recent studies of the postcolonial Gothic have focused on late twentieth- and twenty-first-century authors, particularly novelists and people of color. While this emphasis remains a vital and culturally necessary avenue for scholarship, what has yet to be thoroughly examined, however, is the extent to which postcolonial voices existed within narratives of nineteenth- and early twentieth-century Colonial Gothic fiction. Tabish Khair has claimed that, "in much of Gothic literature, or literature with Gothic elements, the colonies and the colonised remain eerily half-present throughout the nineteenth century and the early twentieth century" (2009, p. 37). The works included in *Women's Colonial Gothic Writing* complicate such a view. In recognizing the importance of nineteenth- and early twentieth-century Colonial Gothic writing by women, we can begin to trace a broader postcolonial Gothic tradition that started during, not after, the first colonial encounters. In structural terms, both women's Gothic and postcolonial Gothic often refuse to provide narrative closure. Protagonists are refused happy endings and the supernatural is frequently left unexplained as the spectral trouble—like the cultural disorder that it symbolizes—refuses to be laid to rest. Ghosts, dead bodies, and wandering souls (both living and dead) are forced to exist and suffer together in a sort of colonial purgatory. If the postcolonial Gothic is about repression and the haunted traumas of the colonial project, women's Colonial Gothic written within the historical moment of the British Empire seeks to give these typically unspoken traumas a voice. By utilizing a women's Gothic tradition that critiques the fear, trauma, and violence that exists within the everyday world and transfers those anxieties to colonial regions, these narratives uncover hidden (repressed) histories of colonialism, especially women's experience within the colonial system. Women's Gothic written during the height of empire emphasizes the colonial subject's constant struggle between the familiar/unfamiliar, the natural/supernatural worlds, and the tenuous safety of the domestic space that is constantly being invaded—not by the indigenous, racial Other that is such a part of other Gothic narratives but, instead, by disease, destitution, and distrust. In doing so, these narratives memorialize what official history has forgotten.

Reconsidering Women's Colonial Writing

Nupur Chaudhuri and Margaret Strobel discuss the tendency to ignore or not fully appreciate the role Western women played within the imperial system. They claim, "In general, theories about colonialism have stressed its 'masculine' nature, highlighting the essential components of domination, control, and structures of unequal power. The colonial experience itself, expressed in terms of political and economic power and dominance, has been a major focus of historical study" (Chaudhuri and Strobel 1992, p. 3). With this narrow focus, critical studies on empire have "reinforced the common belief among imperialists that colonies were 'no place for a white woman'" (ibid., p. 3). When the focus turns to the involvement of Western women in the colonies, it tends to be centered on negative representations, such as "racist attitudes of white women and their luxurious lifestyle compared to their sisters at home" (ibid., p. 3). In recent years this has become less of a problem, as scholars have paid more attention to women's socio-historical involvement in empire, yet there is still a large gap in our understanding of how women wrote about empire, particularly in their fiction. According to Sara Mills, focusing more attention on gender allows us to realize that "conventional modes of imperialism cannot accommodate the variety of activity that took place within the imperial context" (1994, p. 30). Mary Louise Pratt's influential concept of the "contact zone" (1992, p. 4) is important here as it offers a more inclusive examination of the variety of colonial relations, and acknowledges the complexities inherent in those encounters. By bringing gender concerns into critical discussions surrounding imperialism, we can bring women's experience back into the history of empire. For Chaudhuri and Strobel, this emphasis "rejects the notion of empire solely as male space" and "imperial history as solely constituted by what the policy makers in London or in other Western capitals attempted to achieve" (1992, p. 4).

Yet, how to read women's colonial writing—and, indeed, how to view women's place and responsibility within the imperial system—remains an often-contentious topic. Margaret Strobel has noted, "As participants in the historical process of British expansion, [women] benefited from the economic and political subjugation of indigenous peoples and shared many of the accompanying attitudes of racism, paternalism, ethnocentrism, and national chauvinism" (1991, p. xi). In her discussion of English-Canadian settler narratives, Janice Fiamengo discusses the differing views of women pioneers by modern-day scholars, noting that postcolonial critics find these women's writing troubling because "their attitudes to place and to Native peoples" are "colonizing and harmful." Citing such works as Bill Ashcroft, Gareth Griffiths, and Helen Tiffin's *The Empire Writes Back* (1989), Janet Floyd's *Writing the Pioneer Woman* (2002), and Jennifer Henderson's *Settler Feminism and Race Making in Canada* (2003), Fiamengo locates an opinion which suggests that since women were responsible for home-making—an act that symbolizes literal possession of a space which originally belonged to indigenous people in colonial territories—these women can never completely separate themselves from the imperial mission (2015, p. 273). She concludes, "It remains to be seen now whether such texts may be rehabilitated for a less ideologically determined reading strategy" (ibid., p. 273). Ann Curthoys, in her examination of Australian colonial settlement narratives, recognizes the importance of including differing voices and perspectives within the still-contested history of imperialism. She asserts that "it is notable how *good* non-Aboriginal Australians are at memorialising their own sufferings" and calls attention to competing narratives that portray colonial settlers as either "victims" or "aggressors" (Curthoys 1999, p. 3). Much of this ongoing tension between settlers/invaders and indigenous people has to do with notions of land and ownership rights. Colonial narratives which emphasize the harshness of the landscape on settlers tend to overlook the existence of indigenous people on that land. This emphasis on the colonial experience means that Aboriginal people are "denied a place in history" (ibid., p. 13). The absence of indigenous voices—whether these voices are from Australia, New Zealand, Africa, North America, or Asia—also silences the violent history of imperial oppression and displacement.

More recently, Anna Snaith has suggested that we can simultaneously appreciate women's writing about colonialism while still recognizing the more troubling moral ambiguities that exist within their work. Snaith insists on viewing women's colonial writing as "products of both imperial ideology and anti-colonialism" (2014, p. 8). Indeed, we cannot forget that while many women wrote against empire, they were also a part of it. As Snaith says, colonial women writers "articulate some form of imperial subversion, ranging from full-blown anti-imperialism to a re-balancing of the bonds of empire (or cultural nationalism within an imperial framework)." These women thus "engage, even if implicitly, with topical debates concerned with colonial nationalism in a changing empire" (ibid., p. 17).

Women's Colonial Gothic writing provides a key area from which to examine the complexities of women's literary involvement in empire. Women writers of the Gothic and supernatural have long used the genre's subversive qualities to critique the status quo and existing power structures. Beginning in the early nineteenth century, they used ghosts and haunted houses to comment on gender and economic inequality in Great Britain. As women gradually increased their use of the Gothic and the social supernatural throughout the remainder of the century, they also took advantage of increased opportunities for women to travel, whether in the more traditional roles of wives, sisters, and daughters who accompanied emigrating men, or as independent single women who dared to explore foreign lands by themselves. As these women traveled, they took their love of writing with them and, as they encountered the inherent problems with colonialism in distant lands, turned their pens toward these issues. Denied the right to actively take part in governing and determining imperial policies, women used their firsthand experiences to critique what many of them saw as failed imperial ventures. In doing so, the homegrown concerns of the traditional Gothic were pushed beyond its Eurocentric borders and into colonial territories.

Women's Colonial Gothic Writing, 1850–1930 begins with an exploration of two Canadian émigrés, the more well-known Susanna Moodie and the lesser-known Isabella Valancy Crawford, and how these women utilized traditional European Gothic traditions and transformed these Gothic tropes based on their unique experiences in colonial Canada. Chapter 2, "Susanna Moodie, Colonial Exiles, and the Frontier Canadian Gothic," focuses on reading Canadian literature through a Gothic lens, which is, according to Gerry Turcotte, "a fairly recent phenomenon" (1998, p. 288). Yet, by looking at nineteenth-century fiction from the frontier, we begin to recognize that Gothic concerns have long been a part of Canada's colonial past. Susanna Moodie (1803–1885), considered to be the most famous Canadian woman writer of the nineteenth century, emigrated from England with her husband and daughter to Ontario in 1832. In *Roughing It in the Bush; Or, Life in Canada* (1852), she discusses the idea that Canada may be too new for ghosts. However, the frontier that she describes is no less haunted by her own anxieties as an unwilling English émigré faced with an unforgiving new "home." In many ways, Moodie's memoir, which was meant to serve as a guide for new settlers moving to Canada, reads like a Gothic narrative of forced captivity in a strange, foreign land. Fears of disease, wild animals, and a general sense of disorientation permeate the text. Moodie is less well-known for the short stories which preceded the publication of her 1852 memoir. One of the grimmest of these tales, "The Well in the Wilderness," which appeared in 1847 in Moodie's own short-lived venture, the *Victoria Magazine*, transfers the anxiety of settler life described in *Roughing It in the Bush* to a fictional setting. Much like Moodie herself, the family arrives in the unsettled Canadian wilderness unprepared for the harsh realities of frontier life. The violent attack on the mother at the end of the story is only one tragedy in a long chain of suffering that includes financial hardship, disease, hunger, and ultimately, death. An unrelenting fatalism runs throughout Moodie's emigration-themed fiction, which lends itself particularly well to Colonial Gothic concerns of exile and isolation.

Chapter 3, "Gothic Romance and Retribution in the Short Fiction of Isabella Valancy Crawford," shows the progression of women's Gothic in Canada from the early prose of Susanna Moodie to later reimaginings of Gothic conventions and the role of the heroine. Isabella Valancy Crawford (1850–1887) was born in Dublin and immigrated to Ontario with her parents as a child. After the death of her father, Crawford supported herself and her mother by writing, and became one of the first professional writers in Canada. Her short fiction appeared in numerous magazines, including *Frank Leslie's Popular Monthly* and *Illustrated News*, as well as Toronto's *The Globe* and *The Evening Globe*. Yet, the rediscovery of Crawford's writing in recent years is largely centered on her poetry collection *Old Spookes' Pass, Malcolm's Katie and Other Poems* (1884) and her frontier novel *Winona; Or, The Foster-Sisters* (1873). In her short fiction, Crawford frequently turns to darker themes and the harsh realities of life in Canada. Much like her contemporary, Susanna Moodie, Crawford's stories present vulnerable settlers who are forced to immigrate because of sickness and financial hardships. The frontier landscape has a menacing, unforgiving quality, and in Crawford's short fiction, we see the first attempts to develop a language that could adequately describe the Canadian wilderness. "In the Breast of a Maple"—which exists as an undated, unpublished manuscript in the Lorne Pierce Collection (Queen's University, Kingston, Ontario) adopts the traditional Gothic romance plot of stolen inheritance and transfers it to the Canadian frontier. In the story, the de Meury sisters must survive the advances of a lecherous man who hopes that the money and property which he stole from the women's father years before will drive the older sister to marry him out of financial desperation. Both the villainous man and the surrounding wilderness, with its "supernatural stillness," must be overcome in order for the sisters to reclaim their rightful inheritance. Crawford also deployed this blend of Gothic romance and grim, frontier realism in "Extradited," which she published in the *Globe* on September 4, 1886. As with "In the Breast of a Maple," this story features another strong woman, but Crawford rejects the romance that is found in the former tale. In "Extradited," a wife and mother chooses financial security over love and forgiveness as she ensures the capture and eventual death of a reformed criminal who has previously saved her young son from drowning. Though the woman sees herself as a "heroine of duty," Crawford presents the rural landscape as a place that turns once generous people into hardened survivors.

These gender concerns move to a much different cultural climate in Chapter 4, "Generations of the Female Vampire: Colonial Gothic Hybridity in Florence Marryat's *The Blood of the Vampire*," which moves south from the nineteenth-century Canadian frontier in order to explore the Colonial Gothic through issues of race and vampirism. Florence Marryat's (1833–1899) novel has recently been rediscovered as an important contribution to nineteenth-century vampire fiction. The story concerns the young and beautiful Harriet Brandt, who discovers that she is a psychic vampire doomed to destroy those closest to her. While *The Blood of the Vampire* is an important work within the female vampire tradition, recent scholarship on Marryat's work has tended to overlook its importance within the Colonial Gothic tradition. Indeed, colonial concerns are central to the novel. Because Harriet's ancestry is rooted in the Caribbean, her vampiric qualities connect her to the folkloric tradition of the soucouyant, the Caribbean female vampire. As early as the eighteenth century, stories of these creatures were passed down from Afro-Caribbean locals to English and French plantation owners. What is key to this tradition is how the soucouyant is usually characterized—as a black woman driven by excessive, dangerous sexuality who challenges boundaries by invading the domestic space of her victims. This chapter argues that this tradition is integral to understanding the Colonial Gothic nature of Marryat's text. As a mixed-race native of Jamaica who eventually travels to Europe, Harriet Brandt essentially becomes a version of the soucouyant in England.

The discussion of race relations between the British and colonial peoples and the need for greater understanding between races continues in Chapter 5, "Mary Kingsley and the Ghosts of West Africa." Mary Kingsley (1862–1900), who has traditionally been read under the more constrictive label of "travel writer," was an accomplished ethnologist and folklorist. When she decided to embark on an extended tour of West Africa in 1893 after the deaths of her parents, Kingsley found a social purpose that would continue for the rest of her life. In addition to recording various aspects of West African life and customs in *Travels in West Africa* (1897), Kingsley also became interested in the spiritual customs of West Africans. Two of her influential essays, "Black Ghosts" (1896) and "The Forms of Apparitions in West Africa" (1899), are concerned with bringing African ghost stories and the practice of fetish to the attention of her British audiences in an attempt to show the similarities in the spiritual beliefs of the two cultures.

Chapter 6, "The African Stories of Margery Lawrence," looks at a more ominous side of colonialism, one that counter-balances and troubles the more positive outlook forwarded by Mary Kingsley at the turn of the twentieth century. In a career spanning more than forty years, Margery Lawrence (1889–1969) published best-selling novels and supernatural fiction that frequently highlighted an often troubled past and its effect on the living. "Death Valley" (1924) is set within colonial Rhodesia. The story concerns a group of British men who are supposed to be surveying a section of African jungle, but who are actually hunting for ivory. Lawrence echoes Joseph Conrad's *Heart of Darkness* as she describes a cabin in a section of jungle that the local Africans call "Death Valley." The cabin is haunted by a "white devil," a British man who committed unspeakable atrocities and whose restless spirit attacks anyone who enters his cabin, suggesting the haunted, continuously troubled impact of British settlement within Africa. "The Dogs of Pemba" (1926) concerns Hugh Kinnersley, the brutish Commissioner of Pemba, who abuses his African servants and abandons his African mistress when his wife arrives from England. In a perverted reflection of his own mistreatment of the local people, Kinnersley is transformed into a dog-like beast. "The Curse of the Stillborn" (1925) was inspired by Howard Carter's 1922 discovery of King Tutankhamun's tomb and the subsequent Western fascination with all things Egyptian. The story centers on the wife of a missionary who insists on giving a Christian burial to a stillborn Egyptian child, despite warnings from the child's grandmother. In the end, the supernatural power of ancient Egypt achieves a terrifying triumph over British Christianity and its proselytizing mission. Each of these stories complicates earlier versions of the imperial Gothic by making the Western (white) protagonists both the victims *and* villains of the narratives. These stories, written well into the twentieth century, likewise show the continuing impact of colonization on British women's writing.

Chapter 7, "Colonial Gothic Framework: Haunted Houses in the Anglo-Indian Ghost Stories of Bithia Mary Croker," continues the supernatural themes discussed in Lawrence's African stories but shifts focus to an Anglo-Indian colonial setting. The chapter delves into the cultural world of the British Raj, and the tensions which existed between Indians and their Anglo-Indian British colonizers. As Britain's "Jewel in the Crown," India endured one of the longest colonial occupations in history, and the years of close contact between these two cultures led to violent conflicts such as the Indian Rebellion of 1857, a traumatic event that haunted both the Indians and British for decades. In "If You See Her Face" and "The Red Bungalow," Bithia Mary Croker (c. 1850–1920) uses Anglo-Indian bungalows and Indian palaces as sites for haunting and, through these troubled homes, she shows that the domestic can be a reflection of wider socio-political contentions outside the home. Seeing the spirits in both stories, and thus coming face-to-face with the dehumanizing effects of imperialism, proves devastating for the Anglo-Indians who must experience a haunted colonial environment that remains a site of historical and cultural trauma.

The tensions which arise between colonizer and colonized in British India, and the extent to which the British themselves are largely to blame for these problems, is a major concern in Chapter 8, "Animal Gothic in Alice Perrin's *East of Suez*." In these stories, the vengeful revenants of Croker's stories are replaced with dangerous, frightening animals. Though perhaps best-known today for her romance novels set in India, Alice Perrin (1867–1934) gained initial fame writing Anglo-Indian ghost stories that are far more subversive than her novels. "Caulfield's Crime," which is an earlier imagining of the Gothic concerns present in Lawrence's "The Dogs of Pemba," focuses on the repercussions of violence against Indians. The story concerns an Englishman who has an intimate knowledge of India but who misdirects this cultural potential by abusing his power, and ultimately becomes the victim of a reincarnated Indian spirit who returns from the grave to seek revenge over a violent, needless death. Such a needless death is also a major concern in "A Man's Theory," as the bad judgment of the seemingly infallible British colonial father causes the death of his son. The concluding story in *East of Suez*, "The Biscobra," also centers on the possibility of reincarnation but, instead of a surly military man, the narrative focuses on Frank Krey and his young wife, Nell. "The Biscobra" concerns itself with the interior domestic space and its invasion by the surrounding natural environment.

Chapter 9, "The Past Will Not Stay Buried: Female Bodies and Colonial Crime in the Australian Ghost Stories of Mary Fortune," moves the Gothic into Australia. The Irish-born Mary Fortune (c. 1833–1911) moved to the Australian goldfields with her young son after leaving Canada in the mid-1850s. Fortune turned her firsthand experiences witnessing the darker side of Australian colonial life into a lifelong writing career, becoming a pioneering detective story writer. Using the pseudonym "Waif Wander," Fortune wrote hundreds of stories for the *Australian Journal* from 1867–1908. Yet, even though Fortune has received renewed scholarly interest, there is scant attention paid to the use of murdered female bodies in her fiction, and the ghosts which subsequently appear after these violent acts. As revenants, these women return to the world of the living for revenge. This chapter focuses on three of Fortune's Gothic stories: "Mystery and Murder" (1866), "The Illumined Grave" (1867), and "The Old Shaft" (1886). In the stories, Fortune uses ghosts and gruesome deaths to comment on the failure of the domestic space as a place of safety and the wider issue of violence against women in colonial Australia.

Violence against women and their precarious existence in colonial Australia remains a major focus in Chapter 10, "Fear and Death in the Outback: Barbara Baynton's *Bush Studies*." Barbara Baynton (1857–1929) is best-known for the unflinching portrayal of Australian settler life she depicted in *Bush Studies* (1902). At a time when Australian nationalism was at a high point, Baynton wrote against much of the popular literature of the day and questioned the ultimate success of colonialism, particularly regarding the treatment of women in remote "bush" settings. The two stories which bookend *Bush Studies*, "A Dreamer" and "The Chosen Vessel," are also two of the most disturbing stories in the collection. Both narratives critique the supposed comfort and happiness of women in colonial Australia by placing the respective protagonists in hostile and isolated exterior landscapes. Yet, these women are equally unsettled within the home, as Baynton calls attention to how these structures can be sites of other forms of trauma as they fail to provide a safe space for women.

Chapter 11, "Katherine Mansfield and the Troubled Homes of Colonial New Zealand," is, in many ways, a continuation of the themes in Baynton's fiction. "The House," one of Katherine Mansfield's (1888–1923) rare forays into the ghost story genre, focuses on a woman who desperately desires domestic bliss and financial security within the home of her dreams. However, the woman can only briefly experience such happiness after she dies on the front porch of the house. "The Woman at the Store" (1912) centers on the haunted, unforgiving landscape of a remote and unpopulated countryside inhabited by wayward settlers. This landscape has a devastating effect on the story's title character, a lonely woman whose physical and emotional isolation culminates in the murder of her husband in front of their neglected child. Another desperate woman is at the center of "Millie" (1913). In this story, a neglected wife has conflicted feelings for a young suspected murderer who she finds injured and hiding on her husband's property. Although Millie initially sympathizes with the man and sees his situation as similar to her own isolation, loneliness, and desperation, she ultimately becomes complicit in his eventual capture.

The works selected for this book are meant to encourage further discussion of women's involvement with the Colonial Gothic genre. As such, this group provides a representative sampling of women's literary contributions to this area, but is by no means exhaustive. In my selections, I have tried to combine more well-known authors such as Susanna Moodie, Mary Kingsley, and Katherine Mansfield with lesser-known writers such as Isabella Valancy Crawford, Margery Lawrence, and Alice Perrin. Likewise, I have selected some authors whose works may not be readily identified as "Gothic," or whose work in the Gothic genre has been the subject of critical neglect. Even the works chosen for discussion in each chapter are just a sampling of each woman's literary output. Many other Colonial Gothic works could have been discussed if space were not an issue. For instance, Florence Marrayat wrote "Little White Souls," an Anglo-Indian ghost story, while Margery Lawrence penned "The House of the Dancing Feet," also an Anglo-Indian supernatural tale. What I hope this book accomplishes is a renewed appreciation for how nineteenth- and early twentieth-century women who were connected to the British Empire faced the challenges of colonialism through their writing. All their Colonial Gothic work is scary, but it is a scariness—even when ghosts or unexplained forces appear—that is firmly based in the real. Though these narratives are set in different regions across the empire, their anxieties are embedded in something that is both unique to a specific location and yet manages to transcend geographical space. Ghosts are often thought to be rooted to a particular place but, in the Gothic literature of empire, they can also travel, making the empire a very haunted place indeed.

BIBLIOGRAPHY

Brantlinger, Patrick (1988), *Rule of Darkness: British Literature and Imperialism, 1830–1914*, Ithaca and London: Cornell University Press.

Carpenter, Lynette, and Wendy K. Kolmar (1991), "Introduction," in *Haunting the House of Fiction: Feminist Perspectives on Ghost Stories by American Women*, Knoxville, TN: University of Tennessee Press, pp. 1–25.

Chaudhuri, Nupur, and Margaret Strobel (1992), "Introduction," in *Western Women and Imperialism: Complicity and Resistance*, Bloomington: Indiana University Press, pp. 1–15.

Curthoys, Ann (1999), "Expulsion, Exodus and Exile in White Australian Historical Mythology," *Journal of Australian Studies* 23.61: 1–19.

Davison, Carol Margaret (2003), "Burning Down the Master's (Prison)-House: Revolution and Revelation in Colonial and Postcolonial Female Gothic," in Andrew Smith and William Hughes (eds.), *Empire and the Gothic: The Politics of Genre*, Basingstoke: Palgrave Macmillan, pp. 136–154.

Edmundson Makala, Melissa (2013), *Women's Ghost Literature in Nineteenth-Century Britain*, Cardiff: University of Wales Press.

Fiamengo, Janice (2015), "English-Canadian Narratives of Settlement," in Cynthia Sugars (ed.), *The Oxford Handbook of Canadian Literature*, Oxford: Oxford University Press, pp. 260–276.

Hanson, Clare (1989), "Introduction," in Clare Hanson (ed.), *Re-reading the Short Story*, Basingstoke: Palgrave Macmillan, pp. 1–9.

Harrington, Ellen Burton (2008), "Introduction: Women Writers and the Outlaw Form of the Short Story," in Ellen Burton Harrington (ed.), *Scribbling Women and the Short Story Form: Approaches by American and British Women Writers*, New York: Peter Lang, pp. 1–14.

Hay, Simon (2011), *A History of the Modern British Ghost Story*, Basingstoke: Palgrave Macmillan.

Hughes, William, and Andrew Smith (2003), "Introduction: Defining the Relationships Between Gothic and the Postcolonial," *Gothic Studies* 5.2 (November): 1–6.

Jackson, Rosemary (1981), *Fantasy: The Literature of Subversion*, London and New York: Methuen.

——— (1989), "Introduction," in Jessica Amanda Salmonson (ed.), *What Did Miss Darrington See? An Anthology of Feminist Supernatural Fiction*, New York: The Feminist Press, pp. xv–xxxv.

Khair, Tabish (2009), *The Gothic, Postcolonialism and Otherness: Ghosts from Elsewhere*, Basingstoke: Palgrave Macmillan.

Kulperger, Shelley (2009), "Familiar Ghosts: Feminist Postcolonial Gothic in Canada," in Cynthia Sugars and Gerry Turcotte (eds.), *Unsettled Remains: Canadian Literature and the Postcolonial Gothic*, Waterloo, ON: Wilfrid Laurier University Press, pp. 97–124.

Lawn, Jennifer (2006), "From the Spectral to the Ghostly: Postcolonial Gothic and New Zealand Literature," *Australasian-Canadian Studies* 24.2: 143–169.

Liggins, Emma, Andrew Maunder, and Ruth Robbins (2011), *The British Short Story*, Basingstoke: Palgrave Macmillan.

Luckhurst, Roger (1996), "Impossible Mourning in Toni Morrison's *Beloved* and Michèle Roberts's *Daughters of the House*," *Critique* 37.4: 243–260.

McClintock, Anne (1995), *Imperial Leather: Race, Gender, and Sexuality in the Colonial Contest*, New York: Routledge.

Mighall, Robert (1999), *A Geography of Victorian Gothic Fiction: Mapping History's Nightmares*, Oxford and New York: Oxford University Press.

Mills, Sara (1994), "Knowledge, Gender, and Empire," in Alison Blunt and Gillian Rose (eds.), *Writing Women and Space: Colonial and Postcolonial Geographies*, New York: Guilford Press, pp. 29–50.

Moody, Nickianne (1996), "Visible Margins: Women Writers and the English Ghost Story," in Sarah Sceats and Gail Cunningham (eds.), *Image and Power: Women in Fiction in the Twentieth Century*, London and New York: Longman, pp. 77–90.

Ng, Andrew Hock-soon (2007), *Interrogating Interstices: Gothic Aesthetics in Postcolonial Asian and Asian American Literature*, Oxford and New York: Peter Lang.

Pratt, Mary Louise (1992), *Imperial Eyes: Travel Writing and Transculturation*, London: Routledge.

Procter, James, and Angela Smith (2007), "Gothic and Empire," in Catherine Spooner and Emma McEvoy (eds.), *The Routledge Companion to Gothic*, New York: Routledge, pp. 95–104.

Rudd, Alison (2010), *Postcolonial Gothic Fictions from the Caribbean, Canada, Australia, and New Zealand*, Cardiff: University of Wales Press.

Smith, Andrew, and William Hughes (2003), "Introduction: The Enlightenment Gothic and Postcolonialism," in Andrew Smith and William Hughes (eds.), *Empire and the Gothic: The Politics of Genre*, Basingstoke: Palgrave Macmillan, pp. 1–12.

Snaith, Anna (2014), *Modernist Voyages: Colonial Women Writers in London, 1890–1945*, Cambridge: Cambridge University Press.

Stott, Rebecca (1989), "The Dark Continent: Africa as Female Body in Haggard's Adventure Fiction," *Feminist Review* 32 (Summer): 69–89.

Strobel, Margaret (1991), *European Women and the Second British Empire*, Bloomington: Indiana University Press.

Turcotte, Gerry (1998), "English-Canadian Gothic," in Marie Mulvey-Roberts (ed.), *The Handbook to Gothic Literature*, Basingstoke: Macmillan, pp. 288–292.

——— (2009), *Peripheral Fear: Transformations of the Gothic in Canadian and Australian Fiction*, Brussels: Peter Lang.

Uglow, Jennifer (1990), "Introduction," in Richard Dalby (ed.), *The Virago Book of Ghost Stories: The Twentieth Century*, London: Virago, pp. ix–xvi.

Wallace, Diana, and Andrew Smith (2009), "Introduction: Defining the Female Gothic," in Diana Wallace and Andrew Smith (eds.), *The Female Gothic: New Directions*, Basingstoke and New York: Palgrave Macmillan, pp. 1–12.

Wisker, Gina (2016), *Contemporary Women's Gothic Fiction: Carnival, Hauntings and Vampire Kisses*, Basingstoke: Palgrave Macmillan.

CHAPTER 2

Susanna Moodie, Colonial Exiles, and the Frontier Canadian Gothic

In her discussion of class and gender in North American frontier Gothic, Pattie Cowell observes that British Gothic fiction of the late eighteenth and early nineteenth centuries works to reestablish "a threatened social order," whereas American Gothic narratives resolve themselves "by creating an alternative order" (1993, p. 126). This creation of a new order is characterized by the destabilizing of the self in relation to its Gothic frontier setting. Selfhood thus becomes "a hybrid of circumstances of time and place" (ibid., pp. 128–129). Characters in these early American Gothic works, which Cowell notes are usually British, "struggle to return to the world they have always known, a world of traditional and orderly relations of class and gender" (ibid., p. 129). Considering these ideas with the Canadian Gothic in mind opens yet another avenue that serves to further complicate this need to return to some sense of place because, in addition to issues of class and gender, narratives of the Canadian frontier are also concerned with ideas of nationality and nationhood. By its unsettled nature, the frontier—whether American or Canadian—constantly resists efforts to return to any state of normalcy because normalcy remains undefined and unreachable. Because of the pull of Britishness on the Canadian émigré and nebulous questions surrounding English–Canadian identity, Canadian Gothic is not as defined as American identity that seeks to establish what Cowell terms "an alternative order." There is a consistent pull towards the Old Country, especially for an unwilling émigré such as Susanna Moodie, and this pull means that Canadian Gothic wilderness narratives are caught somewhere in a liminal space between being able to reestablish the social order (that is such a part of early British Gothic) and creating a new order. Considering early British Gothic novels by Ann Radcliffe, Horace Walpole, and Clara Reeve, Cowell claims, "Because the function of the British gothic plot is to return to the stable order with which the novel began, *both* class and gender hierarchies must be kept safely and harmoniously in place" (1993, p. 130). Yet, in her Gothic-influenced works, Susanna Moodie disrupts these conventions. After residing in the Canadian wilderness, people are forever altered, families are separated, and nothing can be as it once was.

One of the reasons that Moodie scholars have consistently struggled with labelling her work, particularly *Roughing It in the Bush* (1852), is because of its intermixture of genres. Michael Peterman notes that because *Roughing It* includes "elements of poetry, fiction, travel writing, autobiography, and social analysis, it eludes definition" (1983, p. 81). Alec Lucas surveys varying descriptions of Moodie's memoir, from a "personalized social history" (1989, p. 146), autobiography, anti-pastoral, and a novel *manqué* (p. 147), to "local colour fiction" and "women's travel writing" (ibid., p. 148). Like previous critics, Lucas tends to dismiss the importance of Moodie's earlier Gothic-themed fiction in her later writing. He says that "she had to forgo [...] the make-believe of her sentimental and gothic fiction" (ibid., p. 147), and that "only through the autobiographical sketch could she describe and dramatize her setting and her characters" (ibid., pp. 146–147). Likewise, Carole Gerson sees "the virgin territory of the New World" as a place that "represented detachment from the literary associations and cultural resonances conducive to imaginative literature" (1989, p. 42). John Thurston sees *Roughing It* as a narrative full of unresolved issues of self and language. He says that, throughout the text, Moodie tries to restore a unified self that relies on both an English self and an English literary tradition that gives her, as a writer, access to the short story, romance, and lyric genres (Thurston 1987, p. 200). However, the lack of tradition Moodie finds in Canada thwarts her attempts at presenting her readers with any unified form, while at the same time disrupting her sense of self in a strange land. In the absence of her English home, surrounded by strange places and strange people, Moodie had to find a new way of adequately describing her life through the written word. For Thurston, this exploration of colonial experience is the major strength of *Roughing It*: "Moodie was exactly the person needed to articulate the contradictions at the root [...] of the

Canadian consciousness" (ibid., p. 203). The text's "contradictions, its irresolutions, its generic amorphousness, its open-endedness, its disunity" give us a more authentic description of lived experience (ibid., p. 203). When Moodie's work is read within a Gothic context, these perceived inadequacies and contradictions become narrative strengths that serve to reflect the fractured nature of the emigrant experience.

According to Margot Northey, in her seminal study of the Gothic in Canadian fiction, the reluctance of critics to fully appreciate the existence of a Gothic tradition within Canada has to do with the fact that "by and large critics overplay the realistic side of Canadian fiction, frequently associating its achievement with the growth of realism" (1976, p. 3). Seeking an interpretive mode that enlightens our reading of early as well as contemporary Gothic works, Northey explores the critical possibilities within the term "Gothic," stating:

> "Gothic" refers here to a subjective view of the dark side of life, seen through the distorting mirror of the self, with its submerged levels of psychic and spiritual experiences. Non-realistic and essentially symbolic in its approach, the gothic opens up various possibilities of psychological, spiritual, or social interpretation. Its mood is pre-eminently one of terror or horror. (ibid., p. 6)

It is this sense of "horror" and the distortion of the self that frames Moodie's work as Gothic. Yet, she finds the source of this horror not in the supernatural, but in the unrelenting reality of her everyday existence as a settler.

Susanna Strickland was already a published author when she married John Wedderburn Dunbar Moodie in 1831. At first, he wanted to move his new wife to South Africa, but Susanna refused (and even briefly called off their engagement), not wanting to leave her family and friends in England. In a letter dated January 1831 to James and Emma Bird, she is adamant about her decision not to go ahead with the marriage: "I have changed my mind. You may call me a jilt a flirt or what you please, I care not. I will neither marry a soldier nor leave my country for ever and feel happy that I am once more my own mistress" (Ballstadt et al. 1985, p. 55). Another reason for her refusal to emigrate to South Africa was her fear of the wilderness and wild animals, particularly large animals such as elephants, lions, and tigers (Peterman 1999, p. 51). As a compromise, Moodie proposed emigrating to Canada instead, where

Susanna's brother Samuel and her sister Catherine Parr Traill, herself a published author, were already established. In 1832, the Moodies settled on a farm near Port Hope. In 1834, they moved to another farm in Douro Township, near Peterborough, Ontario. After five years in the backwoods, the couple moved with their children to Belleville.[1]

Susanna Moodie's fiction and non-fiction each gain significance when read together. Moodie's *Roughing It in the Bush*—in both style and content—was influenced by her earlier fiction, and many of her short stories were likewise based on the author's own experiences. Whether intentional or not, *Roughing It* reads very much like a Gothic narrative that foregrounds loss, privation, and despair against the backdrop of the Canadian wilderness. Moodie establishes herself as the Gothic heroine of the tale, naïve and well-meaning, at the mercy of nefarious strangers, and trapped in an unforgiving, often hostile, frontier setting—more exile than emigrant. This depiction bears a close resemblance to Ellen Moers's description of the English heroines who populate Ann Radcliffe's fiction, women who represent a "traveling heroinism" that moves beyond the imagined vistas of Italy, and thus gains historical as well as literary importance: "[These heroines] remind us of all the British ladies who in point of fact did set sail for Canada and India and Africa, with their bonnets veils, and gloves, their teacups and tea cozies—ill-equipped for vicissitudes of travel, climate, and native mutiny, but well-equipped to preserve their identity as proper Englishwomen" (1976, pp. 138–139). Likewise, Marian Fowler notes both the sentimental novel and Gothic novel tradition at work in this self-portrayal, particularly with regard to Radcliffe's writing. Since Moodie likely read Radcliffe's novels as a teenager, Fowler says, "In Susanna's case the style and content of Mrs. Radcliffe's novels probably filtered down to her subconscious, to resurface many years later, in *Roughing It in the Bush*, when her own Canadian experiences made the Gothic mode appropriate" (1982, p. 111). Fowler notices the similarities in Radcliffe's heroines and Moodie's situation. They are "exiles in a foreign land, isolated in wild settings and pining for their lost homes" (ibid., p. 111). Likewise, Gothic heroines in the Radcliffe tradition find themselves trapped in some sort of prison, which "exacerbates the heroine's intense emotionalism by excluding all outside social stimuli" (ibid., p. 112). The Canadian wilderness is the colonial prison, and the imposing pines, menacing wildlife, and expanding swamps that encircle Susanna Moodie are just as Gothic as any European castle or dungeon. This environment works to close off Moodie's contact with her previous world in England that formed the basis of her comfort, safety, and identity. This motif also suits Moodie, as she frequently sees herself as a prisoner in her forced exile, forced to live in a strange and often dangerous foreign land. Yet, unlike Radcliffe's heroines, she will never return home. This is where viewing *Roughing It* through the lens of combined genres can increase the value of Moodie's work as social critique of the colonial experience. Reading her work as travel autobiography, Helen M. Buss asserts that Moodie's stance as a traveler in a foreign land is complicated because she must also now live in that land. As a "cultural emissary of the English world, which felt itself superior to the colonial," Moodie must also recognize her new role of a permanent inhabitant of the colonial world (Buss 1993, p. 87). *Roughing It* is thus a more complex form of travel writing, made so because Moodie is no mere tourist. She is an outsider who is permanently trapped in a colony that must also be her home.

From the beginning of *Roughing It*, which Michael Peterman says "set[s] a Poe-like mood of impending doom" (1999, p. 70), Moodie insists on describing the dangers and deprivations of colonial life for new settlers, as opposed to the hopeful dream of emigration and all its supposed opportunities. She calls the prevailing interest among the British in emigrating to Canada an "infection" (2007 [1852], p. 4), and the first chapter starts not with opportunities in a new land, but with a cholera outbreak in Quebec. Homesick, tired, and hungry, Moodie imagines herself a stranger in a land that is supposed to be her home:

> The lofty groves of pine frowned down in hearse-like gloom upon the mighty river, and the deep stillness of the night, broken alone by its hoarse wailings, filled my mind with sad forebodings,—alas! too prophetic of the future. Keenly, for the first time, I felt that I was a stranger in a strange land; my heart yearned intensely for my absent home. Home! the word had ceased to belong to my *present*—it was doomed to live for ever in the *past*; for what emigrant ever regarded the country of his exile as his *home*? (p. 40)

The language used here could be from any Gothic novel, and her depictions of the scenery around her are deliberately distorted. Accurate descriptions of the landscape are less important for Moodie than describing its effect on her. Faye Hammill suggests that "Moodie's appropriation of the Canadian landscape into her imported literary framework is itself a form of colonization, a method of imposing imperial ideologies onto new world territory" (2003, p. 50). These descriptions are her way of maintaining some semblance of control of her situation, even though this is just as fictional as her (unreal) depictions of the natural world around her. Unable to turn back, she must face both the wilderness that awaits her, as well as her own "forebodings" of what her uncertain future holds. She also returns to the idea of intuitions and prophecies that go unheeded and lead to more danger in the future. It is telling that she reverses the hopeful order of past, present, and future in favor of the more ominous future, present, past, suggesting that there is no future, no means of moving forward in this environment. As Christa Zeller Thomas suggests, the opening section of the book "immediately stages a struggle with place and prefigures the narrative's probing of the crisis of exile" (2009, p. 107).

The existence of the émigré is likened to a living death, as the colony becomes a grave that traps the colonist, who, in turn, is doomed to be forgotten by loved ones back home in England:

> After seven years' exile, the hope of return grows feeble, the means are still less in our power, and our friends give up all hope of our return; their letters grow fewer and colder, their expressions of attachment are less vivid; the heart has formed new ties, and the poor emigrant is nearly forgotten. Double those years, and it is as if the grave had closed over you, and the hearts that once knew and loved you know you no more. (Moodie 2007 [1852], p. 123)

Cholera is the first predator in a narrative filled with danger, disease, and death. The poem that begins the chapter "Our Journey Up the Country" foregrounds Montreal as a "plague-stricken spot" that is "rank with pestilence" (p. 42). Its empty streets are as quiet "as a churchyard vault; Aghast and shuddering." In these lines, "Nature holds her breath / In abject fear," and in imagery of wild beasts that Moodie employs repeatedly throughout the narrative, "feels at her strong heart / The deadly fangs of death" (p. 42). The cholera outbreak is described as a "fatal visitation" (p. 43), and the "phantom" that haunts their journey inland (p. 49).

Once established on her farm, the threat of predatory disease is replaced by frontier settlers whose presence serves to trouble the isolated Moodie. One nearby settler is named "Old Satan," while various local women who arrive uninvited at the cabin are described in equally Gothic terms. On one occasion, "the door was suddenly pushed open, and the apparition of a woman squeezed itself into the crowded room" (p. 90). On another, "a cadaverous-looking woman, very long-faced and witch-like, popped her ill-looking visage into the door" (p. 98). According to Marian Fowler, "Susanna instills into her descriptions of these macabre figures her feeling that her new life is unreal, a nightmare from which she will shortly wake" (1982, p. 97). This is also the nightmare of what Kate Ferguson Ellis has called "the failed home" of Gothic literature (1989, p. ix). Moodie's progress through her narrative involves actually being homeless when a settler refuses to move out of their first intended dwelling—thus making Susanna an actual Gothic wanderer in search of a place to call her own—then moving into a cabin with no front door, to having a door with no functioning lock. All these scenarios suggest the Moodie family's precarious existence in the Canadian wilderness in a series of houses that are not safe or secure, further complicating the concept of "home" for the exiled Susanna. For D. M. R. Bentley, this sense of continued displacement is a hallmark of emigration. Instead of being "a journey of excursion and return," these travels become "an intermediate (and mediating) stage in a process of frequently reluctant removal from a cherished home and usually arduous relocation in an unfamiliar place" (Bentley 1989, p. 95). The very nature of emigrant writing resists the "return to home" motif that is such an integral part of Gothic romance.

Moodie's fear of wild animals is a major cause of unrest in the narrative. Her descriptions of these animals, particularly wolves, highlight her helplessness and symbolize the danger of the backwoods that, for Moodie, keeps her a prisoner in her own rudimentary home. The wild animals that surround her keep her further cut off from civilization and serve to emphasize her isolation in the Canadian backwoods. Seeing *Roughing It* as a work in the anti-pastoral tradition, Lucas claims, "Another strength derives from its setting, for the backwoods is no mere backdrop. It is a living frame of reference in the age-old struggle between human beings and nature" (Lucas 1989, pp. 153–154). In passages that describe animals, Moodie also falls victim to an overactive imagination that makes her feel more endangered than she really is. In these descriptions, she again returns to the Gothic-infused language that is earlier used to describe her death-in-life as an exile from her English homeland, as well as the predatory nature of contagious disease. At one point, when her husband must leave her alone in the cabin to conduct business in a nearby settlement, Moodie states, "for the first time in my life I found myself at night in a house entirely alone."[2] Becoming "too superstitious and nervous," she drags a heavy box in front of the door and thinks about "several ill-looking men" who had passed the house earlier and who she fears will return in the night to find her "alone and unprotected" (Moodie 2007 [1852], p. 192). Too frightened to venture outside for more firewood and on her last candle, Moodie is soon faced with the dark both indoors and out. She hears the "wild beasts," "the howling of a pack of wolves," and the "discordant screams" of geese (p. 193). Her fear of her own weakness and inability to defend herself is reflected in what she perceives as the physical weakness of her cabin structure. She imagines that the wolves will "break through the frail windows, or come down the low, wide chimney, and rob me of my child" (p. 194). She describes her increasing terror at these sounds: "I listened till the beating of my own heart excluded all other sounds. Oh, that unwearied brook! how it sobbed and moaned like a fretful child;—what unreal terrors and fanciful illusions my too active mind conjured up, whilst listening to its mysterious tones!" (p. 193). Seen at a distance, Moodie recognizes that her "too active" mind created these fears, but at the time, her terror was real.

On another occasion, Moodie joins a small group traveling through "the heart of a dark cedar swamp" where her mind becomes "haunted with visions of wolves and bears" and she hears only the "wild howl" of a wolf that breaks the otherwise "sepulchral silence of that dismal-looking wood" (p. 286). When she claims that, in England, those with superstitious inclinations "would people [the area] with ghosts," a fellow traveler claims:

> There are no ghosts in Canada! [...] The country is too new for ghosts. No Canadian is afeard of ghosts. It is only in old countries, like your'n, that are full of sin and wickedness, that people believe in such nonsense. [...] Now ghosts, as I understand the word, are the spirits of bad men, that are not allowed by Providence to rest in their graves, but, for a punishment, are made to haunt the spots where their worst deeds were committed. (pp. 286–287)

Though the speaker directs his critique toward Canada and its native inhabitants, his description reflects Susanna Moodie's own situation. By telling her that "no Canadian" is afraid of ghosts, after just hearing her thoughts on the haunted aspect of the country, Moodie is singled out because her firm belief in ghosts and hauntings is not truly Canadian. Her belief in the supernatural marks her as a person with connections to England, the "old country," which further distances her from what is supposed to be her new, adopted home. Furthermore, Moodie herself, in her separation/exile from England, is aligned with those unsettled beings who do the haunting. As she has previously remarked, as an émigré who has been forced to leave her beloved family and homeland, she is likewise doomed by "Providence" to not rest in an English grave, close to those she loves most.

Moodie closes her narrative of emigration, with its relentless descriptions of disease, danger, and despair in what she calls "the prison-house" of Canada (p. 539), on an equally solemn and foreboding note, while she also presents herself as a survivor who is forever scarred physically and emotionally by her ordeal:

> For seven years I had lived out of the world entirely; my person had been rendered coarse by hard work and exposure to the weather. I looked double the age I really was, and my hair was already thickly sprinkled with grey. I clung to my solitude. I did not like to be dragged from it to mingle in gay scenes, in a busy town, and with gaily-dressed people. I was no longer fit for the world; I had lost all relish for the pursuits and pleasures which are so essential to its votaries; I was contented to live and die in obscurity. (pp. 524–525)

In *Strange Things* (1995), Margaret Atwood describes how the ominous tone of Moodie's narrative makes it a fitting example of Canadian Gothic writing:

> Moodie's book was written as a *warning* to prospective immigrants, especially those of her own class. She emphasizes hardship and catastrophe—people were always stealing things from her or stuffing dead skunks up her chimney, or the house was catching fire in the middle of the winter. People in her books go mad, commit murder, get lynched; she leans more towards drama and Gothic effects than towards food preparation. (1995, pp. 96–97)

According to Atwood, this sense of alienation and displacement was made even stronger because the early women settlers in Canada "were not in the North woods of their own volition. They were there because circumstances and fate—namely their husbands—had dragged them there" (ibid., pp. 95–96).[3]

Susan Glickman has commented on the ambiguous nature of *Roughing It in the Bush*, which refuses to be held to any one genre: "we must remember we are reading neither a novel, from which we may expect some overall coherence of design and point of view, nor a genuine journal […] but something in between" (2007 [1989], p. 595). Glickman sees this in-betweenness as a particular strength, saying that "it is exactly this discontinuity, tension, *lack* of resolution, that makes *Roughing It in the Bush* such a fascinating book." It is at once "part documentary, part psychological parable" and "above all an authentic account of a woman trying to cope not only with a new world, but, more importantly, with a new self" (ibid., p. 602). Likewise, John Thurston has remarked on how the more traditional ways of reading Moodie's emigration narrative tend to limit its cultural effectiveness. He stresses that "seeing it as an apprenticeship novel or a Gothic romance can no longer account for its interest." Instead, the work "needs to be opened up to its history and its discontinuities traced to the dispersed social and psychological energies it tries to contain" (Thurston 1996, p. 134). I would argue that maintaining an emphasis on the work's Gothic qualities, particularly its Colonial Gothic aspects, leads us to appreciate how the many disunities of the text can highlight the disconnected experience of emigration. Susanna Moodie needed a language of fractured existence, fear, and isolation to tell her story and to relate her experience, and she found such language by utilizing the Gothic mode. By drawing on a Gothic tradition that also frequently foregrounds individual perception in the form of a tortured, long-suffering narrator, Moodie was able to establish herself as a heroine who emerges sadder but wiser at the end of her story. This is made clear to her readers in the epigraph: "I sketch from Nature, and the picture's true; / Whate'er the subject, whether grave or gay, / Painful experience in a distant land / Made it mine own."

Signs and portents are connected to the uncertain future of the émigré throughout Moodie's fictional and non-fictional writing. In *Roughing It*, she laments not listening to the "mysterious warnings" of her soul. She remembers "how sternly and solemnly this inward monitor warned me of approaching ill, the last night I spent at home; how it strove to draw me back as from a fearful abyss, beseeching me not to leave England and emigrate to Canada" (p. 203). The belief in extrasensory perception and other supernatural occurrences was a lifelong interest for Moodie. As a young girl, Susanna and her sisters reveled in stories of their family home, Reydon Hall, being haunted, and they later became involved in the new phenomenon of phrenology through their acquaintance with the brothers John and Robert Childs (Peterman 1999, pp. 23, 39–40). Moodie also wrote about the supernatural in such tales for *La Belle Assemblée* as "Sketches from the Country No. 1—The Witch of East Cliff," published in July 1827, "A Dream," published in August 1828, and "Sketches from the Country. No. 5.—Old Hannah; or, The Charm," which appeared in January 1829.

She, along with her husband and her sister Catharine, became involved in the Spiritualist movement, which began in America in the late 1840s with the spirit communications of Kate and Maggie Fox of New York.[4] Susanna met Kate Fox in person in 1855 and describes a séance in a letter to Richard Bentley:

> Since I last wrote you, I have had several visits from Miss Kate Fox the celebrated Spirit Rapper, who is a very lovely intellectual looking girl, with the most beautiful eyes I ever saw in a human head. Not black, but a sort of dark purple. She is certainly a witch, for you cannot help looking into the dreamy depths of those sweet violet eyes till you feel magnetized by them. (1985, p. 157)[5]

In her letters, Moodie mentions coming into contact with former friends and acquaintances via her husband's "Spiritoscope": "a board running upon two smooth brass rods with an index that pointed to the alphabet in order to save the trouble of culling over the alphabet" (1985, p. 180).[6] Catharine Parr Traill also served as a spirit medium for the family on several occasions. Initially a confirmed skeptic, Moodie could not deny the supernatural manifestations that she herself claimed to witness. Ballstadt, Hopkins, and Peterman note: "The rationalist in her was always struggling with the romanticist, eager to test the powers of the mind; her early prose and poetry, as well as *Roughing It in the Bush*, give ample evidence of her experiments and interest in the occult and the irrational" (1985, p. 120). Thomas Hodd likewise sees a connection with Moodie's interest in Spiritualism and her longer fiction, namely *Mildred Rosier, A Tale of the Ruined City*, serialized in the *Literary Garland* in 1844, and *Monica; or, Witchcraft*, which appeared in the magazine in 1846. In both works, Moodie "demonstrates not only her awareness of gothic conventions" but "is also careful to point out that her characters, while perceived as witches by others, have more in common with mediums than with their folkloric ancestors" (Hodd 2014, p. 122).

For Hodd, Moodie's involvement with the Spiritualist movement "formed part of a continual quest for spiritual understanding that she had been expressing in her creative work since the 1820s" (ibid., p. 126).

Moodie's supernatural tale, "The Witch of East Cliff" (1827), combines her interest in otherworldly forces, witchcraft, and the occult, with one of her earliest examinations of the effects of an isolated, foreboding landscape on the imagination, a theme that she would rely on for many descriptions of the Canadian backwoods in *Roughing It*. Set in England, it tells the story of Joel Skelton and his encounter with the local witch, Rachel Lagon. Accepting a bet to visit the witch, and subsequently accepting her dare for him to look into her shed, Skelton recalls how he saw a pile of fishing nets rise up from a corner of the shed, after which the devil appears to him with a "black head and fiery eyes" (Moodie 1827, p. 18). Yet, the most Gothic description of Skelton's encounter with the witch's spell comes after he leaves the shed. Skelton assumes he is alone and feels thankful for having escaped the witch when he hears something quickly approaching behind him:

> I turned round to ascertain who it might be; but no language can express my terror, on beholding a jet black steed, with a flowing mane, and tail of fire streaming in the blast, advancing at that furious pace towards me. The earth trembled beneath his hoofs, and his course was marked by a blue track of light from the pine forest. Oh, how I wished, in that extremity of fear, that the ground beneath my feet would yawn and cover me—that I could hide myself in the bowels of the earth! (p. 18)

Alone and vulnerable on the isolated heath, Skelton is unable to protect himself from the demonic beast and only narrowly escapes death after the horse throws him into a nearby stream that is covered with ice.

A comparable situation can be found in Moodie's novel *The World Before Them* (1868). The orphaned young woman, Dorothy Chance, finds herself alone on a remote stretch of heath at midnight. The narrator makes it clear that though Dorothy finds herself frightened by her isolation, her belief in the supernatural also has a positive influence: "This fear of the invisible world, so inherent in simple natures, has been implanted for a wise purpose. It keeps alive a consciousness of the immortality of the soul, which otherwise might be disregarded by those who are separated by poverty and distance from coming to the knowledge of revealed truth" (1868, vol. 1, p. 158). The statement also has its roots in Moodie's own belief in extrasensory perception as a means of staying connected to distant loved ones in England while she lived in Canada. Communicating through spiritual means strengthened an otherwise fragile connection with those she loved and missed. Dorothy crosses the heath and enters a hollow where her mother died, a place local inhabitants say is haunted by the ghost of the dead woman. She becomes terrified when she senses the presence of an apparition, and this fear is compounded by her physical surroundings:

> her eyes, as if under a terrible fascination, were fixed upon the clump of furze that crowned the little ridge above, that looked so black and shadowy when all around was bright as day. While she stood, pale with horror, her eyes wide open, her quivering lips apart, the white teeth chattering together, and her limbs relaxed and trembling, a low wailing sound crept through the purple heath, the furze bushes shivered as if instinct with life. (ibid., p. 161)

Like Joel Skelton, Dorothy has no one to comfort her (besides a faithful dog) and loses consciousness after witnessing the supernatural visitation. In both her early stories and later novel, Moodie finds no comfort or solace in the natural environment; it serves only to heighten the fear experienced by the respective protagonists. This treatment of the unforgiving aspects of the natural world, away from towns and people, represents a recurring theme in Moodie's writing, a theme that would reach its pinnacle in "The Well in the Wilderness."

In a letter of November 25, 1852 to Richard Bentley, Moodie sent along her story, which would be published in his *Miscellany* the following year. Moodie describes the story and its inspiration, saying:

> "The Well in the Wilderness," is a real story. And its very truthfulness, gives it a horrid interest.
> The facts, on which this little sketch was founded, were told me by a person who knew the younger members of the Steels family; and the story made such as impression on my mind, that during a severe attack of ague, I used to rave about it during the hot fit, and I wanted my daughter to write it down for me to get it out of my head. This *I did*, as soon as I recovered, but it would have been more effective as the *nightmare* of my fever. (1985, p. 129)

The nightmarish quality of the story is reflected again in Moodie's epitaph, in which she seemingly speaks to someone who has "urged her to forget" the horror of the incident:

> In vain you urge me to forget—
> That fearful night—it haunts me yet;
> And stampt into my heart and brain,
> The awful memory will remain;
> Yea, e'en in sleep, that ghastly sight,
> Returns to shake my soul each night. (p. 87)

The story is the most horrific and unflinching piece of fiction Moodie wrote and the closest she came to Gothic horror. In many ways, it can be seen as the culmination of all her fears of the wilderness which she expressed in more restrained tones throughout *Roughing It* and in her earlier *La Belle Assemblée* sketches.[7]

First published in Moodie's own short-lived *Victoria Magazine* in November 1847, "The Well in the Wilderness; A Tale of the Prairie—Founded Upon Facts" centers on the emigration of the Steele family from England to Canada.[8] More specifically, Richard Steele, his wife Jane, and their four children must leave England because the family is unable to make a profit from farming. The property, containing a "snug little cottage" and "twenty-five acres of excellent arable land" (1991 [1847], p. 87) had been in the Steele family for many generations and represents both status and stability for the family. Yet, each year, the farm fails to make a profit large enough to support them, forcing them to emigrate. Early in the story, Moodie suggests that the family will pay an even higher price by leaving England through several ironic comments that gain tragic meaning by the story's end. On her birthday, Annie, the only daughter, refuses to sulk over having no presents for her birthday, saying instead that her family's love is "worth the wealth of the whole world" (p. 88). Steele responds by adding, "Annie is right […] we are all here to night, well and strong, aye, and rich, in spite of our homely fare, in each other[']s affections" (p. 88). Moodie wants her readers to hold this moment in their minds, a moment seemingly frozen in time, when the family was poor, but safe and happy. More importantly, she stresses to her readers that the family is together, a fact that will change as soon as their journey to North America begins.

Before the family sets sail, Jane, whose words echo those of Moodie herself, mourns her fate: "We have no longer a home in England. I was born here Richard [...] and it is so hard, to tear one's self away" (p. 89). Richard likewise reveals his own sadness at being forced to sell his family land, a break that also signals a loss of his sense of heritage. He says that selling the farm is "riving my heart asunder, to part with the roof which sheltered an honest race for so many years; but duty demands it of me, and now the debt is paid" (p. 89). But the family's debt is not yet paid for the purposes of Moodie's narrative, a story that serves as a stark warning about the consequences of emigration, forced or otherwise. On the voyage over, there is a scarlet fever outbreak onboard ship, and two of the youngest Steele brothers die along with several other children. These deaths also take a physical and emotional toll on the surviving members of the family. Jane becomes "wasted and worn to a shadow," while Annie "looked the ghost of her former self" (p. 91). The weakening of Annie will lead to greater tragedy later in the narrative, but the narrator insists that "human love" "lives in the present, lingers over the past, and cannot bear to give up, that which now is, for the promise of that which shall be" (p. 91). However, this sentiment is undercut by the end of the story.

The family settles in Illinois, though all the descriptions in the story are clearly based on what Moodie had witnessed living in the Canadian wilderness. Setting the story outside of Canada was in some way a coping mechanism for Moodie, who, writing the story while living in what she considered to be a dangerous wilderness, and herself having a husband and small children, preferred not to set such a tragic story literally so close to home. In the descriptions of the place where the Steeles settle, however, Moodie relives her own anxieties over being so isolated during her family's earliest days in Canada. The narrator describes how the family "began to think, that they had acted too precipitately in going so far back into the woods, unacquainted as they were with the usages of the country. But repentance came too late; and when at length, they reached their destination, they found themselves at the edge of a vast forest [...] no human habitation in sight, or indeed existing for miles around them" (p. 92). The family also realizes that they have chosen to settle in an area with no natural stream and must rely on getting their water from a distant well that lies "in the centre of a jungle" (p. 95). Although the water is "delicious," "clear as crystal," and "cold as ice"

(p. 93), the environment surrounding the water source is foreboding and unwelcoming. Returning from the well, the eldest brother describes its location:

> 'tis an ugly place […] I should not like to go to that well, at early day, or after night-fall […] 'Tis in the heart of a dark swamp, just about a hundred yards within the forest, and the water trickles from beneath the roots of an old tree, into a natural stone tank; but all around is involved in frightful gloom. I fancied that I heard a low growl, as I stooped to fill my pail, while a horrid speckled snake glided from between my feet, and darted hissing and rattling its tail into the brake. Father you must never let any of the women go alone to that well. (p. 93)

An outbreak of sickness descends on the family again, and both Annie and her brother are stricken with fever. In her delirium, Annie begs for water and seeing that there is none in the cabin, and the men are out working, Jane decides to go to the well, again ironically thinking to herself that "in reality there is nothing to fear" (p. 94). This, again, is Moodie indirectly suggesting to her readers that, in fact, someone thinking he or she is safe in the wilderness is actually what puts that person in potential danger. Thus, in a fictional story, Moodie is vindicating her own cautiousness. To her thinking, being scared all the time kept her and her children alive.

When Steele returns in the evening and finds that his wife has not returned from the well, he immediately goes in search of her. As he nears the well, his own fears increase until he reaches the spot and discovers his wife: "as he drew near the spot, his ears were chilled with a low deep growling, and the crunching of teeth, as if some wild animal was devouring the bones of its prey" (pp. 95–96). But this is not an "as if" scenario. On the contrary, this reality exists both within the action of the fictional story, as well as outside the story, as it is presumably based on a real event. Moving closer to the well, Steele sees, "a pair of luminous eyes glared like green lamps at the edge of the dark wood; and the horrid sounds which curdled the blood of the yeoman, became more distinctly audible" (p. 96). Steele manages to shoot the panther and it falls "across the mangled remains of his victim" (p. 96).[9] By lingering on the details of the horrific scene, Moodie makes sure both Steele and her readers face this reality: "It was not fear that chained him to the spot, and hindered him from approaching his dead enemy. It was horror. He dared not look upon the mangled remains of his wife […] How could he recognize in that crushed and defiled heap, his poor Jane" (p. 96). A neighbor then arrives and instructs his sons to bury Jane's "disfigured and mutilated body, before the feelings of her husband and children, were agonized by the appalling sight" (p. 97). Yet, the "quiet lovely spot" under "a wide spreading chestnut tree" does not lessen the horror of Jane's death. The site becomes "the nameless grave where the English mother slept" (p. 97), and time seemingly forgets Jane Steele. The remote settlement becomes "a prosperous village" and "Richard Steele died a wealthy man" who is buried beside his wife "in the center of the village church-yard" (p. 97). Yet, the peace and tranquility of the story's end feels hollow when weighed against the violent events of the story. The safety and comfort of the villagers are only achieved through the sacrifice of earlier settlers. Jane Steele, and many like her, will never partake of the village's prosperity.

John Thurston sees this as one of Moodie's most hopeless, desolate stories, claiming, "The one time she tried to bring her fiction to her New World home she produced a shocking image of loss of faith in God's ability to engineer happy plots for immigrating heroines [...] she unravels European romance and replaces it with American tragedy—writing was her way of questioning decisions about her life that she felt she had had no choice but to make" (1996, p. 107). In "The Well in the Wilderness," Susanna Moodie asks what price is paid for progress, and is such progress worth the lives of people like Jane? Writing amidst the Canadian wilderness in the 1840s, before the growth of so many of the prosperous villages imagined in her story, her answer would most likely have been no.

In their study of the Canadian postcolonial Gothic, Cynthia Sugars and Gerry Turcotte claim that "gothic discourse is used to mediate forgotten histories and, in some instances, initiate forms of cultural mourning (signalling a loss of cultural memory/history resulting from colonialism or migration or, alternatively, because of a perceived illegitimacy in one's tenancy of the land)" (2009, p. xi). In other words, Gothic is a way of describing what is lost or what must be reimagined in the process of emigration. The stable life, the status quo that existed on the home shores of Britain, becomes the unknown, disjointed new life of the colonial settler. In the case of Susanna Moodie, her descriptions of the danger and violence that awaits emigrants in the backwoods of Canada are representations of both "forgotten histories" and "cultural mourning"—what (and who) had to be sacrificed for the sake of a modern and civilized British colony.

Notes

1. Susanna Moodie and her family were part of what is known as the "Great Migration" from the British Isles to Canada from c. 1815–1850. The growing numbers of English, Irish, Scottish, and Welsh emigrating to Upper Canada during this period was influenced by an agricultural and economic depression that impacted Britain following the Napoleonic Wars. The competition for decreasing job opportunities was made worse by a large population of discharged British soldiers returning from the Napoleonic Wars and the War of 1812 who were looking for new employment prospects. For more on British emigration to Canada during this period, see Helen Cowan's *British Emigration to British North America* (University of Toronto Press, 1961), Elizabeth Jane Errington's chapter, "British Migration and British America, 1783–1867," in Phillip Buckner's *Canada and the British Empire* (Oxford University Press, 2008, pp. 140–159), Errington's *Emigrant Worlds and Transatlantic Communities* (McGill-Queen's University Press, 2007), and Lucille H. Campey's *Seeking a Better Future: The English Pioneers of Ontario and Quebec* (Dundurn Press, 2012).
2. Gillian Whitlock and Christa Zeller Thomas suggest that John Dunbar Moodie's frequent absences throughout *Roughing It* are described by Susanna as another way to foreground her vulnerability in the backwoods. This, too, fits with her role as Gothic heroine. In the dramatized world she creates, the absence of Moodie as the male protector—the "hero" in Susanna's narrative—puts her in even more potential danger.
3. Herself a pioneer in the Canadian Gothic genre, Margaret Atwood has used Susanna Moodie and her "ghost" as inspiration for her book of poetry, *The Journals of Susanna Moodie* (1970), as well as Moodie's account of Grace Marks in *Life in the Clearings Versus the Bush* (1853) for her historical novel, *Alias Grace* (1996).
4. According to Ballstadt, Hopkins, and Peterman in their edition of Susanna Moodie's letters, she was well-read in the contemporary theories of the Spiritualist movement. In addition to numerous reports of spirit manifestation that appeared in Canadian newspapers, as well as the New York newspapers the *Albion* and *Tribune*, Moodie read several books on the subject, such as John W. Edmonds and George T. Dexter's *Spiritualism* (1853), Nathaniel Tallmadge's edition *The Healing of the Nations* (1855), Robert Hare's *Experimental Investigation of Spirit Manifestations, Demonstrating the Existence of Spirits and Their Communion with Mortals* (1855), E. W. Capron's *Modern Spiritualism: Its Facts and Fanaticisms, Its Consistencies and Contradictions* (1855) (Ballstadt et al. 1985, pp. 118–121).

5. According to Ballstadt, Hopkins, and Peterman, the Fox sisters lived near Belleville before moving to New York. The eldest Fox sister, Elizabeth Ousterhout, lived in Consecon, and during one of Kate and Maggie Fox's trips to visit their sister in Canada, they met Susanna Moodie (1985, p. 119).
6. The Spiritoscope was invented by Robert Hare (1781–1858), a chemistry professor at the University of Pennsylvania, and described in his *Experimental Investigation of the Spirit Manifestations, Demonstrating the Existence of Spirits and Their Communion with Mortals* (1856).
7. The importance of drawing fiction from real life was the subject of Moodie's prose essay "A Word for the Novel Writers," which appeared in the *Literary Garland* in August 1851. Near the beginning of the essay, Moodie claims, "Most novels, or romances, particularly those of the modern school, are founded upon real incidents; and like the best heads in the artist's picture, are drawn from life, and the closer the story or painting approximates to nature, the more interesting and popular will it become" (p. 348).
8. The *Victoria Magazine* was founded in September 1847 as a cheaper alternative to John Lovell's Montreal-based *Literary Garland* (1838–1851), which had published many pieces by Susanna Moodie. The Moodies envisioned the magazine as one which would interest working-class Canadians (Ballstadt et al. 1985, pp. 73, 78–80). Although they sought to publish local Canadian authors, the Moodies and other members of the Strickland family supplied most of the content. By August 1848, after twelve issues, the magazine ceased publication due to financial difficulties (Ballstadt et al. 1985, p. 73; Peterman 1999, pp. 137–138).
9. Susanna Moodie was most likely describing the cougar, or what was called the "American lion." According to *Cassell's Popular Natural History* (vol. I, London [n.d.]), "In the northern districts it inhabits the swamps and prairies, living chiefly on different species of deer, on which it is said sometimes to drop down from a tree, which it had ascended to watch their path; or it makes inroads on the bogs of the squatter, who has gone to the unopened country. Other kinds of food, however, are sought after, and taken without much discrimination" (ibid., p. 122).

Bibliography

Atwood, Margaret (1995), *Strange Things: The Malevolent North in Canadian Literature*, Oxford: Clarendon.
Ballstadt, Carol, Elizabeth Hopkins, and Michael Peterman (eds.) (1985), *Susanna Moodie: Letters of a Lifetime*, Toronto and London: University of Toronto Press.

Bentley, D. M. R. (1989), "Breaking the 'Cake of Custom': The Atlantic Crossing as a Rubicon for Female Emigrants to Canada?" in Lorraine McMullen (ed.), *Re(Dis)covering Our Foremothers: Nineteenth-Century Canadian Women Writers*, Ottawa and London: University of Ottawa Press, pp. 91–122.

Buss, Helen (1993), *Mapping Our Selves: Canadian Women's Autobiography in English*, Montreal and Kingston: McGill-Queen's University Press.

Cowell, Pattie (1993), "Class, Gender, and Genre: Deconstructing Social Formulas on the Gothic Frontier," in David Mogen, Scott P. Sanders, and Joanne B. Karpinski (eds.), *Frontier Gothic: Terror and Wonder at the Frontier in American Literature*, Rutherford, NJ: Fairleigh Dickinson University Press, pp. 126–139.

Ellis, Kate Ferguson (1989), *The Contested Castle: Gothic Novels and the Subversion of Domestic Ideology*, Urbana and Chicago: University of Illinois Press.

Fowler, Marian (1982), *The Embroidered Tent: Five Gentlewomen in Early Canada*, Toronto, ON, Canada: Anansi Press.

Gerson, Carole (1989), *A Purer Taste: The Writing and Reading of Fiction in English in Nineteenth-Century Canada*, Toronto and London: University of Toronto Press.

Glickman, Susan (2007 [1989]), "Afterword," in *Roughing It in the Bush*, Toronto: McClelland & Stewart, pp. 593–602.

Hammill, Faye (2003), "'Death By Nature': Margaret Atwood and Wilderness Gothic," *Gothic Studies* 5.2 (November): 47–63.

Hodd, Thomas (2014), "'Not Legitimately Gothic': Spiritualism and Early Canadian Literature," in Janice Fiamengo (ed.), *Home Ground and Foreign Territory: Essays on Early Canadian Literature*, Ottawa, ON, Canada: University of Ottawa Press, pp. 115–135.

Lucas, Alec (1989), "The Function of the Sketches in Susanna Moodie's *Roughing It in the Bush*," in Lorraine McMullen (ed.), *Re(Dis)covering Our Foremothers: Nineteenth-Century Canadian Women Writers*, Ottawa and London: University of Ottawa Press, pp. 146–154.

Moers, Ellen (1976), *Literary Women*, Garden City, NY: Doubleday.

Moodie, Susanna (1827), "Sketches from the Country. No. 1—The Witch of the East Cliff," *La Belle Assemblée*, New Series No. 31 (July): 15–19.

——— (1851), "A Word for the Novel Writers," *Literary Garland* 9 (August): 348–351.

——— (1868), *The World Before Them*, Vol. 1, London: Richard Bentley.

——— (1991 [1847]), "The Well in the Wilderness," in John Thurston (ed.), *Voyages: Short Narratives of Susanna Moodie*, Ottawa: University of Ottawa Press, pp. 87–97.

——— (2007 [1852]), *Roughing It in the Bush; Or, Life in Canada*, Toronto, ON, Canada: McClelland & Stewart.
Northey, Margot (1976), *The Haunted Wilderness: The Gothic and Grotesque in Canadian Fiction*, Toronto: University of Toronto Press.
Peterman, Michael (1983), "Susanna Moodie (1808–1885)," in Robert Lecker (ed.), *Canadian Writers and Their Works: Fiction Series 1*, Downsville, ON: ECW.
——— (1999), *Susanna Moodie: A Life*, Toronto, ON, Canada: ECW Press.
"The Puma, or American Lion" [n.d.], *Cassell's Popular Natural History*, Vol. 1. London.
Sugars, Cynthia, and Gerry Turcotte (2009), "Introduction: Canadian Literature and the Postcolonial Gothic," in Cynthia Sugars and Gerry Turcotte (eds.), *Unsettled Remains: Canadian Literature and the Postcolonial Gothic*, Waterloo, ON, Canada: Wilfrid Laurier University Press, pp. vii–xxvi.
Thomas, Christa Zeller (2009), "'I Had Never Seen Such a Shed Called a House Before': The Discourse of Home in Susanna Moodie's *Roughing It in the Bush*," *Canadian Literature* 203 (Winter): 105–121.
Thurston, John (1987), "Rewriting *Roughing It*," in John Moss (ed.), *Future Indicative: Literary Theory and Canadian Literature*, Ottawa, ON, Canada: University of Ottawa Press, pp. 195–204.
——— (1996), *The Work of Words: The Writing of Susanna Strickland Moodie*, Montreal and Kingston: McGill-Queen's University Press.

CHAPTER 3

Gothic Romance and Retribution in the Short Fiction of Isabella Valancy Crawford

For years, what little has been written about Isabella Valancy Crawford has been focused on her reputation as a poet.[1] The scarcity of criticism on Crawford's fiction has also been caused by the lack of scholarly attention to the Canadian short story itself, which tends to be overshadowed by the development of the American short story in the early nineteenth century. In his survey of Canadian short fiction, Reingard M. Nischik notes that it did not become a "national genre" until the 1890s, and that it was not until the twentieth century that Canadian short stories "joined the realm of world literature" (2007, p. 1). Alexander MacLeod likewise argues that the "marginalized form of the short story has been consistently central to the major aesthetic and cultural shiftings of Canadian literature" throughout the colonial and Confederation eras (2015, p. 430). Yet, when Crawford's work is included in studies of Canadian fiction, the mentions are often brief or dismissive. As early as 1909, Lawrence J. Burpee noted that although Crawford had "won a certain amount of popularity with her stories," they "were more or less pot-boilers" (p. 2).[2] Nischik lists her name with those of Rosanna Leprohon, Susan Frances Harrison, Gilbert Parker, and Edward William Thomson as "other notable" nineteenth-century Canadian writers of short fiction, mentioning that they are known "for a few of their less formulaic stories reprinted in anthologies" (2007, p. 4). Michelle Gadpaille, in her study of the Canadian short story, admits that Crawford is among two women writers (along with Susan Frances Harrison) who are "worthy of mention," among nineteenth-century Canadian short fiction authors. However,

© The Author(s) 2018
M. Edmundson, *Women's Colonial Gothic Writing, 1850–1930*,
Palgrave Gothic, https://doi.org/10.1007/978-3-319-76917-2_3

Gadpaille's description of Crawford's work is far from flattering. Judging Crawford on the fact that she supported herself by writing, Gadpaille concludes that her short stories "reveal an amateurish command of structure, an extreme artificialy of language in narrative and dialogue, and a penchant for romantic twaddle" (1988, p. 11). In contrast, Clara Thomas claims that Crawford "was a powerfully gifted and tragically solitary woman-artist of the nineteenth century" (1979, p. 135), and compares her life and work to those of the Brontë sisters, most especially Emily Brontë. In her collection of Crawford's short stories, published in 1975, Penny Petrone asserted that, though her poetry was well-known, Crawford's prose had been "totally disregarded" by critics (1975, p. 9).[3]

The importance of Crawford's work in the genre of short fiction has recently received a much more complete appraisal with the work of Len Early and Michael Peterman, particularly their edition of her *Collected Stories*.[4] Not only do they gather the most complete collection of Crawford's fiction to date, but they also attempt to more fully appreciate how Crawford navigated the publishing world of the 1870s and 1880s, as well as the many ways her fiction goes beyond popular conventions of short fiction from the period. Beginning in 1873, Crawford began publishing with Frank Leslie, who was at the time a leading periodical publisher in New York.[5] Michael Peterman insists that "Crawford was well aware of the publishing realities of her time" and "was also playfully attuned of the romantic excesses and the narrative thinness of the literary material that Leslie required" (2005, p. 80).[6] He asserts that, despite these hindrances, Crawford "often found ways to be creative" (ibid., p. 74). According to Peterman, reading Crawford's short fiction "reveals a young woman who weighed her literary options carefully, reached out for the most reliable sources of income in her time, wrote copiously, and succeeded in certain of the marketplaces available to her" (ibid., p. 74). Early and Peterman note that Crawford's short fiction has been ignored for many years due not only to the fact that popular magazine fiction has only recently been accepted as worthy of scholarly attention, but also due to the "lack of 'Canadian content' in most of her stories" (2009, p. xiv). These factors have placed her fiction in what they call "a critical no man's land" because of "its publication context, non-Canadian settings, and use of a model commonly regarded as inferior and pejoratively associated with female writers and readers" (ibid., p. xiv).

What makes her work much more than the often-formulaic fiction that populated the pages of such newspapers as Frank Leslie's—and another way in which she managed to escape the stylistic conventions of such publications—was her creative use of the Gothic romance, a form of literary escapism that dates to Horace Walpole's *The Castle of Otranto* (1764). In her survey of the Gothic romance, Edith Birkhead discusses the stock conventions of the genre, which include heroes, heroines, villains, imprisoned women, and tyrannical fathers, along with disguised identities, forbidden love, and travel through ominous landscapes (1963, pp. 20–24). Tracing the Gothic romance into the nineteenth century, Birkhead sees the Gothic chapbooks that were so popular early in the century as the precursors of later Gothic short stories and tales of terror (ibid., p. 186). Many of these stories "are Gothic novels, reduced in size," pieces of entertainment that cater to the same emotions that transfixed readers of the previous century: "this type of story makes a strong appeal to human beings who like to know how much of the terrible and painful they can endure, and who yet must ultimately be reassured" (ibid., pp. 187, 191).

Critics have claimed that Crawford's best work was done when she incorporated Canadian content, but her Gothic stories show an adept understanding of the creative possibilities of the Gothic genre that had its roots in the European tradition of her Anglo-Irish background.[7] Crawford's interest in "reports," such as the ghost stories related by her landlady Mrs. Hay, as well as her recording of various "Dreams and Manifestations," come from a long tradition of such stories of apparitions, dating back to Daniel Defoe's "The Apparition of Mrs. Veal" (1705), considered to be the first modern ghost story, and continuing through the nineteenth century, with such notable works as Catherine Crowe's *Ghosts and Family Legends* (1859) and Andrew Lang's *Cock Lane and Common-Sense* (1894).[8]

In addition to her interest in the supernatural, Crawford's work in the Gothic mode allows her to foreground strong women protagonists that resist the usual trappings of the weak and helpless women from earlier Gothic narratives of the late eighteenth and early nineteenth centuries. In this way, they become later reimaginings of Ann Radcliffe's central women figures who were "simultaneously persecuted victim and courageous heroine" (Moers 1976, p. 91). Ellen Moers discusses "heroinism" "as a massive force for change in literature," one that was developed by women writers and "was born, like so much else that was revolutionary, in the last decades of the eighteenth century and the first of the nineteenth" (1976, p. 125). In the novels of Radcliffe, women could enjoy a freedom not found in other novels of the period as heroines could partake in adventures that were previously limited to male heroes (ibid., p. 126). These were women who were very much on their own—whether voluntarily or not—and free to make their own decisions. This freedom functions through both outdoor and indoor travel. As Moers notes, "indoor travel" was even "more possible for women [...] For indoors, in the long, dark, twisting, haunted passageways of the Gothic castle, there is travel with danger, travel with exertion—a challenge to the heroine's enterprise, resolution, ingenuity, and physical strength" (ibid., pp. 128, 129). Yet, the "strength of sensibility" (ibid., p. 135) that is at the heart of Radcliffe's formation of the heroine in Gothic fiction was reversed by the male writers who followed her: "For most of them [...] the Gothic heroine was quintessentially a defenseless victim, a weakling, a whimpering, trembling, cowering little piece of propriety whose sufferings are the source of her erotic fascination" (ibid., p. 137). Moers suggests, however, that in the hands of women writers, the tradition of Radcliffean heroinism continued, expanded, and even "flourished," later in the nineteenth century:

> The Victorian woman writer's interest in Mrs. Radcliffe, long after her kind of mannered and genteel Gothic fiction had vanished from the literary mainstream, is a minor but interesting sign that women's literature flourished on its own traditions. More significant is the whole thrust in women's writings toward physical heroics, toward risk-taking and courage-proving as a gauge of heroinism, long after male writers had succumbed to the prevailing antiheroic, quiescent temper of the bourgeois century, and admitted, with whatever degree of regret or despair, that adventure was no longer a possibility of modern life. (ibid., p. 131)

Isabella Valancy Crawford was one of the inheritors of the Radcliffean Gothic and, along with other women authors of her generation, both in the colonies and on the British Isles, was integral to shaping the heroine as a progressive literary figure, a character with a will and agency of her own.

Yet, Crawford, in her dependence on the romance formula, also inherited a literary tradition that has been the continued subject of critical contempt. Laurie Langbauer begins her study of women and romance by admitting, "Whether conceived as a mode of erotic wish-fulfillment, or as a prose form auxiliary to the novel, romance is thought somehow proper to women and usually derided accordingly" (1990, p. 1). She continues by discussing how women writers were confined by both their gender and their chosen genres, stating, "Women and romance are constructed within the male order and the established tradition of prose fiction that grows out of and upholds that order; they are constructed as marginal and secondary in order to secure the dominance of men and novels" (ibid., p. 2). But if this is what was expected of Isabella Valancy Crawford—herself an unconventional nineteenth-century woman who chose a career over marriage—she would find ways to subvert these literary and cultural expectations, and use the supposedly formulaic, predictable, and outworn popular romance plot to her advantage. In this way, Len Early and Michael Peterman suggest that "Crawford's stories dramatize a persistent anxiety about and inclination to question dominant nineteenth-century codes of gender." Many of her stories "simultaneously affirm and destabilize conventional notions of frail and timid femininity through an insistence on the courage, initiative, and activity of their protagonists" (Early and Peterman 2009, p. xxii). By focusing on the inner lives and struggles of unconventional heroines, Crawford continues the tradition of earlier women writers who use the Gothic and supernatural as a means of questioning the status quo. Edith Birkhead notes that the Gothic romance in its earliest days "was full of sentimentality" and ultimately "did not reflect real life" (1963, p. 223), but she also recognizes subtle changes in the genre later in the nineteenth century, namely in the work of Charlotte Brontë. With Brontë's novels, "a more robust heroine, who thinks clearly and yet feels strongly, has come into her own" (ibid., p. 224). This change in the heroine is part of what Robert B. Heilman has termed the "new Gothic." In his examination of the novels of Charlotte Brontë, Heilman describes a type of nineteenth-century Gothic where heroines are "'unheroined,' unsweetened" (1958, p. 119) as these characters are given "a new sense of the dark side of feeling and personality" (ibid., p. 119). Much like Brontë, Crawford found "new ways to achieve the ends served by old Gothic," and, while keeping certain romantic and melodramatic conventions, she also "moves deeply into the lesser known realities of human life" through an "intense exploration of feeling that increases the range and depth of fiction" (ibid., pp. 121, 123, 127).

Heilman's description of the literary power of the Gothic novel is also a fitting summation of how combining the Gothic with romance gave

Crawford the ability to put her heroines in a variety of situations that would never be experienced in non-Gothic settings:

> In the novel it was the function of Gothic to open horizons beyond social patterns, rational decisions, and institutionally approved emotions; in a word, to enlarge the sense of reality and its impact on the human being. It became then a great liberator of feeling. It acknowledged the non-rational—in the world of things and events, occasionally in the realm of the transcendental, ultimately and most persistently in the depths of the human being. (ibid., p. 131)

This idea of a modernized Gothic heroine who represents a more confident version of womanhood reflects the contested views of femininity in literature and society at the time Crawford was writing. Eliza Lynn Linton, in her now (in)famous 1868 essay, "The Girl of the Period," urged women to reject independence and ambition, and to "come back again to the old English ideal, once the most beautiful, the most modest, the most essentially womanly in the world" (p. 340). Yet, many women refused to "come back again," in both their lives and their written work. Writing in 1886, Crawford's fellow Canadian Sara Jeannette Duncan happily bid goodbye to "the heroine of old-time, drifting fast and far into oblivion," who "was the product of an age that demanded no more of femininity than unlimited affection and embroidery." For Duncan, this change in the portrayal of the heroine was a direct result of women writers' increasing awareness of their own autonomy: "The advent of the blue-stocking suggested the introduction of brains into [the heroine's] composition [...] The novel of to-day is a reflection of our present social state. The women who enter into its composition are but intelligent agents in this reflection, and show themselves as they are, not as a false ideal would have them" (pp. 771–772). This chapter explores four stories by Crawford that show her mastery of the Gothic romance: "The Perfect Number Seven" (1880), "Sèvres Fulkes" (1885), "Extradited" (1886), and "In the Breast of a Maple" (c. 1887). The women at the heart of each story show the progression of the Gothic heroine into a more modern, self-actualizing figure who finds ways to resist traditional notions of femininity and who exhibits a greater agency in deciding her own future.

"The Perfect Number Seven" was first published in *Frank Leslie's Chimney Corner* on November 6, 1880. It was reprinted in 1883 in both *Frank Leslie's Pleasant Hours* (without Crawford being named as author) and in *Frank Leslie's Popular Monthly*. The story is, according to Early and Peterman, "a remarkable repertory of romance conventions." Events such as "a violent storm, a corpse that turns out to be alive, a return from the sea—[are] given a Gothic seasoning of vampirism and grave-robbing, and then transposed, astonishingly, to the key of refined social comedy" (Early and Peterman 2009, p. xix). Crawford's description of the scene that opens the story harkens back to Susanna Moodie's Gothic descriptions of a threatening natural environment, and, in its ominous characteristics, seems to exhibit some sort of supernatural, otherworldly feel:

> A night of shudders and shivers. The trees trembled; the ferns and grasses writhed snakily; a faint mist on the sky made the dim stars shudder; the wind quivered fitfully, and the sea crept up and down, to and fro on the ghostly beach like a frightened beast, shivering and listening for the stronger-fanged beast which represents its doom. (Crawford 2009a [1880], p. 292)

In its description of "a frightened beast" being preyed upon by an unknown, stronger opponent, Crawford prefigures the crime that is at the heart of the story's action: the kidnapping (in the form of robbing a grave of a woman who has been buried prematurely) and near murder of a young woman by two men who intend to use her body for dissection.

The description of the night on which the crime takes place reflects the horrific nature of the crime itself, while also relying upon the Gothic convention of nothingness and absence:

> The night was ghastly without magnificence, quiet without peace, dark without solemnity. The land was a phantom, the ocean a spectre, the sky an uncertainty. Nothing seized the glance but the revolving light of the lighthouse. No sound individualized itself but the shriek of a night-hawk wheeling, harpy-like, high in air. (p. 292)

Like the "ghastly" night that surrounds her, the introduction of the woman's body is also lacking in positive substance. She is described as something barely recognizable as a woman, as "the rigid thing [...] here and there a fold in its dark draperies indicated the bust of a woman, the taper limbs, a shrouded profile" (p. 292). Her "rigid" appearance also lacks the essential signs of life that fool the men into thinking she is dead. When Florian, one of the two men responsible for robbing her grave, is tasked with taking her body out to sea for disposal, he imagines the "dead" body moving: "its motion lent a secret sinister movement to the form stretched at his feet; it seemed about to arise and confront him, and his ghastly face streamed with drops of real anguish as he bent over it. Twice he made an effort to touch the silent thing; twice his hand dropped nerveless to his side" (pp. 293–294). Florian's fear and refusal to touch the woman's body contrast with his attraction to her by the end of the story.

As he continues out to sea, Crawford emphasizes the horrific nature of the crime and the sense of guilt felt by Florian. As he counts the rotations of the lighthouse lamp, his fear increases. Its light is "like some terrible opal full of supernatural meaning" and "sent a ghastly finger pointing across the sullen water at the frail boat" (p. 294). The boat "leaped on the hideous red like a sentient thing half slain by terror," with "blood licking the sides of the boat and spreading itself on the ocean for the black heaven to take note of" (p. 294). At the end of this intense countdown to the disposal, Florian must look directly upon the woman's body: "He lifted the sullen folds of black, and bent over a little marble face, with open, glassy eyes, blue, parted lips, and some tresses of fine, fair hair blowing over it [...] this morsel of fine clay daintily wrapped in snowy cashmere and satin, to which clung the odors of violets and tuberoses" (pp. 294, 295). Yet, this fragility belies the power that this woman will have over Florian's life after she returns from the dead.

As Florian lifts her body, Crawford ironically plays with the convention of the romantic embrace. Her head lies upon his breast "embracing and embraced" (p. 295). Her fragility is emphasized by Crawford's play of "form" and "foam": the "white form" and "ghostly garments" of the woman is set against "the ghastly foam, like froth from the very waves of death" (p. 295). When she moves in response to his action, he feels a fear greater than before, as if her living body is worse than her dead one. Her return to life happens simultaneously with the arrival of a storm at sea. According to Early and Peterman, "Although sensational events such as storm, flood, and wreck are to be expected, these outward catastrophes mirror the emotional turbulence of the relationships in which Crawford's lovers find themselves. The stories repeatedly suggest that powerful psychic forces subsist beneath the surface of decorum" (2009, p. xx). These psychic forces between Florian and the woman that influences him, almost against his will, to attempt to save her life at the peril of his own are joined with a physical contact that, with its erotic connotations of vampirism, also challenges "the surface of decorum." Florian decides to feed the woman with his own blood in order to sustain her life. Although he admits that his choice is "a trifle repulsive," he continues to act upon the lifeless body, saying, "Thank heaven, I have plenty of the vital fluid in my veins, and she shall never know that I transformed her into an unconscious vampire" (p. 296). This transfusion of blood seemingly connects the two because later in the narrative, when Phil questions Florian's recognition of Pollie, he insists, "who should know her again if I did not—I, with my life-blood in her veins" (p. 309). After Florian gives his blood to Pollie, he, too, becomes weakened and loses consciousness. The two then continue their "embrace": "His head drooped forward until it rested on the lily face his life had gone to flush with the flame of returning animation [...] the two silent, beautiful young forms lying dumb and motionless, drenched by the bitter, death-white spray" (p. 297). After the two are rescued by a passing ship, Pollie and Florian remain separated, and after realizing that she is covered in blood and that her throat has been cut (not realizing of course that most of the blood is Florian's), she regains her memory of the night she was taken from her grave, only waking in time to remember seeing a man cut into her neck.

In the second half of the story, Crawford continues to play with the conventions of romance and the comic Gothic. Thinking Florian has drowned at sea, Phil, his partner in crime, falls in love with Fairy Mosler, a widowed coquette who is related to Pollie. As with Florian, Phil remains haunted by his crime and tries to burn down the "shanty" where they brought Pollie's body for the dissection. He calls the place "a nerve centre of torment" and admits that "six months of Paris have failed to lay the ghost" of his guilt (p. 306). When Florian miraculously returns from the dead, much like Pollie, Phil is anxious for his friend to meet his fiancée. However, when he enters the room where he thinks Fairy is, it turns out to be Pollie instead. In a case of switched identities and subsequent confusion, the previous scene in the boat repeats itself, as Pollie faints at the sight of Phil and Florian, with the latter catching her in his arms once again: "his [arms] seemed to grow round her, and she moved upon his breast and fixed her amethyst eyes on him [...] involuntarily putting her hand to her throat" (p. 309). The moment then merges into morbid comedy, as, after Pollie regains consciousness and says, "*that* is the man who bought my body to—to cut up" (p. 309), Phil responds by saying that "it was all strictly professional." He tells Fairy, "I think the most hopeless moment of my life was when she woke from her death-like trance under the dissecting-knife, and I thought I had cut her throat when she relapsed into that fearful swoon" (p. 309). However, wanting to end her playfully Gothic tale—full of plot twists, near deaths, mistaken identities, and romance rituals—with an equally Gothic happy ending, Crawford allows Florian and Pollie to fall in love and to live happily ever after. The final scene of the two is reminiscent of their first deathly embrace, as "the ghostly rustle of a dress" is heard as they walk together and "his beautiful head [is] bent close to hers" (p. 310).

In the story, Crawford cleverly reverses several stock Gothic conventions. Eve Sedgwick has noted that two of the most important of these conventions are the "unspeakable" and the "live burial" (1986, pp. 4–5). In putting her hands to her throat at the story's dramatic climax, Pollie is expressing what she cannot speak. It is only after she wakes (yet again) from a fainting spell that she can describe the victimization of her body. Likewise, her live burial, which Sedgwick describes as symbolic of "the repression of the libido" and as a typical punishment for illicit sexual activity (ibid., p. 5), leads to the reverse, a happy marriage to her former tormentor-turned-savior-turned-lover. Pollie's burial and resurrection—her literal and figurative resurrection—leads to the moral reawakening of Florian. The image of the two at the end of the story harkens back to the scene of the pair in the boat, when Florian saved Pollie by sacrificing his body to save hers. Yet, by the end, it is Florian's head that is bent toward Pollie, and she has now saved him from a death-in-life existence by her love and forgiveness.

"Sèvres Fulkes" was published in *Frank Leslie's Popular Monthly* in September 1885. The entire action of the story takes place in the Rockby Asylum for the Insane and involves hidden identities, secret crimes, and, mostly importantly, a heroine who outsmarts the story's villain in order to save her estranged husband's life.[9] The story is also one of Crawford's most modern in terms of her descriptions of the conditions in a late nineteenth-century mental hospital, her characterization of the asylum's "new physician" Dr. Warring and his advanced theories on mental illness, as well as her inclusion of "telephone-tubes," "cablegrams," and telegraphs. The two patients are described to readers in the opening paragraphs through their case files. George Arleigh is a wealthy 27-year-old American diagnosed with "acute paroxysmal dementia" whose case has been "impossible to diagnose thoroughly [...] owing to unfamiliar symptoms" (Crawford 2009b [1885], p. 443). The title character, John Fulkes, is a 30-year-old American who "considers himself a Sèvres vase" and is a "harmless monomaniac" (p. 443).[10] However, in his misdiagnosis, Crawford begins to examine how appearances can be deceiving, especially Fulkes's "harmless" nature.

During one of Arleigh's attacks, Crawford captures the hellish atmosphere of the asylum and the pain suffered by incurable patients. As Dr. Warring approaches George's room, he hears "horrible outcries like nothing human" which "continued in one sheet of awful sound" (p. 443). As he enters the room, Warring sees "Case 100," as Arleigh is known, "struggling furiously in the grasp of four keepers—shrieking, foaming, convulsed; horrible and terrible" (p. 443). Arleigh's case continues to puzzle Warring, who knows that the patient will die unless he finds the underlying cause of the illness. Arleigh's own description of his condition emphasizes his suffering: "Imagine to yourself seven devils entering into you, and expressing their diabolism through your physical being, while your mind is clear enough to take accurate note of every throe and convulsion" (p. 444). What neither Arleigh nor Warring realize, however, is that the "devil" who expresses his "diabolism" through the suffering of George Arleigh is Fulkes, who in actuality is Harley Ferrers, a cousin who is secretly poisoning his relative in order to gain his inheritance. Crawford's descriptions of the duplicitous "Fulkes" manage to fool both characters and readers throughout the first half of the story, and, on subsequent readings, her craftiness in simultaneously describing and disguising Fulkes's true intentions become even more apparent. Fulkes is alone with Arleigh immediately before his attack, reading to his "poor friend [...] when he began to jerk" (p. 444). While outwardly being "very fond of the invalid" (p. 444), Fulkes also cleverly uses his supposed glass delusion to disguise his identity in order to fool his ailing cousin. To keep himself from "breaking," Fulkes is wrapped "from head to heels" in cotton, with "a thinner layer, with holes for sight and breath" covering his face (p. 444). He even develops a multi-layered lie that elicits even greater sympathy from his victim. Arleigh tells Warring, "That man is the best of good-natured fellows. Have you seen behind his odd mask yet? No! his face is terribly disfigured by some accident, and they say it was this misfortune developed the hereditary taint in him—he hid his face at first from morbid shame, now he conceals it to preserve its enamel beauty from mishap, poor fellow" (p. 445). Yet, his fragile condition, the thinness of his "mask," also reflects the tenuous nature of Fulkes's plan. He tells Warring, "You see how careful I am, don't you?," with the dual meaning of needing to be "careful" in his present situation (p. 444). In other words, Fulkes cannot risk being uncovered, literally and figuratively.

Disguised identity and feigned illness with ulterior motives is not confined to Fulkes, however, who is ultimately undone by a woman who manages to beat him at his own game. George's wife, Tolla Arleigh, arrives at the hospital under the name of Miss Grey, who supposedly is there to sing to the patients "in all sweet charity and pity" (p. 446). Yet, Tolla's function in the story is as a foil to Fulkes, and her mission to save her husband is an inversion of Fulkes's efforts to kill him. As Len Early and Michael Peterman note, Crawford's "'little women' consistently prove themselves courageous and resourceful, rescuing their powerful masculine counterparts from physical danger" (2009, p. xxi). Tolla's initial description as a frail, helpless woman is in keeping with Crawford's tendency to portray outwardly fragile but inwardly strong heroines. She is described as "a slight, girlish, dusky-eyed creature, in a primrose satin down to her slender ankles, a string of pearls round her beautiful bare throat, with a bunch of yellow Japanese primroses in her dark hair. A delicate and dainty dusky creature" (Crawford 2009b [1885], p. 446). Crawford intensifies Tolla's helplessness by making her blind. On her way to Arleigh, she "clings" to Warring's arm: "Her eyes, large and lustrous, were widely opened and fixed in a peculiar stare, and she had a trick of putting one small hand out in a groping fashion very pitiful to see" (p. 446). Much like Fulkes assuming the guise of a Sèvres vase, her beauty and perceived fragility bely her intelligence and ability to dissemble in order to fulfill her scheme.

The story she tells Warring helps to build the tragic romance of the plot. The two were married secretly, against the wishes of Arleigh's father, and, after the couple "quarreled about some trifle," Arleigh left Tolla, who subsequently fell ill and went blind (p. 447). She conveniently regains her sight after being reunited with her husband and proceeds to do what the doctors cannot. Warring, who represents an advanced view of medicine, maintains that Arleigh is not insane and that his condition is nervous rather than mental. Yet, he confesses to Tolla that despite consulting with other physicians, he cannot discover the true cause of his patient's sickness. Upon hearing Warring's incomplete diagnosis, Tolla confidently proclaims that she will make the difference in his case and will save her husband's life, saying, "Doctor, he will recover, now that *I* have found him [...] I *will* find out what you sages cannot" (p. 447).

Feigning blindness again, Tolla nurses her husband and is able to more closely observe Fulkes, who confesses to her, "Sometimes I think I should feel myself happier if I regained the ordinary osseous formation and cellular tissues [...] become a mere human being, in fact, instead of a priceless work of art" (p. 448). Crawford uses Fulkes's glass delusion ironically, considering, as Timothy J. Reiss says, that the delusion was often based on a desire of the sufferer to be honest and transparent (2003, pp. 32–38). Under the influence of Tolla, Fulkes almost drops his pretense in an indirect way of admitting his guilt. On some level, he would be "happier" being a "human being" again. Tolla's ability to put Fulkes at ease through her seeming helplessness is what ultimately leads to his downfall, allowing the romance plot to prevail. Without his knowing, she sees him put poison in Arleigh's tea (with a black powder, presumably from India, that is unknown to the doctors) and reveals her knowledge of Fulkes's entire scheme:

> "*I saw you do it*," she said, laughing, and flaming her eyes round on him in triumph. "I did not go blind a second time. I wanted to watch my treasure, and I dissembled. How confidently you stole behind me just now! How securely you dropped your poison over the blind girl's shoulder! Ah, Harley Ferrers, was there ever a more cunning plot than to follow the cousin who had quarreled with his wife and made *you* his heir, into the asylum, to finish your work, unsuspected, and secure his wealth. I knew your voice; you could not always disguise it. I watched you day and night; I waited, and you have been delivered into my hand." (Crawford 2009b [1885], p. 449)

Yet, this passage reveals that it is not just her pretended lack of sight that allowed Tolla to discover Fulkes's secret. She is also able to recognize his voice, making his many layers of cotton, his "mask," useless. She, too, planned her revenge carefully. For good measure, upon being figuratively "uncovered" by Tolla, Fulkes, still wrapped in cotton, is struck by lightning and suffers the painful death he had envisioned for Arleigh: "Wreaths of smoke puffed from him in yellow rings, a hundred tongues of flame made a horrible aureole round him. The lightning had fired his disguise of cotton-wool, and for a second he stood a pillar of flame, then rushed furiously through the open French window, blind in his savage agony" (p. 449).

The final paragraphs reaffirm Tolla's role in saving her husband when others could not. Fulkes's plan was successful "until Tolla's love-sharp eyes and ears penetrated his disguise, and enabled the valiant, tender creature to wrest his deadly secret from him" (p. 449). Crawford makes it clear to her readers that, in her version of the romance plot, the heroine saves the hero and defeats the villain. Tolla ensures her own happy ending not through chance or forces beyond her control, but through intelligence and cunning. According to Gerald Lynch and Angela Arnold Robbeson, in their study of the Canadian short story, the nineteenth-century romance was a particular achievement of women "who thrived on the margins of patriarchal society" (1999, p. 4). This point-of-view thus allowed stories by women to be more than "'merely' sketches, or effusive romances, or amateurish (and therefore dismissible) in any sense. They are fully realized short stories as accomplished and important in their historical-cultural contexts as any that came before or afterwards" (Lynch and Robbeson 1999, p. 4). Along with recognizing the importance of historical and cultural context when considering short stories by women, Crawford's ability to navigate and succeed in the publishing world of her day is worth noting. Len Early claims that Crawford's "best stories resist, subvert, and enliven the clichés of romance and melodrama through her command of irony, handling of perspective, and poet's sense of language" (2011, p. 112). Her stories "reveal a versatile imagination that draws upon a broad and eclectic range of materials to transform the popular modes in which she chose—or was obliged—to work" (ibid., p. 122). In the best examples of her short fiction, Early notes that Crawford's use of "evocative landscapes, reverberant allusions, and an adroit manipulation of genre allow her to extend the scope of typical story-paper fiction and imbue it with depth and significance" (ibid., p. 122).

"Extradited" was published in Toronto's *Globe* in September 1886 and is the most anthologized of all Crawford's stories.[11] Most scholars also consider it her best. Even Michelle Gadpaille, who had an overall negative view of Crawford's fiction, admitted that "in spite of a ragged narrative" and an "infelicitous way with words," "the dramatic intentions of the plot and the characterization of the wife (the men are mere stereotypes) are memorable" (1988, pp. 11, 12). Indeed, the most interesting element in the story is Crawford's complex portrayal of Bessie, young wife to the Irish-Canadian Sam O'Dwyer. The story's setting is one of early settler life in Upper Canada, and the O'Dwyers are making a clearing in the woods in order to establish a farmstead. Yet, in their new life, Bessie feels loneliness and privation. She is not used to the rough living that she must endure as Sam's wife, but she also feels that her husband does not put his family first. When she tries to embrace him at the beginning of the story, he "pushed her away mechanically" (Crawford 2009c [1886], p. 450), and asks instead about their hired man, Joe. Bessie firmly tells her husband, "I didn't marry Samuel O'Dwyer to have a hired man set before me and my child" (p. 450), a statement that will have ramifications for the rest of the story. When Sam learns that Joe is wanted for robbery and has a one thousand-dollar reward on his head in America, he intends to shield his friend from the law, but Bessie thinks instead of her child. It is a combination of her role as wife and mother that establishes Bessie's complexity and multi-dimensional characterization:

> Many of her exceedingly respectable virtues were composed mainly of two or three minor vices; her conjugal love was a compound of vanity and jealousy; her maternal affections an agreement of rapacity and animal instinct. In giving her the child, nature developed the she eagle in her breast. She was full of impotent, unrecognized impulses to prey on all things in her child's behalf. (pp. 451–452)

Yet, this mother's instinct is also accompanied by a continual disappointment in her physical surroundings, as well as a disappointment in her husband. This unhappiness encloses Bessie, who feels she must fight against the impotence that her marriage and child have placed upon her. The narrator tells us that "by training and habit she was honest, but her mind was becoming active with the ingenuity of self-cheatry" (p. 452). A former "pretty schoolmistress" from a well-to-do family, Bessie grows to resent her uneducated husband and feels "hedged in by the grim fence of routine knowledge and imperfect education" (p. 452). This sense of imprisonment extends to her home as well, with its "floor of hewn planks [...] the wooden benches, the coarse table, the log walls [which] started through the gloom like bleak sentinels of the great Army of Privation" (pp. 450, 452).

Having no qualms about turning Joe in to get the reward, Bessie plans to invest the money for her child, telling herself, "I'll bank every cent of it for Baby [...] I'm glad I know my duty as a parent—Sam would never see things as I do—and a thousand dollars is a sight of money" (p. 452). Yet, Bessie underestimates how differently she and her husband view the situation. When Bessie refuses to let Joe near her child, Sam lashes out at her, telling her that she should be thankful for all the help Joe has given them over the past two years. He leaves her no voice in the situation, telling her unequivocally that not only will they protect Joe at any cost, but that he plans to take them all to South America. He claims that, next to Bessie and the baby, Joe "is in the core of [his] heart" (p. 455). Yet, his actions say otherwise. Sam unilaterally decides to leave everything the family has worked for, not to mention taking Bessie away from her family, all in order to place the needs of Joe above their own. In his world, Bessie has no say in her future; she will trade her bleak prospects in Canada for an even more uncertain future in South America. Michelle A. Massé's discussion of "marital Gothic" is particularly useful in an examination of the gradual disintegration of the O'Dwyer's marriage. Massé describes this form of Gothic arising out of late eighteenth- and early nineteenth-century novels which resolves terror, horror, and danger through the conventional happy ending: a marriage between the novel's heroine and hero that represented "a sacramental expulsion of horror" (1992, p. 20). In these narratives, "perfect love supposedly has cast out fear, and perfect trust in another has led to the omission of anxiety" (ibid., p. 20). But, in later nineteenth-century fiction, these conventional happy endings were complicated as a way of reflecting the social entrapment of women in unhappy marriages. According to Massé, "horror returns in the new home of the couple, conjured up by renewed denial of the heroine's identity and autonomy. The marriage that she thought would give her voice (because she would be listened to), movement (because her status would be that of an adult), and not just a room of her own but a house, proves to have none of these attributes" (ibid., p. 20).

Yet, Bessie is too clever to fully give into Sam's attempt to silence her. She sends a secret note to her father, and, in so doing, takes control of her own future and that of her child's. When two detectives come to extradite Joe back to America, Sam again chooses his friend over his family. The decision is made for them when the baby jumps from Bessie's arms and falls into the stream near the house. Joe jumps into the water to save the child, which leads to his death:

With one sublime effort he flung the child on the bank, and then with the force of a battering-ram the first of Piner's logs crashed upon him. It reared against him like a living thing instinct with rage, and wallowing monster-like led its barky hordes down the rushing stream, rolling triumphantly over a bruised and shattered pigmy of creation, a man. (Crawford 2009c [1886], p. 458)

In this description, Crawford stresses the powerlessness of everyone involved in the situation. Joe is killed by the very logs that he and Sam depended on for their livelihood, and Sam, unable to swim, stands helpless on the bank, unable to save his friend from either the law or the logs. Bessie, too, is frustrated is her ultimate goal. Like herself, the logs seemingly have their own "instinct." Because he is killed, she loses the reward money. She is also instructed by one of the detectives to keep her plan to collect the reward to herself because Sam "ain't got no idee of dooty to speak of" (p. 458). This duty and her desire to be rid of Joe, according to Penny Petrone, is influenced by Bessie's "need for self-assertion" (1977, p. 114). In an underlying message/warning to Bessie, he tells her to keep quiet because of Sam's fondness for Joe, the detective seemingly understanding the tension that existed among the three. Suggesting that Bessie might be in danger if her husband learns the truth, he tells her that Sam "might cut up rough [...] You best keep dark, ma'am" (Crawford 2009c [1886], p. 458). This secret thus becomes another obstacle in the couple's relationship, with the last line of the story telling readers that Bessie saw herself "as an unrewarded and unrecognized heroine of duty" (p. 458).[12] The words "unrewarded" and "unrecognized" extend beyond her attempt at getting the reward money to secure a financial future for her child. Readers are left to see her life and happiness similarly "unrewarded," and her autonomy in her marriage "unrecognized" and non-existent.

Penny Petrone notes that "Extradited" describes "a frontier crisis" that contrasts two different mindsets: "one dictated by the head, which would rise above the poverty and struggles of pioneer living, and the other dictated by the heart which puts financial security second to the warmth and affection of the spirit" (1975, p. 12). Perhaps we should consider Bessie as somewhere in between. Though she does indeed wish to "rise above" her current lifestyle, her motives are complicated by motherhood and a love for her child that causes her to make difficult decisions that she deems necessary for their future well-being.

According to Len Early, instead of succumbing to the clichéd conventions of melodrama, Crawford "undertakes direct psychological analysis and pivots on the issue of moral choice central to classic realistic fiction" (2011, p. 121). Yet, moral crises are not solely confined to the realist mode. I would argue that, following Simon Hay's concept of a "naturalist supernatural" (2011, p. 92), Crawford is creating a form of "naturalist Gothic." In discussing the term, Hay claims that, in the late nineteenth-century, the ghost story "turn[ed] away from realism's project of explaining the social and historical networks of causation that make up society, and instead explain[ed] the psychological causes of individual actions" (ibid., p. 92). As an "unrewarded and unrecognized heroine of duty," Bessie exists as a particularly useful example of what many women were forced to sacrifice in order to survive in an unforgiving Canadian frontier setting. Though fictional, her struggles are very real and reflect the difficult decisions that settlers faced each day. This subject harkens back to the bleak picture of early settler life that became such a prominent theme in Susanna Moodie's fiction and non-fiction. The harshness of emigrant life was equally a part of Isabella Valancy Crawford's own life. She lived through the deaths of her siblings in Ireland and Canada, and endured her father's financial scandals and alcoholism which left the family destitute and almost constantly on the move. Canada helped to give Crawford her poetic voice but, in her fiction, it was not always the land of opportunity. The Gothic mode allowed her to show readers that loneliness and despair come in many forms, and heroines of duty, particularly colonial ones such as Bessie, rarely achieve happy endings.

"In the Breast of a Maple" is thought to be the last story Crawford wrote before her death in 1887, and exists as an unpublished manuscript among her papers in the Lorne Piece Collection at Queen's University in Kingston, Ontario.[13] The story employs the social comedy that Crawford used to positive effect in the second half of "The Perfect Number Seven," but transfers the setting to the wilderness of Lower Canada with its focus on two French-Canadian families. "In the Breast of a Maple" also relies on the conventions of Gothic romance to enhance its comic effect, and draws a well-defined heroine that defies previous interpretations of the stock character.

Marie de Meury is introduced to readers as she vigorously chops down the titular maple tree. She is a strong, physical woman who no longer timidly stands apart from nature (a theme used repeatedly in the writing of Susanna Moodie), but who instead bends it to her will: "Mademoiselle de Meury's fine jaw became steel, her raven brows contracted, she fixed her moccasined feet in the snow as a pine strikes its roots into the earth. She threw out her arms in a noble curve, and again, bright as a sharp young moon, her heavy axe head buried itself in the trunk of the maple" (Crawford 2009d [1887], p. 480). As the descriptive passage continues, Crawford describes Marie's physical beauty as a complement to her strength: "Her broad bosom swelled at the power of the stroke, proud crimson dappled her cheeks and then settled into the level, satin-red of a rose, her large nostrils swelled and grew fixed as marble, one snowy tooth longer than its fellows bit into her full under lip, her steady black eyes looked implacably at her sturdy foe, the maple" (p. 480). Her beauty is a distinctly Canadian beauty, and she is a product of the environment around her in her "clinging woolen skirt," with her face showing "the white glitter of an icicle" (p. 480). She is "like a large strong rose born to bloom in, rejoice in, and perfume the cold crystal Canadian air" (p. 483). Yet, her masculine qualities are balanced with her feminine ones, as "her knuckles grew large as a man's as she grasped the handle of her axe" (p. 480). Marie's positioning within the forest and her efforts in felling the tree make her a more active agent in her physical setting. The regular swings from her axe "built echoing edifices of sound" that beat back "the supernatural stillness of the forest" (p. 481). This oneness with her surroundings is also reflected in her knowledge of native folklore when she mentions the "Mu-se-gisk, an Indian spirit of the air" (p. 481).[14]

Marie's unconventional beauty draws the attention of the story's villain, Monsieur Dalmas, who muses that "an adorable woman with an axe in her hand is an anomaly" (p. 480). Throughout the story, he remains both drawn to and fearful of Marie's beauty and strength. Crawford shows her knowledge of the Gothic romance through the romantic clichés with which he constantly plies Marie: "have compassion on your slave who adores you! [...] the impetuous adoration of a heart pierced by your charms" (p. 482). Dalmas observes most of the action of the story cowering behind a tree, and his commentary provides much of the comedy. In his anger and frustration at Marie's refusal of his advances, he thinks to himself, "Adorable and ferocious wood nymph [...] she could not be always armed with an axe" (p. 483). His ugliness—he is described variously with "a fur collar [that] surrounded his little bald head, his thin nose protruded like a snipe's bill from its recesses" (p. 482) and later as "an ugly little yellow fog, the sweat rolling down his face and body in streams (p. 484)—is contrasted with the beauty of the heroines and hero of the story. In addition to Marie, Dalmas's son Jean, is handsome and in love with Marie's sister, Lucille, a character who comes closest to retaining the qualities of the eighteenth-century Gothic heroine. Her health fades after Jean leaves to seek his fortune, and she is described, in stark contrast to her sister, as a "slender figure flitting with the gentle step of a ghost in and out through the trees" (p. 481). During Jean's prolonged absence, she had duly "pined herself to a charming little phantom in her uncertainty" (p. 484).

To these playful modern imaginings of the Canadian Gothic romance, Crawford adds her own twist on the lost inheritance trope. After the maple tree falls and Jean is chopping off the limbs, they discover a pocketbook that belonged to Marie and Lucille's father. The lost pocketbook contained the receipt that was the only evidence that de Meury had paid off a mortgage due to Dalmas. The father had died shortly after losing his pocketbook in the snow, a death followed soon thereafter by their mother, thus leaving the sisters to "battle" their hardship "with all the pride and courage of their race" (p. 484). Dalmas, in turn, refused to acknowledge the receipt and took possession of the de Meury family home in order to force Marie into a financial desperation that would eventually lead to her accepting his marriage proposal. The finding of the receipt foils his plans and increases his fears of Marie. Dalmas, who, as the quintessential Gothic villain, has some of the best lines of intentionally over-the-top dialogue in the story, is forced to conclude, "that Amazon will insist on my retirement to the penitentiary" (p. 484). Continuing the theme of Marie's connection with her natural environment, her ascendancy over Dalmas's control is highlighted when she "screamed like an eagle" and "her head reared like a stag's" after finding the pocketbook (pp. 484, 485). Most importantly, the receipt frees the de Meury sisters from financial destitution, restores the possession of their ancestral home, and ensures Lucille's marriage to Jean.

Marie's reward is somewhat different, however. As heroine, she is rewarded not with marriage but with financial independence. Penny Petrone claims that though many of Crawford's characters are stereotypical and lack dimension, her heroines, on the other hand, "are often portrayed with spunk, with physical and moral strength, emotional and intellectual independence" (1975, p. 13). This is particularly true for the protagonists of "In the Breast of a Maple" and "Extradited":

Although Marie de Meury's characterization lacks subtlety, her attitude towards men and marriage at a time when any marriage was considered better than none is an independent one. Bessie O'Dwyer's stubbornness in resisting her husband's wishes for the sake of her son's financial security is symbolic of attempts by frontier mothers to make life less harsh for their children. (ibid., p. 13)

Both women are described by Crawford as "eagles" who protect themselves and those closest to them. The heroines in her stories not only become more complex through this emphasis on intelligence and self-preservation, but also retain their humanity in their efforts to preserve and remain true to their individual sense of duty and justice. In many ways, Bessie O'Dwyer and Marie de Meury can be read as literary reimaginings not only within the larger tradition of the Gothic heroine from her demure beginnings in the eighteenth century, but also as progressions in Isabella Valancy Crawford's career as a writer of short fiction. The creation of Pollie in "The Perfect Number Seven" and Tolla Arleigh in "Sèvres Fulkes" allowed Crawford to craft and refine her own changing versions of the heroine, and that character's importance in a modern Gothic romance, characterizations that eventually led to the creation of the even more progressive portrayal of Bessie and Marie. These later heroines also showcase Crawford's ability to create more complex Canadian frontier heroines, distinct colonial characters that emerge and benefit from the conventions of a British literary tradition.

In their edition of Crawford's short fiction, Len Early and Michael Peterman admit that her work "is undeniably uneven," considering that she worked at a fast pace in order to support herself and her family in the competitive world of nineteenth-century mass market newspapers and magazines. Ultimately, however, they conclude that her short stories "deserve critical attention and respect":

> At their best, they exhibit her characteristic flair for poetic language, ironic detachment, and sympathetic humour, and they reveal her shrewd sense of the short story's possibilities during the era in which she wrote. That she was fundamentally serious about her forays into fiction is suggested by the fact that she continued to publish it under her own name rather than pseudonymously or anonymously, both common practices in the world of nineteenth-century periodicals. (Early and Peterman 2009, p. xxxi)

In attempting to rescue Crawford's reputation as a fiction writer, Early and Peterman assert that her short fiction is an important part of a Canadian literary tradition which provides a link between the earlier stories of writers like Susanna Moodie and later Canadian writers of the twentieth century (2009, p. xxxi). Lorraine McMullen and Sandra Campbell call these nineteenth-century women literary "pioneers," both in gender and genre, "who were aspirants to wider fictional and worldly horizons" (1993, p. 11). Isabella Valancy Crawford's heroines are also pioneers. The conventions of romance and melodrama allowed Crawford to put her heroines in extreme situations and environments, mental and physical places that test these characters' strength and fortitude, and to showcase their ability to resist the inevitable victimhood that awaited female characters who populated earlier Gothic texts, particularly those written by men. The circumstances that formed Isabella Valancy Crawford's life played a direct role in these fictional portrayals and her work within the Gothic romance. Her story is also one of survival. Forced to emigrate with her family from Ireland as a young girl, she carried a literary tradition with her. And when she was forced to support herself and her family through writing, she used that tradition both to creative and financial advantage. In so doing, Crawford gives us a new type of Gothic romance, one that relies on progressive heroines who survive, find their voice, and grow stronger against all odds, much like the writer herself.

Notes

1. Even though Crawford is still mainly known as a poet, her overall reputation as a socially-engaged writer is still very much overlooked by critics. In addition to Crawford's biographers and editors, Katherine Sutherland has recently commended Crawford for her political engagement in helping to form a national literature for Canada through her examination of female sexuality and her more nuanced descriptions of indigenous culture, especially compared to earlier Canadian writers of the nineteenth century. Sutherland calls these aspects of Crawford's writing "politically progressive, even radical" (2008, p. 125). See her chapter "Re-evaluating the Literary Reputation of Isabella Valancy Crawford" in Jennifer Chambers's *Diversity and Change in Early Canadian Women's Writing* (Cambridge Scholars, 2008), pp. 120–138.
2. Though not as critically dismissive of her fiction, contemporary tributes to Crawford in the years following her death also tended to focus on her poetry. See, for instance, E. J. Hathaway's 1895 article "Isabella

Valancy Crawford" in *The Canadian Magazine*, which gives a brief overview of her work as a fiction writer before moving on to a more extended examination of her poetry (pp. 569–572). The following year, Thomas O'Hagan, in his survey article "Some Canadian Women Writers," devoted a paragraph to Crawford's work as a poet, saying: "Her death [...] was a distinct loss to Canadian literature [...] No Canadian woman has yet appeared quite equal to Miss Crawford in poetic endowment" (p. 782).

3. Despite being an early champion of Crawford's fiction, Petrone, in her unpublished doctoral thesis, finds most of the short stories, including 'Sèvres Fulkes" and "In the Breast of a Maple," lacking in plot development, characterization, style, and structure. Petrone singles out "Extradited" as the one Crawford story that "remains worthy of serious critical attention" (1977, p. 108).

4. Early and Peterman rightly note that they "use the term 'collected' rather than 'complete' [...] recognizing that other published short stories by Crawford may remain as yet untraced" (2009, p. xxxii).

5. Crawford's first published seven stories, poems, and a serialized novel with George-Édouard Desbarats's Montreal newspapers *The Hearthstone* and *The Favorite* but, according to Early and Peterman, found the experience "disappointing" (2009, p. xi), which led her to pursue future opportunities with Leslie's publishing company. Crawford was one of many Canadian writers who published their work in the United States. For more on the commercial incentives for Canadian authors to publish across the border, see Nick Mount's *When Canadian Literature Moved to New York* (University of Toronto Press, 2005). Crawford herself expressed her frustration with Canadian publishers in a letter of February 19, 1887 published posthumously in *Arcturus*:

> I feel that I should wish to introduce myself to your notice as a possible contributor to the pages of *Arcturus*. Of course the possibility is remote as by some chance no contribution of mine has ever been accepted by any first-class Canadian literary journal. I have contributed to the *Mail* and *Globe*, and won some very kind words from eminent critics, but have been quietly "sat upon" by the High Priests of Canadian periodical literature. I am not very seriously injured by the process, and indeed there have lately been signs of relenting on the part of the powers that be, as I was offered an extended notice of my book [*Old Spookses' Pass, Malcolm's Katie, and Other Poems*] in the columns of the—and the—. This proposal I declined (I suppose injudiciously), as I think it might have been given at first, instead of coming in late in the day, and at the heels of warm words from higher literary authorities. (p. 84; Farmiloe 1983, p. 60; Galvin 1994, p. 74)

6. For more on Frank Leslie's success in the world of newspaper publishing, see Joshua Brown, *Beyond the Lines: Pictorial Reporting, Everyday Life, and the Crisis in Gilded Age America* (University of California Press, 2002), pp. 24–29. Circulation for *Frank Leslie's Illustrated Newspaper* was, at one time, as many as 200,000 readers (Brown 2002, p. 28). By the 1860s, it was maintaining a circulation of around 70,000 (ibid., p. 62). According to Brown, "By the 1870s Frank Leslie's Publishing House [...] employed between three and four hundred people, including seventy engravers" (ibid., p. 62).
7. Crawford would have had access to a wide range of reading material throughout her life. According to Early and Peterman,

   > By the time she began to publish she was well versed in the Bible, Longfellow, Tennyson, Shakespeare, Dickens, Byron, Thomas Moore, Milton, and Thackeray, along with a retinue of other large or lesser literary names (Goethe, Louisa May Alcott, Agnes Strickland, Washington Irving) even as she had gained a working knowledge of art history [...] music [...] mythology, and history, likely through books available to her in her father's library or through the kindness of family friends. (2009, p. xii)

   After moving to Toronto, Crawford became a member (for a two-dollar yearly fee) of the Mechanics' Institute in June 1876. The Institute contained a library, reading rooms, a lecture hall, and a music hall. After the passage of the Free Library Bylaw in 1883, the Institute transitioned into a public library the following year (Farmiloe 1983, p. 50; Galvin 1994, pp. 61–62).
8. The handwritten manuscripts of "Mrs. Hay's Ghost" and "Dreams and Manifestation" are part of the Crawford Papers in the Lorne Pierce Collection, Queen's University Archives.
9. Crawford's inspiration for the Rockby Asylum was most likely the Toronto Lunatic Asylum, also known as the Provincial Lunatic Asylum, and 999 Queen Street, which opened in 1850 and was located only a few blocks from her residence in a boarding house at the corner of King and John Streets. The hospital was a popular tourist site. Susanna Moodie visited the asylum in 1852 and described it in *Life in the Clearings Versus the Bush* (1853). Crawford directly mentions "the Asylum" in Chapter 10 of her novel *Winona; or, The Foster-Sisters*, which was serialized in the Montreal periodical *The Favorite* from January 11 to March 29, 1873.
10. "Glass delusion" was originally discovered in the Early Modern era and discussed throughout the nineteenth century as a form of hypochondriacal melancholia. Two of the more famous cases of those suffering from the delusion were the French king Charles VI, and Princess Alexandra of Bavaria, who believed that she had swallowed a glass piano. In *Clinical*

Lectures on Mental Diseases (1883), Thomas Smith Clouston describes the symptoms: "The patient's depressed feelings all centre round himself, his health, or the performance of his bodily or mental functions [...] he cannot think because his brain is made of lead; he is made of glass, and will break if roughly handled. There are no limits to the fancies of the hypochondriac or the hypochondriacal melancholic" (p. 55). An 1891 article on "Mental Delusions" in *The World of Wonders: A Record of Things Wonderful in Nature, Science and Art* cites a physician, Dr. Millengen, who described a patient "who, believing he was a fragile glass vessel, would not sit down for fear of cracking himself" (p. 147). For more on the delusion, see Gill Speak, "An Odd Kind of Melancholy: Reflections on the Glass Delusion in Europe (1440–1680)," *History of Psychiatry* 1.2 (1990), and Timothy J. Reiss's chapter, "Essences of Glass, Histories of Humans," in *Mirages of the Selfe: Patterns of Personhood in Ancient and Early Modern Europe* (Stanford University Press, 2003), pp. 26–64.

11. According to Penny Petrone, the story may have been based on a real incident. Five months before "Extradited" was published, on April 14, 1886, the *Globe* included an article titled "The Extradition Difficulty" about a hired worker's murder. What became known as "The Keppel Tragedy" then appeared on the front page of the newspaper on April 24, 1886 (Petrone 1977, p. 126).

12. In his article, "Isabella Valancy Crawford and an English Canadian Sodom," Richard Dellamora reads Sam and Joe's relationship as homosexual, lending another layer of secrets to the story. He claims, "'Extradited' is a story about secrets and their construction within a genealogical narrative. Strong beyond his frame, sensitive, and well educated, Joe is haunted by a secret that remains nameless until near the end of the story. Bessie works to expose this secret in order to disarm a second secret that is yet more disturbing: namely the disruption of the family by Sam and Joe's entanglement" (Dellamora 2002, p. 20). In this interpretation, Bessie becomes representative of "the civilizing function of woman" in an otherwise uncivilized colonial setting (ibid., p. 19).

13. A letter dated January 31, 1887 from the editor of the *Pictorial Times* to Crawford suggests that the story would have been published had she lived: "Your story 'From the Heart of a Maple' is very acceptable, but for the present we are limited by space to short sketches not exceeding beyond 2 or 2 ½ columns. We might use your contribution a little later on [...] and if you chose to leave with us till then, we shall be happy to publish it" (Isabella Valancy Crawford Papers, Lorne Piece Collection, Douglas Library, Queen's University, Kingston, Ontario).

14. The Mu-se-gisk is mentioned in Charles G. Leland's *The Algonquin Legends of New England, Or, Myths and Folk Lore of the Micmac, Passamaquoddy, and Penobscot Tribes* (1884). In telling the Micmac

(Mi'kmaq) and Passamaquoddy story of the origins of Glooskap the Divinity, Leland includes the following description: "Now it happened in after-days that Glooskap came to see his uncle, and the child cried. 'Dost thou know what he says?' exclaimed the Master. 'Truly, not I,' answered Mikchich, 'unless it be the language of the Mu-se-gisk (P., Spirits of the Air), which no man knoweth'" (Leland 1884, p. 57).

Bibliography

Birkhead, Edith (1963 [1921]), *The Tale of Terror: A Study of the Gothic Romance*, New York: Russell & Russell.

Burpee, Lawrence J. (1909), *A Little Book of Canadian Essays*, Toronto: Musson.

Clouston, Thomas Smith (1883), *Clinical Lectures on Mental Diseases*, London: J. & A. Churchill.

Crawford, Isabella Valancy (2009a [1880]), "The Perfect Number Seven," in Len Early and Michael Peterman (eds.), *Collected Short Stories of Isabella Valancy Crawford*, London, ON: Canadian Poetry Press, pp. 292–310.

——— (2009b [1885]), "Sèvres Fulkes," in Len Early and Michael Peterman (eds.), *Collected Short Stories of Isabella Valancy Crawford*, London, ON: Canadian Poetry Press, pp. 443–449.

——— (2009c [1886]), "Extradited," in Len Early and Michael Peterman (eds.), *Collected Short Stories of Isabella Valancy Crawford*, London, ON: Canadian Poetry Press, pp. 450–458.

——— (2009d [1887]), "In the Breast of a Maple," in Len Early and Michael Peterman (eds.), *Collected Short Stories of Isabella Valancy Crawford*, London, ON: Canadian Poetry Press, pp. 480–485.

Dellamora, Richard (2002), "Isabella Valancy Crawford and an English Canadian Sodom," *Canadian Literature* 173 (Summer): 16–32.

Duncan, Sara Jeannette (1886), "Saunterings," *The Week* 28 (October): 771–772.

Early, Len (2011), "Border Crossings in Isabella Valancy Crawford's Story-Paper Fiction," *Canadian Literature* 209 (Summer): 109–125.

Early, Len, and Michael Peterman (2009), "Introduction: Isabella Valancy Crawford and the Nineteenth-Century Short Story," in Len Early and Michael Peterman (eds.), *Collected Short Stories of Isabella Valancy Crawford*, London, ON: Canadian Poetry Press, pp. xi–xlv.

Farmiloe, Dorothy (1983), *Isabella Valancy Crawford: The Life and Legends*, Ottawa, Canada: The Tecumseh Press.

Gadpaille, Michelle (1988), *The Canadian Short Story*, Toronto: Oxford University Press.

Galvin, Elizabeth McNeill (1994), *Isabella Valancy Crawford: We Scarcely Knew Her*, Toronto, ON, Canada: Natural Heritage/Natural History.

Hathaway, E. J. (1895), "Isabella Valancy Crawford," *The Canadian Magazine* 5 (October): 569–572.
Hay, Simon (2011), *A History of the Modern British Ghost Story*, Basingstoke: Palgrave Macmillan.
Heilman, Robert B. (1958), "Charlotte Brontë's 'New' Gothic," in Robert C. Rathburn and Martin Steinmann, Jr. (eds.), *From Jane Austen to Joseph Conrad: Essays Collected in Memory of James T. Hillhouse*, Minneapolis: University of Minnesota Press, pp. 118–132.
Langbauer, Laurie (1990), *Women and Romance: The Consolations of Gender in the English Novel*, Ithaca and London: Cornell University Press.
Leland, Charles G. (1884), *The Algonquin Legends of New England, Or, Myths and Folk Lore of the Micmac, Passamaquoddy, and Penobscot Tribes*, Boston: Houghton Mifflin.
Letter from Editor of *Pictorial Times* to Isabella Valancy Crawford. Isabella Valancy Crawford Papers, Lorne Piece Collection, Douglas Library, Queen's University, Kingston, ON.
Linton, Eliza Lynn (1868), "The Girl of the Period," *Saturday Review* 25 (14 March): 339–340.
Lynch, Gerald, and Angela Arnold Robbeson (1999), "Introduction," in Gerald Lynch and Angela Arnold Robbeson (eds.), *Dominant Impressions: Essays on the Canadian Short Story*, Ottawa: University of Ottawa Press, pp. 1–8.
MacLeod, Alexander (2015), "The Canadian Short Story in English: Aesthetic Agency, Social Change, and the Shifting Canon," in Cynthia Sugars (ed.), *The Oxford Handbook of Canadian Literature*, Oxford: Oxford University Press, pp. 426–447.
Martin, Mary F. (1972), "The Short Life of Isabella Valancy Crawford," *Dalhousie Review* 52 (Autumn): 390–400.
Massé, Michelle A. (1992), *In the Name of Love: Women, Masochism, and the Gothic*, Ithaca and London: Cornell University Press.
McMullen, Lorraine, and Sandra Campbell (1993), "Introduction," in Lorraine McMullen and Sandra Campbell (eds.), *Aspiring Women: Short Stories by Canadian Women*, Ottawa: University of Ottawa Press, pp. 1–11.
"Mental Delusions" (1891), *The World of Wonders: A Record of Things Wonderful in Nature, Science, and Art*, London: Cassell.
Moers, Ellen (1976), *Literary Women*, Garden City, NY: Doubleday.
Moodie, Susanna (1989 [1853]), *Life in the Clearings Versus the Bush*, Toronto: McClelland & Stewart.
Nischik, Reingard M. (2007), "The Canadian Short Story: Status, Criticism, Historical Survey," in Reingard M. Nischik (ed.), *The Canadian Short Story: Interpretations*, Rochester, NY: Camden House, pp. 1–39.
O'Hagan, Thomas (1896), "Some Canadian Women Writers," *Catholic World* 63 (September): 779–795.

Peterman, Michael (2005), "Writing for the Illustrated Story Papers in the 1870s: Individuality and Conformity in Isabella Valancy Crawford's Stories and Serialized Fiction," *Short Story* 13.1: 73–87.

Petrone, Penny (1975), "Introduction," in Penny Petrone (ed.), *Selected Short Stories of Isabella Valancy Crawford*, Ottawa: University of Ottawa Press, pp. 9–16.

——— (1977), *The Imaginative Achievement of Isabella Valancy Crawford*, Diss., University of Alberta.

Reiss, Timothy J. (2003), *Mirages of the Selfe: Patterns of Personhood in Ancient and Early Modern Europe*, Stanford: Stanford University Press.

Sedgwick, Eve Kosofsky (1986), *The Coherence of Gothic Conventions*, New York and London: Methuen.

Sutherland, Katherine (2008), "Re-evaluating the Literary Reputation of Isabella Valancy Crawford," in Jennifer Chambers (ed.), *Diversity and Change in Early Canadian Women's Writing*, Newcastle: Cambridge Scholars Publishing, pp. 120–138.

Thomas, Clara (1979), "Crawford's Achievement," in Frank M. Tierney (ed.), *The Isabella Valancy Crawford Symposium*, Ottawa: University of Ottawa Press, pp. 131–136.

CHAPTER 4

Generations of the Female Vampire: Colonial Gothic Hybridity in Florence Marryat's *The Blood of the Vampire*

Published in 1897 (the same year as its more famous counterpart, Bram Stoker's *Dracula*), Florence Marryat's *The Blood of the Vampire* has been recently rediscovered as a significant contribution to nineteenth-century vampire fiction. Yet, while the novel—along with Sheridan Le Fanu's *Carmilla* (1872), Mary Elizabeth Braddon's *Good Lady Ducayne* (1896), and Mary E. Wilkins Freeman's "Luella Miller" (1902)—is now established as an important work within the female vampire tradition, recent scholarship on Marryat's work has tended to overlook its connection to Gothic hybridity. The story concerns the young and beautiful Harriet Brandt, a psychic vampire doomed to destroy those closest to her. However, instead of making her protagonist the outright villain of the tale, Marryat chose to embed Harriet's cursed lineage and doomed fate within the British society in which she seeks acceptance.[1] With this idea in mind, the "blood" referenced in the title has little to do with the traditional notion of a vampire's lust for blood but, instead, with Harriet's mixed-race Jamaican ancestry. This "terrible parentage" includes a type of inherited vampirism which begins when her grandmother, the black mistress of a white judge in Barbados, is bitten by a vampire bat while pregnant with Harriet's mother. The daughter, in turn, is described as "a fiend," "a revolting creature," and as "a fat, flabby half caste." And although Harriet desperately tries to identify herself through her white father's line, he, though of "pure" English blood, is equally vilified in the narrative because of his vivisection and torture of slaves while living in Jamaica.

In January 1898, a negative review of the novel in *The Speaker* claims that though Marryat was "trying hard to be fashionably 'creepy' […] this vampire is no more terrifying to grown-up minds than would be the turnip-bogey of our childhood" (p. 29). The reviewer concludes by stating that "instead of being, as it is intended to be, appalling and blood-curdling," the novel "produces an impression of tediousness and disagreeable sensationalism" (ibid., p. 30). Considering Marryat's intention as a writer, Greta Depledge has argued that she, instead of relying on a more traditional portrayal of a monstrous female vampire, "has presented us with a 'heroine' who encodes many late nineteenth-century concerns such as transgressive women and sexuality, race, and ideas of heredity" (2010, p. xi). Significantly, in the context of Colonial Gothic, the novel also expands the traditional vampire trope through its concern with the negative effects of colonialism on Harriet and how her character represents contemporary anxieties about biracial women "passing" as white. These racist tendencies are echoed in *The Speaker*, as the anonymous review concludes, "Harriet Brandt is herself a victim of heredity, exercising her fatal gifts unconsciously and instinctively, rather than of *malice prepense*. The illegitimate daughter of a barbarous, vivisecting man of science and of a voluptuous Creole slave, she is scarcely likely to attain any high degree of moral perfection" (*The Speaker*, p. 30). After years living in Anglo-Indian society, Marryat would have been no stranger to prevailing theories of racial inferiority and the perceived negative effects of racial intermixture. In 1854, she married Thomas Ross Church, an ensign in the 12th Madras Staff Corps stationed in Penang. Marryat remained in the region until 1860, when she returned to England. In 1868, she published *Gup: Sketches of Anglo-Indian Life and Character*. Yet, this biographical aspect is often overlooked in critical discussions of Marryat's vampire novel. The British fear of miscegenation was particularly prevalent as the mixed-race children of empire increasingly sought to intermingle with white British society, in Britain itself and in the colonies. Indrani Sen has noted that biracial women symbolized "deep-rooted colonial anxieties" (2002, p. 86). Because they contained a mixture of "black" and "white," biracial women were thought to be inferior to both Indian and British women. Sen claims, "the factors of race, class and sexuality inflected the cultural constructions of Eurasian women with greater sensuality, weaker will power and, by inference, more proneness to 'immorality' than the 'native' woman" (ibid., p. 48). With these perceived "weaker" genetic qualities, these mixed-race women were viewed as a threat to the cultural and racial superiority of the British because they had the ability to attract, marry, and produce children with British men without having to reveal themselves as biracial: "European in her appearance as she is, the Eurasian woman, in a sense, signifies the black 'face' behind a near-white 'mask' and the marriage of the white man with the almost-white Eurasian woman is seen as a more immediate threat to Anglo-Indian imperial and ethnic identity" (ibid., p. 88). This attitude also points to deeper gender anxieties, as genetic deficiencies that derived from racial mixing were believed to originate in the Indian mother rather than the English father.

In the novel, Harriet desperately tries to distance herself from any connection with her maternal Afro-Caribbean background. She tells her friends, "my father was English, his name was Henry Brandt, and my mother was a Miss Carey—daughter of one of the Justices of Barbadoes!" (Marryat 2010 [1897], p. 13). In similar terms to Sen's ideas of anxieties surrounding a biracial woman's ability to pass as white, H. L. Malchow describes how vampires add another layer of cultural complexity to traditional "white seductresses" such as Haggard's She-Who-Must-Be-Obeyed and Stoker's Arabella, noting:

> there is also lurking in the vampire the powerful suggestion of an explicitly racial obsession—that of the "half-breed." Both vampire and half-breed are creatures who transgress boundaries and are caught between two worlds. Both are hidden threats—disguised presences bringing pollution of the blood. Both may be able to "pass" among the unsuspecting, although both bear hidden signs of their difference, which the wary may read. (1996, p. 168)

Robert J. C. Young claims nineteenth-century writers (such as the Brontë sisters, Conrad, and Haggard) "write almost obsessively about the uncertain crossing and invasion of identities: whether of class and gender [...] or culture and race" (1995, p. 2), an idea which suggests that this continuing involvement with nebulous identity is "*the* dominant motif of much English fiction" (ibid., p. 3). Young continues by describing the cultural power of the term "hybrid" from the nineteenth century to today, noting, "In the nineteenth century it was used to refer to a physiological phenomenon; in the twentieth century it has been reactivated to describe a cultural one" (ibid., p. 6). Young recognizes the major treatises of race as "contradictory, disruptive and already deconstructed," which leads the concept of hybridity to "[suggest] the impossibility of essentialism" (ibid., p. 27). Connecting nineteenth-century racial theory to a contemporary emphasis on the cultural ramifications of such theories and recognizing hybridity's refusal to fit into neatly defined categories allows a unique comparison to the structure of Gothic texts, which themselves often resist easy categorization. This comparison leads us to consider texts dealing with hybridity as distinctly Gothic in nature.

Genetics and heredity are at the heart of Marryat's novel, and the inescapable nature of the two form the foundation to Harriet's tragedy. Significantly, it is a doctor who warns people against any association with Harriet, putting Harriet's social "health" in jeopardy by frightening away would-be friends and acquaintances. This warning operates on two levels. Phillips reveals what he considers a real danger posed by Harriet's close connection with others, but this "taint" is based largely on Harriet's parentage and her racial mixture.[2] In prescribing that those nearest her should distance themselves from Harriet as they would from a person with a contagious disease, the doctor is essentially labeling her friendship as toxic and unhealthy. The nature of this advice reflects the power male doctors had over public conceptions of illness in the nineteenth century and beyond. As Athena Vrettos notes, "the doctor's claim to medical and scientific legitimacy" could be seen as "a symbol of masculine authority" (1995, p. 91). Indeed, the doctor and his diagnosis directly influence how Harriet is viewed by the society around her. Recalling his time in Jamaica, Dr. Phillips tells Margaret Leyton about Harriet's "terrible parentage" (Marryat 2010 [1897], p. 67). After being expelled from a hospital in Switzerland for performing experiments in vivisection, Harriet's father settles on his family plantation in Jamaica. In the case of Harriet's father, Marryat transplants vivisection to the colonies, a geographical context that allows her to address the horrors of slavery. Dr. Phillips tells Ralph Pullen that Brandt performed his experiments "simply for his own gratification and for no use that he made of them in treating his fellow creatures" (p. 77). Phillips recalls that Brandt would "decoy diseased and old natives into his laboratory, after which they were never seen again" (p. 77). After the bones of Brandt's victims are discovered, the servants gather together, kill both Brandt and Harriet's mother, and set fire to the plantation.

Phillips's description of Harriet's mother is equally derogatory. He calls her "the most awful woman I have ever met" (p. 76) and uses an atavistic description that is assumed to mirror her inward degeneration. He says:

> She was the daughter of a certain Judge Carey of Barbadoes by one of his slave girls and Brandt took her as his mistress before she was fourteen. At thirty, when I saw her, she was a revolting spectacle. Gluttonous and obese—her large eyes rolling and her sensual lips protruding as if she were always licking them in anticipation of her prey. (pp. 76–77)

His earlier description of the mother to Margaret is even more contemptuous and links the woman's outward appearance with her deranged personality:

> She was not a woman she was a fiend, a fitting match for Henry Brandt! To my mind she was a revolting creature. A fat, flabby half caste who hardly ever moved out of her chair but sat eating all day long until the power to move had almost left her! I can see her now with her sensual mouth, her greedy eyes, her low forehead and half-formed brain, and her lust for blood. It was said that the only thing which made her laugh was to watch the dying agonies of the poor creatures her brutal protector slaughtered. But she thirsted for blood, she loved the sight and smell of it, she would taste it on the tip of her finger when it came in her way. (p. 68)

Bram Dijkstra suggests that, in late nineteenth-century society, women who behaved in immoral or non-normative ways represented a threat to subsequent generations because their perceived "tendency to atavistic reversion [...] brought out the beast in man" (1986, p. 335). In other words, the woman was ultimately to blame for any "monstrous" offspring, an idea that was frequently applied to children who were the products of miscegenation. Dijkstra continues by saying, "The conjoining of bestial woman with the remnant of the beast in man could only spawn human animals, evil creatures from the distant past coming back to haunt civilization" (ibid., p. 335). Just as he blames Harriet's mother for her daughter's weaknesses, Phillips claims that the woman's degenerate nature is, in turn, a direct result of her mother being bitten by a vampire bat while she was pregnant. Though Malchow claims that "Marryat's introduction of the supernatural, the vampire bat's bite" is "nearly superfluous" (1996, p. 170), we should consider the transmission of vampire blood from the grandmother into the mother as another layer of hybridity. There is not only a mixture of human races, but a combination of animal and human as well. It is also significant that Marryat chooses "half caste," a word most frequently used to describe biracial children who were products of Indo-British unions. A derogatory term, it not only highlighted racial impurity, but also implied that the mixed-race person was a social outcast. Both Harriet's grandmother and mother were no doubt put in a similar situation as a result of their relationships with white men, with each woman being pulled from her own cultural group, yet not fully being accepted by white society either.

Though not actually a part of present events in the narrative, these women are in many ways present in the way they haunt both Harriet herself, as well as her past, present, and future. And although Harriet desperately tries to distance herself from the maternal side of her family, the genetic "curse" of these women continues to possess her. Considering the importance of the maternal in Marryat's novel points again to the importance of the vampire bat bite. The unwelcome violence of the animal's attack that penetrates the woman's body is symbolic of the equally violent sexual predation that she experienced as a young girl, a literal slave to the whims of a powerful white English judge. In her discussion of vampires and the maternal in Le Fanu's *Carmilla*, Angelica Michelis sees the anxieties of Gothic fiction in the late Victorian period as directly linked to the idea of the "open body," a body representative of "the social body as invaded by what is not 'proper' to it." Michelis states that "the vampire can thus be read as a trope for the relationship between mother and infant, as being representative of the ambiguous process of splitting, productive and destructive at the same time" (2003, p. 16). In Marryat's narrative, following the bite, the woman's death after delivering her daughter signals the beginning of a line of female (self) destruction within the narrative. The grandmother dies giving birth, her daughter dies at the hands of slaves, and Harriet kills herself in an effort to finally free herself from her ancestral curse. After describing both parents as terrible people, Phillips refuses to blame Harriet's father for any of her perceived shortcomings as a product of an interracial union. And later, the narrator echoes Phillips's sentiment when Harriet is described as "inherit[ing] a very fair amount of brains from her scientific father" (Marryat 2010 [1897], p. 149). Eschewing any negative paternal hereditary influence, Phillips describes Harriet's deficiencies as a direct result of her mother's hereditary line, telling Pullen:

> The girl is a quadroon, and she shews it distinctly in her long-shaped eyes with their blue whites and her wide mouth and blood-red lips! Also in her supple figure and apparently boneless hands and feet [...] I can tell you by the way she eats her food, and the way in which she uses her eyes, that she has inherited her half-caste mother's greedy and sensual disposition. (p. 77)

This represents three generations of women who are blamed for genetic qualities over which they have no control. Phillips remotely "diagnoses" each woman based on his own racial prejudices and anxieties. His words are telling of his fears of the sexuality the women represent. They possess "sensual," "supple," and lustful qualities, but, according to Phillips, who Depledge sees as Marryat's representation of "the patriarchal, authoritarian stance that was emblematic of late nineteenth-century medical practice" (2010, p. xxvii), these qualities can only lead to negative, destructive behavior. In fact, though Marryat was viewed by many of her contemporaries as little more than a popular writer of superficial romances, churning out a novel per year, her portrayal of Dr. Phillips and his views are very realistic when compared to medical treatises on the perceived dangers of racial mixing during the nineteenth century. For instance, as early as 1817, John Williamson, in his *Medical and Miscellaneous Observations Relative to the West India Islands*, warned:

> There are, however, many circumstances connected with the customs of the country, which the young European should avoid conforming to. Associations with black women, who become, by perseverance, companions, as well as bed-fellows, independent of other considerations, are too repugnant to a reflecting and honourable mind to be reconciled to; at least, it may be presumed that, when it does, degradation has found admission; and, from one step to another, it is to be feared, will reach those practices, by which so many fine young men have been ruined in Jamaica. (Williamson, vol. 2, p. 253)

Seen as both creators and destroyers of subsequent generations, Harriet's mother and grandmother receive no sympathy in the narrative for their victimization. Harriet's mother is "taken" as a mistress at only fourteen. Her youth and biracial heritage presumably do not allow her a say in her future. Likewise, Harriet's grandmother is only seen as a pregnant slave who, like her daughter, is the mistress of a white man. Although Harriet's friends try to be sympathetic regarding her parents, with Margaret proclaiming, "it is not the poor girl's fault," Phillips counters with an unsympathetic opinion that he presumably bases on scientific theory, saying, "The bastard of a man like Henry Brandt, cruel, dastardly, godless, and a woman like her terrible mother, a sensual, self-loving, crafty and bloodthirsty half-caste—what do you expect their daughter to become?" (Marryat 2010 [1897], p. 69). Like her mother and grandmother before her, Harriet's "curse" also forces her into the role of outcast based on both her race and gender. Phillips says, "She possesses the fatal attributes of the Vampire that affected her mother's birth—that endued her with the thirst for blood which characterised her life—that will make Harriet draw upon the health and strength of all with whom she may be intimately associated—that may render her love fatal to such as she may cling to!" (p. 79). Yet, this fatalness and Harriet's (unintentional) killing of several white people in the narrative serves as retribution for the past deaths of Harriet's black ancestors as slaves on West Indian plantations, particularly black women who were doubly victimized as slaves and concubines. According to Bram Dijkstra, through the figure of the vampire and femme fatale, women could deny "man's ownership rights" (1986, p. 334). This idea is relevant to how Harriet, the daughter of slaves, subverts the white ownership that killed her grandmother and previous generations. Her control over and killing of her husband is a perverted reversal of the slave/master, black/white paradigm.[3]

Marryat's emphasis on race also connects her novel to the soucouyant, a female vampire that is a part of Caribbean folklore.[4] Skin is an integral part of these tales, as it points to both the indeterminacy of the soucouyant's appearance and the demonic nature of a powerful black, female supernatural being. A major part of the power of the soucouyant is her ability to shed her skin and thus to transform her identity from "woman" to "monster." This shedding allows its own hybridity, as the soucouyant is often described as "something at once animal and human" (Anatol 2015, p. 43). In her supernatural form, which is typically represented as a fireball, she transcends all bodily restrictions. The soucouyant lives apart from other members of the community. According to Giselle Liza Anatol, "Her home on the edge of the geographical limits of her community therefore parallels her position on the cusp of society. [...] The soucouyant occupies a literal *and* metaphorical space outside the accepted boundaries; the woman is made monstrous by her repudiation of social norms [...] she travels outside the domestic sphere as well as the physical landscape occupied by ordinary humans" (2015, pp. 44, 45). This anxiety over reverse colonization—itself a major trope of the imperial Gothic—is also the subject of an important soucouyant tale in Gérard Besson's *Folklore and Legends of Trinidad and Tobago* (2001), which describes a character named Désirée who lives in Paramin, Trinidad. Accepting a bet from a member of her community, Désirée flies to London in a single night and steals a gold spoon from Queen Victoria. In her discussion of the soucouyant, Anatol recognizes the anticolonial message in this particular folktale, noting that Désirée's story represents "a challenge to colonial authority in its plot element of procuring gold from the British Empire and bringing it back to the Americas, from whence it was likely stolen in the first place" (ibid., p. 45). This fear of an African invasion of Britain can also be traced to popular fears over vampires. In the nineteenth century, according to Teri Ann Doerksen:

> Vampire texts, which became increasingly popular as the images of the Dark Continent proliferated, provided an exploration of illicit sexuality shrouded first in the construction of metaphorical "creatures of darkness," to replace the inhabitants of Darkest Africa, and second in the displacement of the kind of penetration involved in literal sexuality into the metaphorical realm of a somewhat different kind of "penetration." (2002, p. 140)

The destructive potential of African supernatural power—indigenous practices that were transported along with the human cargo on slave ships and subsequently established on the islands—was also reflected in contemporary accounts by the British in the West Indies. In *Obeah: Witchcraft in the West Indies* (1889), Hesketh Bell calls the belief in vampires "one of the most deeply-rooted of all the West Indian superstitions" (p. 161). This belief in the "loogaroo" is founded on women's presumed intimacy with evil forces. These women "have made a pact with the devil," in exchange for "occult power," and must harvest human blood to repay their debt to "the arch fiend" (p. 166). Eden Phillpotts's *In Sugar-Cane Land* (1894) discusses the practice of obeah and the Jumby, a ghoul-like creature, but when he moves on to discuss the "loup-garou," the Grenadian version of the soucouyant, Phillpotts's description mentions a specific African origin for the creature:

> Another Ethiopian monster, akin to the vampire or wer-wolf, is the loup-garou. These have similar vile tendencies as the Jumbies. Loups-garou, however, are addicted to habits which render them assailable. They always take off their skins when at work, to be cooler no doubt, and they invariably hide these coverings at the root of a silk-cotton tree. If anybody finds a skin, he can put the loup-garou who owns it in an extremely awkward position; because, if not returned, the owner catches a chill and grows faint and poorly from exposure, and ultimately fades away altogether. (pp. 166–167)

Likewise, Charles Dance in *Chapters from a Guianese Log-Book* (1881) focuses primarily on female supernatural entities and their destructive natures. In the section "Superstitions on the Coast," Dance describes the "Water Mamma," a mermaid creature worshipped by "the offspring of the old African slaves" (1881, p. 78), who lures people away from their families. Other female spirits are tied more specifically to the sexual nature of their physical bodies. "Long bubbies" are female ghosts whose "right breast [is] elongated or lengthened at pleasure [and] with which they threaten certain night walkers and flog others" (ibid., p. 79). "Cabresses" are the ghosts of dead courtesans who "visit dancing houses and other places of public resort" (ibid., p. 79). These ghosts reenact their actions in life but, in the afterlife, become more powerful and deadly through their ability to punish men. They "seem to enjoy the amusements, join in them, attach themselves to some reckless lovers of pleasure, and luring them to some desolate spot, break their necks or press them to death in the moments of dalliance" (ibid., p. 79). The soucouyants of Guyana are described in equally gendered terms but, unlike the other female spirits, are unnatural because they subvert the role of protective mother by preying upon children:

> These old women, by the recitation of some absurd lines, are said to be empowered to take off their skin, which they fold up and hide in a convenient place. They then anoint their skinless bodies, and assume superhuman powers. They fly through the air; they enter closed rooms, and suck the life-blood of infants. During the time that they remain without their skin, a lurid halo surrounds them. If the wrapped-up and hidden skin can be found and pickled while the owner of it is skimming the air high overhead, or, like a vampire bat, gorging and disgorging infant blood, it ceases to be of use when the hag attempts to replace it, for it burns the skinless body; and the charm being only for one aerial trip each night, the old wretch is bound to be discovered in the morning. (ibid., p. 81)

The soucouyant folktale, with its focus on a predatory female, provides another perspective from which to view Harriet. Phillips tells Harriet that she is "more of the *drawing* than the *yielding* order," but again this is linked back to her "inheritance" when the doctor claims that this characteristic "is a natural organism" (Marryat 2010 [1897], p. 162). Yet, Phillips founds his diagnosis of Harriet based partly on his knowledge of the supernatural incident involving her grandmother's pregnancy and this no doubt affects his vampiric description of Harriet's genetic "disease":

> I think it is my duty to warn you that you are not likely to make those with whom you intimately associate stronger either in mind or body. You will always exert a weakening and debilitating effect upon them so that after a while, having sapped their brains and lowered the tone of their bodies, you will find their affection, or friendship for you visibly decrease. You will have, in fact, *sucked them dry*. (p. 162)

That Harriet has this effect on men and women within the narrative shows her similarities with other female vampires of the fin de siècle—most notably, Sheridan Le Fanu's lesbian vampire Carmilla, but also the overtly sexual portrayal of the female vampire in Philip Burne-Jones's painting "The Vampire" (1897). This work, in turn, inspired Rudyard Kipling to write "The Vampire," a poem that eschews any supernatural content in an attempt to show the extent to which sexually-liberated (living) women are just as dangerous as their undead counterparts. As Carol Senf notes, the "growing awareness of women's power and influence" meant that "writers in the nineteenth century often responded by creating powerful women characters, the vampire being one of the most powerful negative images" (1988, p. 154). In Marryat's novel, this power ultimately proves destructive for Harriet and those she is closest to, even though she is far from being a monster. Her portrayal as a victim, despite the fact that her influence does cause the deaths of multiple characters, including her own husband, is directly connected to her "fatal heritage" (Marryat 2010 [1897], p. 176). Seeing that she is destined to harm others no matter how much she loves them, Harriet sees her death as the only resort. However, this death will be on her own terms. In this way, Harriet's death is an important counterpoint to the death of Lucy Westenra in *Dracula*. After she has been turned into a vampire, Stoker makes it clear that her sexually predatory nature must be contained. This containment is achieved through the male repossession of her body when the "heroes" of the novel drive a stake through her heart and behead her, actions which Elizabeth Signorotti terms "vampire lore's extreme phallic corrective" (1996, p. 624). Harriet, on the other hand, is allowed the freedom to choose her own end.

Despite her doomed heredity, Harriet Brandt is an important instance of the late nineteenth-century femme fatale, but one which is all the more complex because of Harriet's mixed-race identity and contemporary fears over biracial women "passing" as white within British society. In her portrayal of Harriet, Florence Marryat presents another version of the dangerous colonial outsider who lures white British men to their eventual doom, with the most famous figure being Charlotte Brontë's depiction of Bertha Mason, who, according to Rochester, "tricked" him into marrying her by hiding her family history. Yet, when looking at this tradition of the femme fatale and Harriet Brandt's place within it, we should also consider Marryat's earlier depiction of the biracial Lola Arlington in her novel *A Daughter of the Tropics* (1887). In her portrayal of Arlington, a woman with beauty and intelligence whose ultimate downfall is connected to her mixed-race ancestry, Marryat gives us a femme fatale that prefigures Harriet Brandt and a character that shows Marryat's continuing interest in highlighting the tragic destinies of biracial West Indian women who must try to survive within white British society. In the novel, Lola is, like Harriet, beautiful and alluring, a direct result of her mixed-race ancestry: "She was neither dark nor fair. Her dull blue-black hair and full brown eyes were Spanish in colouring and expression, but her delicately-tinted complexion, *piquante* nose, and rather wide and full-lipped mouth, betokened a mixture of English blood. Her speech, also, had not the slightest accent to betray a foreign origin" (Marryat 1887, vol. 1, p. 16). Originally from the West Indies, Lola is the secretary to the playwright Mark Kerrison. Kerrison admits that she "is a talented woman" who is "quick and imaginative" and who helps him write his plays (1: 32). Kerrison's friend, Colonel Escott, newly returned from India, continues to observe Lola and finds hints of her mixed-race background: "on nearer inspection he perceived that there was a slight wave, carefully smoothed down, in her blue-black hair, and that her cheek-bones were rather high, and there was a certain squareness of formation about the upper and lower portions of her face" (1: 35). Escott concludes that "if not faultless, she was a magnificent creature" (p. 35).

As Escott continues to be intrigued by Lola, he learns more about her mysterious past. A friend tells him that she was married to a money lender, "as great a rogue as can be found in the length and breadth of London," who brought her back from Haiti when she was about twenty years old (1: 46). Marryat describes Lola's mother, Madame Clairçine de Pellé, as darker in complexion than her daughter: "Her yellow skin was seamed and wrinkled—her course black hair had turned iron-grey—and the whites of her eyes were almost brown. She was only one stage nearer the possession of negro blood than her daughter; but all her characteristics inclined to those of the less favoured race" (1: 75). Along with this darker skin, Marryat connects darker motives to the mother's character. She encourages her daughter to poison her first husband and, later in the novel, urges Lola to administer a love potion to make Kerrison fall in love with her daughter. Living in poverty with her own grandmother, "Maman," in a slum section of London, Madame de Pellé obviously cares more for what Lola can do for the family financially than for the well-being of her daughter. The two women make a meager living from Maman's work as a fortune-teller. Maman's past in the West Indies is even more mysterious, as she is represented as being closer to the traditional rituals of the islands, rituals possibly involving cannibalism. When Madame de Pellé mentions Maman's witnessing of human sacrifice rituals at "the ceremonies of the Vaudoux" and how she saw the victims burned on altars, Lola responds, "And eaten them too, I daresay" (2: 206). Lola, in turn, "hate[s] and despise[s]" her mother and great-grandmother and "hated herself sometimes for having sprung from so unworthy a beginning, and almost wished she had been born a veritable negress than endued with blood that had a taint upon it" (1: 78). The narrator later tells readers that Lola's mother feels part of this racially-based shame, saying, "She was more than half afraid of her handsome and arrogant daughter, who, she felt, looked down upon her as an origin unworthy of her beauty and her position" (2: 196).

When Escott remarks that her origin "accounts for her colouring," the friend immediately makes a connection between Lola's heredity and her violent tendencies. He claims that her Creole "slave blood" caused her to stab her husband in the arm when Arlington insulted her regarding her mixed race (1: 47). When Escott mentions the possibility of Kerrison someday marrying Lola, Kerrison is adamant that he only cares for her mind and what her talents can do for him in the creation of his plays. As a wife, because of the "black blood in her veins" (1: 57), she cannot seriously be considered as a potential marital partner. Coming from India, Escott says that he has seen many wives "with that flaw in their composition," but Kerrison will hear none of it. He states:

> I have such a horror of it that I would rather marry a woman "with a history!" It is never purged from the system! The taint remains for ever! [...] Wait till you see her in a passion, and then it will come out. She turns green under emotion. But the blood is well diluted. I believe she's an octoroon—seven parts white. Still, it's *there*, and I should never forget it. (1: 57)

Escott tells Kerrison that he does "not share [his] prejudice to such an alarming extent" (1: 57–58), hinting that his time in India has made him more tolerant. He remains a loyal admirer of Lola, and learns more of her tragic story. She tells him that she was "forcibly married" to Arlington at the age of sixteen "without knowing what marriage meant, or what were its duties and its obligations." This marriage then led to "a life of horror, of deceit, and fraud, and chicanery—and I obliged, by threats of violence, to see it all, and appear to approve of it, and make no sign" (2: 17). In a later conversation with her mother, Lola's age at marriage is even younger and her position likened to that of a "slave" to Arlington. Lola blames her mother for this, saying, "You sold me as a child of fifteen to a horrible old Jew with the worst of characters, who initiated me into every sort of crime" (2: 202). Yet, from this traumatized background of use and abuse, Lola learns to rely on her beauty. As *A Daughter of the Tropics* progresses and Lola becomes increasingly entrapped by her scheming, Marryat focuses less on the regal nature of Lola's beauty and intelligence, and places more emphasis on her animal-like qualities. As her crimes begin to backfire, she is like a cornered animal, unpredictable and dangerous. Lola relies on her looks as a form of self-preservation, particularly as she uses her seductiveness to ensure that Colonel Escott continues to support and protect her.

Like Harriet Brandt, Lola is both victim and villain, seemingly forced into her self-destructive actions by a combination of bad parentage, abuse, financial dependency, and a desperate need to be loved. Lola uses Escott to achieve her ends to make Kerrison fall in love with her. Lola seems to truly love Kerrison and will use any means in order to win him.[5] She is described as having "the blind, unreasoning love of an animal" (2: 46) and turns "dark and vindictive" when a rival for Kerrison's affection appears on the scene (2: 52). Despite her machinations, Lola's desire for Kerrison is ultimately tragic because he cannot bring himself to consider her as a wife because of his prejudice against her racial background. She has value to him only insofar as she helps him professionally. When

Kerrison encourages Lola to write and stage her own play, a play which is performed to great success, this high point in Lola's potential career as a writer is immediately undercut when Kerrison accidentally drinks the poison Lola had intended for her romantic rival. Accused of Kerrison's death, Lola retreats to her mother's house, where Escott, still sympathetic, offers help. He arranges for Lola to secretly board a ship bound for Australia but, while Lola waits to set sail, she thinks she hears the police nearing her cabin. She chooses to commit suicide, jumping off the ship and drowning. Like Harriet, Lola feels that killing herself is the only way she can find peace and escape her guilt over accidentally causing the death of the man she loves.

Written a decade apart, both Lola Arlington and Harriet Brandt represent Marryat's attempts to present complex women, women who are simultaneously villains and victims, outcasts whose racial pasts come back to haunt them and those they care about. Significantly, these women—who are both initially well-meaning and self-supportive—meet their demise through a social ostracization and a fatal connection to a man who is the object of their desire. Because of their beauty, both Lola and Harriet represent how "the female body emerged in nineteenth century science and fiction as a particularly dangerous Gothic Other" (Davis 2007, p. 41). This danger is compounded by their biracial status within their respective narratives. Each is a physical and a social threat. Likewise, both Lola and Harriet's amativeness, which, in each narrative is seen as a result of their black, West Indian ancestry, is perceived as dangerous. In her discussion of *The Blood of the Vampire*, Octavia Davis claims, "The surface of Harriet's body exhibits conventional white middle-class feminine delicacy that belies not only the racial and social origins of the 'primitive' Other, but also the latent sexual tendencies that contemporary science defined as regressive" (ibid., p. 44).

Indeed, as both novels progress, and as the women experience an increased romantic desire for a man, Marryat describes them in increasingly animalistic terms, ultimately reinforcing stereotypes about those of mixed-race ancestry and echoing many of the latent fears concerning biracial colonial subjects, particularly women, who managed to assimilate into white British society. Though Harriet tries to distance herself from her West Indian heritage, there are several instances in the novel where she displays the racism inherent in the plantation system. This racist mindset can be seen as another destructive form of "inheritance." She tells Margaret that she loved the plantation overseer, "old Pete," the best because of the freedom he allowed her as a child. Yet, this freedom is connected to a dominating violence that Harriet exhibits against the slaves on her family's plantation. She recalls:

> We had plenty of niggers on the coffee plantation, regular African fellows with woolly heads and blubber lips and yellow whites to their eyes. When I was a little thing of four years old Pete used to let me whip the little niggers for a treat when they had done anything wrong. It used to make me laugh to see them wriggle their legs under the whip and cry! (Marryat 2010 [1897], p. 17)

In her delight at punishing the slaves, Harriet inherits traits from both parents: the vivisectionist father who likewise tortured slaves for his personal pleasure and the mother who enjoyed tormenting them as well. When Margaret is shocked by her blasé attitude, Harriet exclaims, "We think nothing of that sort of thing over there" (p. 17). Her use of the pronoun "we" is one of the few times that she chooses to identify with her West Indian heritage. Harriet's violence toward the plantation children is revisited indirectly later in the novel when Elinor Leyton tells Ralph Pullen that Harriet is so fond of children that she thinks "she would like to eat them" (p. 58)—a comment that associates Harriet with cannibalism and is reminiscent of Lucy Westenra's attacks on children as the Bloofer Lady, but an association that also points back to contemporary descriptions of Caribbean female vampires and their attacks on infants and children.

Harriet's animalistic traits are especially prevalent when she begins to feel a romantic attachment to Ralph Pullen, who later tells Anthony Pennell that he cannot consider Harriet as a wife because "she has black blood in her [...] it would be impossible for any man in my position to think of marrying her! One might get a piebald son and heir!" (p. 143). When Ralph touches her arm, "the animal" is "roused" in Harriet's blood (p. 62). Later, she is described as having "dark eyes [...] looking for their prey" and "restless lips [...] incessantly twitching" (p. 128). And when she finds she cannot control Ralph, she "had not the slightest control over her passions" (p. 89). In this fit of rage, Marryat likens Harriet to an angry dog: "The girl put her head down on the pillow, and taking the corner of the linen case between her strong white teeth, shook it and bit it as a terrier worries a rat!" (p. 90). As Ralph slips from her grasp, Harriet's lineage again comes into play. The narrator says, "All the Creole in her came to the surface—like her cruel mother she would have given over Ralph Pullen to the vivisecting laboratory if she could. Her dark eyes rolled in her passion; her slight hands were clenched upon each other; and her crimson lips quivered with the inability to express all she felt" (pp. 111–112). Susan Zieger likewise points to the racist undercurrents in Harriet's suicide note and claims that the note "reads like eugenic propaganda" (2008, p. 202). She states that Harriet's vampirism is ultimately "a racial defect," and her "vampiric dependency on white life becomes a eugenic threat that the narrative must eliminate" (ibid., p. 216). Zieger notes that though Harriet leaves her inheritance to her friend Margaret Pullen, her bequest is ultimately "a poisoned gift" because it "recirculat[es] the ill-gotten wealth of slave ownership back into the British economy" (ibid., p. 226).

Harriet's regret when she learns of her vampirism also has racial undertones. When she remembers the black wet nurses that died because of their contact with her, Harriet expresses remorse, but not as much as when she recalls the "little white child" Caroline: "Poor little Caroline! I can see her now! So pale and thin and wan she was! […] little Caroline *died*! Pete carried me on his shoulder to see the funeral and I would not believe that Caroline could be in that narrow box" (Marryat 2010 [1897], p. 165). Like her grandmother and mother, the black women who nursed Harriet are consigned to anonymity and remain nameless, while Harriet chooses to focus on the named white child. Zieger claims that in the description of the black wet nurses, Harriet represents the "whiteness that lives off and uses up its black colonized material" (2008, p. 223). On the other hand, in causing Caroline's death, Harriet "functions as the contaminating death of a terrifying proximity to blackness" (ibid., p. 223). Harriet's own conflicted, hybrid identity is likewise reflected in how she chooses to describe those she killed. The "I" who was given to the wet nurse is white, while the person who killed the "little white child" identifies as non-white (ibid., p. 223). By the end of the novel, Harriet, in killing herself, kills both black and white. In terms of ending and narrative choice, Marryat seemingly implies that the threat Harriet represents to society—as both a vampire and a biracial woman capable of reproducing—must be exterminated. Her death echoes the racial qualities of Lucy Westenra's death in *Dracula*. Teri Ann Doerksen has observed, in her discussion of how late nineteenth-century vampire literature mirrored fears of invasion by half-human "savages" from the "Dark Continent," that Lucy's seductiveness and primal urges as a vampire represented "a devolution, an active movement away from the Victorian concept of civilization" (2002, p. 142). As such, her "metaphorical harlotry" and "savagery" signal a reversal in the established social order of Britain. Lucy's transformation into a primitive creature who must satisfy animal urges means that "the colonizer has become the colonized, the natural order has been reversed, and the corresponding threat to English supremacy must be mitigated" (ibid., p. 142). In other words, Lucy must be destroyed by a group of white men whose duty is to uphold that "natural order." Yet, in Marryat's narrative, Harriet kills herself and simultaneously kills both black and white. In so doing, she becomes a microcosm of the cultural battle between both races. The races cannot live as "one" within Harriet's own body, just as they seemingly cannot live in harmony within society at large. Her death is thus a personal and societal tragedy.

What is left at the end of the novel is Harriet's desperate need to be connected to someone who accepts her past. Yet, her genuine love for Anthony Pennell is haunted by a cursed heritage that will not let her be happy. Through her suffering, Harriet must expiate her own sins, as well as those of her parents and the plantation mentality they represent. Though Pennell's death after his marriage to Harriet can be read as a metaphor for the societal deaths of men of the time who married biracial women, the event also serves to heighten the reader's sympathy for Harriet and the impossible situation in which she finds herself. According to Octavia Davis, "Marryat's novel offers no solace and no solutions; instead, it resists contemporary science by dwelling upon the pain Harriet suffers when she unintentionally kills her beloved husband" (2007, p. 52). Harriet has less beauty and intelligence than Lola Arlington, but writing a decade after *A Daughter of the Tropics*, Marryat continues her exploration of how these fatal women fight to survive in an equally-fatal race- and gender-biased society that turns women into monsters. As Malchow has suggested, Harriet's story is similar to the ultimate fate of Mary Shelley's Creature. Indeed, Harriet Brandt is far more like Frankenstein's Creature than she is Dracula. As she struggles with the knowledge of her vampirism, Harriet calls herself "accursed" and exclaims, "My parents have made me not fit to live!" (Marryat 2010 [1897], p. 177). While Marryat probably did not deliberately set out to retell the Frankenstein myth, the two novels share many similarities and comparing them helps to highlight Harriet's role as Gothic outcast. Each character is an amalgamation of different "parts" that cause them to be negatively judged based on their outward appearances.

Both have "fathers" who push the moral limits of science. As a child, Harriet is ignored by her parents. Both characters verbally express their desperate need for friendship, with neither being fully accepted by the societies they seek to join. Harriet accidentally kills a child due to her psychic vampirism which drains the life from the child. Finally, after blaming herself for her husband's death, she kills herself. Her last written words are again similar to Frankenstein's Creature: "Do not think more unkindly of me than you can help. My parents have made me unfit to live. Let me go to a world where the curse of heredity which they laid upon me may be mercifully wiped out" (Marryat 2010 [1897], p. 187). Enslaved by her heritage, Harriet can only escape through death.

By providing a sympathetic portrayal of Harriet Brandt—a portrayal that significantly departs from Charlotte Brontë's femme fatale, the vampiric white Creole, Bertha Mason Rochester—Florence Marryat ultimately complicates the more traditional imperial Gothic narratives of the late nineteenth century, with their xenophobic tendency to vilify and degrade the colonial Other. Though Harriet Brandt's presence does indeed negatively affect the lives of many of the novel's characters, Marryat suggests that the prevailing contemporary attitudes to those of mixed-race ancestry—and the perceived weaknesses that accompanied such racial mixing—become a fatalistic self-fulfilling prophecy for Harriet, who ultimately cannot escape her haunted past and who also cannot live fully within an equally traumatized present. Thus, she becomes the embodiment of the social outcast so long represented by the vampire, a being who is never allowed to be fully part of the world she or he is destined to inhabit.

Notes

1. Marryat's sympathetic portrayal of Harriet could be connected to her own "diagnosis" by a medium as having the qualities of a psychic vampire. In *There is No Death* (1891), Marryat recalls being told in June 1879:

   You are one of the world's magnets. You have nothing really in common with the rest. You draw people to you, and live upon their life; and when they have no more to give, nor you to demand, the liking fades on both sides. It must be so, because the spirit requires food the same as the body; and when the store is exhausted, the affection is starved out, and the persons pass out of your life. You have often wondered to yourself why an acquaintance who seemed necessary to you today you can live perfectly well without to-morrow. This is the reason. More than that, if you continue to cling to those whose spiritual system you have exhausted, they would poison you, instead of nourishing you. You may not like it, but those you value most you should oftenest part with. Separation will not decrease your influence over them; it will increase it. Constant intercourse may be fatal to your dearest affections. You draw so much on others, you *empty* them, and they have nothing more to give you. (pp. 174–175)

2. For more on the novel's relation to the concept of bestial women and contemporary theories of racial degeneration, see Brenda Mann Hammack, "Florence Marryat's Female Vampire and the Scientizing of Hybridity," *SEL* 48.4 (Autumn 2008): 885–896.
3. For an extended discussion of how these issues are addressed in the contemporary writing of Afro-Caribbean women authors through the figure of the postcolonial vampire, see Gina Wisker's "Celebrating Difference and Community: The Vampire in African–American and Caribbean Women's Writing," in Tabish Khair and Johan Höglund's *Transnational and Postcolonial Vampires* (Palgrave Macmillan, 2013), pp. 46–66.
4. Jean Rhys utilized the soucouyant tradition in her work. In *Wide Sargasso Sea* (1966), the former slave, Christophine, tells Antoinette, "Your face like dead woman and your eyes red like *soucriant*" (1999 [1966], p. 70). In Rhys's short story "The Day They Burned the Books" (1968), a servant describes Mrs. Sawyer with similar qualities: "Mildred told the other servants in the town that her eyes had gone wicked, like a soucriant's eyes, and that afterwards she had picked up some of the hair he pulled out and put it in an envelope, and that Mr Sawyer ought to look out (hair is obeah as well as hands)" (1992 [1968], p. 152). More recently, the soucouyant features in Helen Oyeyemi's *White is for Witching* (2009).
5. Throughout the novel, Marryat wavers between describing Lola's feelings for Kerrison as genuine love and a lower form of "passion." These feelings are frequently connected to Lola's race. At one point, the narrator tells readers that Lola "would have laid down her life for Mark Kerrison" (3: 3), but later claims, "The love which she had borne for her employer, and which (though the best feeling she was capable of) was but a morbid and insatiate passion after all" (3: 123). After the accidental death of Kerrison, Marryat reverts to describing Lola's feelings as a type of love that is limited by her racial makeup: "In her low-minded, animal way, she had loved the man" (3: 253).

Bibliography

Anatol, Giselle Liza (2015), *The Things That Fly in the Night: Female Vampires in Literature of the Circum-Caribbean and African Diaspora*, New Brunswick, NJ: Rutgers University Press.

Bell, Hesketh (1889), *Obeah: Witchcraft in the West Indies*, London: Sampson Low, Marston, Searle & Rivington.

Dance, Charles (1881), *Chapters from a Guianese Log-Book: Or, The Folk-Lore and Scenes of Sea-Coast and River Life in British Guiana*, Georgetown, Demerara: The Royal Gazette Establishment.

Davis, Octavia (2007), "Morbid Mothers: Gothic Heredity in Florence Marryat's *The Blood of the Vampire*," in Ruth Bienstock Anolik (ed.), *Horrifying Sex: Essays on Sexual Difference in Gothic Literature*, Jefferson, NC: McFarland, pp. 40–54.

Depledge, Greta (2010), "Introduction," in Greta Depledge (ed.), *The Blood of the Vampire*, Brighton: Victorian Secrets, pp. iii–xxxvi.

Dijkstra, Bram (1986), *Idols of Perversity: Fantasies of Feminine Evil in Fin-de-Siècle Culture*, New York and Oxford: Oxford University Press.

Doerksen, Teri Ann (2002), "Deadly Kisses: Vampirism, Colonialism, and the Gendering of Horror" in James Craig Holte (ed.), *The Fantastic Vampire: Studies in the Children of the Night*, Westport, CT: Greenwood Press, pp. 137–144.

Malchow, H. L. (1996), *Gothic Images of Race in Nineteenth-Century Britain*, Stanford: Stanford University Press.

Marryat, Florence (1887), *A Daughter of the Tropics*, 3 vols., London: F.V. White.

——— (1891), *There is No Death*, New York: Lovell.

——— (2010 [1897]), *The Blood of the Vampire*, Greta Depledge (ed.), Brighton: Victorian Secrets.

Michelis, Angelica (2003), "'Dirty Mamma': Horror, Vampires, and the Maternal in Late Nineteenth-Century Gothic Fiction," *Critical Survey* 15.3: 5–22.

Phillpotts, Eden (1894), *In Sugar-Cane Land*, London: McClure.

Rhys, Jean (1992 [1968]), "The Day They Burned the Books," in *Jean Rhys: The Collected Short Stories*, New York and London: W. W. Norton, pp. 151–157.

——— (1999 [1966]), *Wide Sargasso Sea*, Judith L. Raiskin (ed.), New York: W. W. Norton.

Sen, Indrani (2002), *Woman and Empire: Representations in the Writings of British India (1858–1900)*, Hyderabad: Orient Longman.

Senf, Carol (1988), *The Vampire in Nineteenth-Century English Literature*, Madison: University of Wisconsin Press.

Signorotti, Elizabeth (1996), "Repossessing the Body: Transgressive Desire in *Carmilla* and *Dracula*," *Criticism* 38.4 (Fall): 607–632.
The Speaker (1898), Rev. of *The Blood of the Vampire*, January 1, pp. 29–30.
Vrettos, Athena (1995), *Somatic Fictions: Imagining Illness in Victorian Culture*, Stanford: Stanford University Press.
Williamson, John (1817), *Medical and Miscellaneous Observations Relative to the West India Islands*, 2 vols., Edinburgh: Smellie.
Young, Robert J. C. (1995), *Colonial Desire: Hybridity in Theory, Culture, and Race*, London: Routledge.
Zieger, Susan (2008), *Inventing the Addict: Drugs, Race, and Sexuality in Nineteenth-Century British and American Literature*, Amherst: University of Massachusetts Press.

CHAPTER 5

Mary Kingsley and the Ghosts of West Africa

Mary Kingsley decided to leave her native England for an extended visit to West Africa in 1893 after the deaths of her parents. This initial journey would be followed by subsequent trips between August 1893 and November 1895, when the "Scramble for Africa" was at its peak. As Kingsley became more familiar with the inhabitants of West Africa, her views on ways to govern the region often put her at odds with Britain's official policies. In her writings, she criticized the Colonial Office, which, in her view, frequently took advantage of its power in Africa. Instead, she favored allowing local British tradesmen to establish greater rights in the region and to have the freedom to conduct their business without government interference. She frequently expressed her concern over the rights of indigenous people (and the British tradesmen who lived in the region) to retain some autonomy in their business and cultural affairs, and she herself brought goods to trade with West Africans.[1] Kingsley was raised as an agnostic, so she had little inclination to reform the religious views or customs of the African people with whom she met. She disagreed with the missionaries who tried to change traditional African religious practices into a sanctioned form of Western Christianity.[2] Kingsley recognized that her role as a proper, though unconventional, Victorian lady, as well as a travel writer, provided her a unique perspective from which to launch her social agenda regarding British rule in Africa. In many ways, Kingsley's enlightened political views make her an important transitional figure in British literature, representing both the last days of the Victorian period and the beginning of the modern world. Because of the relative ease with which she traveled in Africa, she understood that the walls dividing continents were breaking down. She saw spiritual matters as a way to show two separate and geographically distant cultures the possibilities and benefits of cultural understanding and mutual respect.

In his study of the imperial Gothic, Patrick Brantlinger classifies three central concerns for such writing: "individual regression or going native; an invasion of civilization by the forces of barbarism or demonism; and the diminution of opportunities for adventure and heroism in the modern world" (1988, p. 230). In similar terms, James Procter and Angela Smith note that within the fiction of Haggard and Kipling "the civilised explorer or servant of empire is constantly threatened by entombment in the landscape or loss of self-control because of disease and excessive heat. Here the colonised culture is given Gothic treatment as being itself the source of barbarism, temptation and horror" (2007, p. 96). Yet, Mary Kingsley uses her descriptions of West African spiritual customs to overturn each of these defining characteristics of imperial Gothic writing in the late nineteenth century. She puts herself in the position of explorer within her non-fiction to show how conventional Gothically-charged narratives of colonial anxiety are complicated when there is a more refined cultural understanding of those being colonized. Kingsley thus positions her writing as a counterpoint to contemporary views that characterized these colonized groups as dark, distant Others who had no definite culture or traditions of their own or whose traditions were overly superstitious and not as "advanced" as Western belief systems. In many colonial narratives, this perceived lack of civilization invites Western explorers to inflict their own culture onto colonized peoples. However, Kingsley's insistence on describing African supernatural customs in terms that her British audience could relate to allows her to refute the usual limitations—defined by Brantlinger—in imperial Gothic writing. Instead of regression or "going native," Kingsley emerges from West Africa a more enlightened, cosmopolitan person. Eschewing the more traditional (typically male) "civilizing mission" of empire, she takes an ethnographic journey through West Africa, proving that there are, indeed, plenty of opportunities to still find "adventure." And in the most important sense, Kingsley uses the spiritual and folkloric beliefs of West Africa to show that instead of "an invasion of civilization by the forces of barbarism or demonism," the African people have a belief system that mirrors that of her British audience. In doing so, Kingsley subverts contemporary narratives of colonial anxiety caused by fears of foreign invasion by the colonial Other and focuses instead on the fear West Africans have in their own ghosts. Her descriptions of apparitions, vampires, and demons are not meant to scare but rather to inform, to foster greater understanding between two cultures. In other words, she uses the language and subject matter of the imperial Gothic against itself in order to explore ideas of inclusiveness and cultural similitude.

Though best remembered today for *Travels in West Africa* (1897) and *West African Studies* (1899), Kingsley observed the spiritual and religious customs of West Africans in two important essays: "Black Ghosts" published in *The Cornhill Magazine* for July 1896, and "The Forms of Apparitions in West Africa," an address to the Society for Psychical Research, which was published shortly afterward in their *Proceedings* (1899). These essays attempt to bridge the gap between African and European cultures by describing spectral superstitions that are common to the people of both continents. Kingsley first seeks to understand the spiritual culture at the root of African belief before she assumes privileged knowledge of the region's past, present, or future. Her studies of West African folklore offer glimpses into imperial Africa at the end of the nineteenth century, and Kingsley's descriptions of supernatural African tribal life serve to bring the distant "dark" colonies into British homes, showing her audience that their own apparitions had much in common with African ghosts. Her detailed descriptions of West African spiritual traditions allowed the British public to begin to recognize how intricate a belief system Africans possessed. In so doing, Kingsley was able to advance her progressive cultural views, which insisted that Africans were no less human than Europeans.

Mary Kingsley was at heart an ethnologist, and, as she traveled in Africa, became increasingly interested in the spiritual life and customs of Africans. Through her study of such customs, she championed the cultures of West Africa. In Kingsley's 1897 address to the Folklore Society, "The Fetish View of the Human Soul," she says that sympathy with Africans allows her to better understand their culture: "It is, I own, no easy thing to understand Fetish: probably it can only be thoroughly done by a white whose mind is not a highly civilised one, and who is able to think black" (1897a, pp. 139–140).[3] For Kingsley, this ability to more fully appreciate local customs requires one to transcend cultural prejudices, though her statement still suffers from racialist undertones. Likewise, to understand the otherworldly, one must expand one's own thoughts above earthly, limited views. That same year, in "West Africa, from an Ethnologist's Point of View," she stated that her "capacity to think in black comes from my not regarding the native form of mind as 'low,' or 'inferior,' or 'childlike,' or anything like that, but as a form of mind of a different sort to white men's—yet a very good form of mind too, in its way" (1897c, p. 65). In many cases, she succeeded in forming lasting bonds with the West Africans with whom she came in contact. A 1901 memorial essay by Kingsley's longtime friend Alice Stopford Green cites an unnamed African, who said, "She thought our thoughts [...] Our inner consciousness was known to her" (quoted in Green 1901, p. 7).

Kingsley's spiritual sense was located primarily in the natural world, and she discussed this type of pantheistic spirituality at length in *Travels in West Africa* and *West African Studies*. Throughout her writings, Kingsley describes the otherworldly attraction of the West African landscape as a kind of "*Belle Dame sans merci*" (1897b, p. 11). In *Travels in West Africa*, she describes this spell as an all-consuming force:

> Nor indeed do I recommend African forest life to any one. Unless you are interested in it and fall under its charm, it is the most awful life in death imaginable. It is like being shut up in a library whose books you cannot read, all the while tormented, terrified, and bored. And if you do fall under its spell, it takes all the colour out of other kinds of living. (Kingsley 1897b, p. 102)

Later, she again warns her readers of the spiritual power of such a place:

> I warn you that with all precaution, the study of African metaphysics is bad for the brain, when you go and carry it on among all the weird, often unaccountable surroundings, and depressing scenery of the Land of the Shadow of Death [...] The fascination of the African point of view is as sure to linger in your mind as the malaria in your body. Never then will you be able to attain to the gay, happy cock-sureness regarding the Deity and the Universe of those people who stay at home. (p. 441)

In other passages, Kingsley describes her interactions with the African landscape as a kind of out-of-body experience:

> I just lose all sense of human individuality, all memory of human life, with its grief and worry and doubt, and become part of the atmosphere. If I have a heaven, that will be mine, and I verily believe that if I were left

alone long enough with such a scene as this or on the deck of an African liner in the Bights, watching her funnel and masts swinging to and fro in the great long leisurely roll against the sky, I should be found soulless and dead. (p. 178)

In this passage, she describes a kind of transcendence that allows her to become one with the environment around her. Even more importantly, Africa inspires this feeling. In a letter of 1899 to Matthew Nathan,[4] which was published in *African Affairs* on the centenary of her birth, Kingsley described herself in even more self-effacing, ghostly terms. She says:

> The fact is I am no more a human being than a gust of wind is. I have never had a human individual life [...] it is the non-human world I belong to myself. My people are mangroves, swamps, rivers and the sea and so on— we understand each other. They never give me the dazzles with their goings on, like human beings do by theirs repeatedly. (*African Affairs* 1963, p. 7)

According to Christopher Lane, "Kingsley sometimes gives herself an ethereal status, as though she were colonialism's revenant [...] an observer of humanity, to which ostensibly she no longer belongs" (2003, p. 100). The more she distanced herself from the Western world, the more unbiased and impartial Kingsley became as an ethnographer, who, according to Dea Birkett, "became one of the most forceful exponents of a non-evolutionary approach" (1989, p. 154). This distancing of perspective allowed Kingsley to view Africans more objectively than many of her contemporary writers. As Cheryl McEwan notes, "[Kingsley's] depictions of west Africans owed less to the ideas of atavism and primitivism (as expressed in the works of Haggard, Conrad, Wells, and Bram Stoker) than they did to late eighteenth-century portrayals [...] Unlike the late nineteenth-century romantics, Kingsley did not wish to see west Africans 'civilized' and Christianized but wished to see their customs protected from Europeanization" (2000, p. 139).

"Black Ghosts," published in *The Cornhill Magazine* in July 1896,[5] tries to bridge the cultural gap which existed between colonizer and colonized near the turn of the twentieth century. In the characteristic humorous way that is such a part of her travel writings, Kingsley begins "Black Ghosts" with the statement: "My own feelings regarding ghosts are those of Dr. Johnson's dear old lady. I do not believe in them, but

I am very much afraid of them" (1896, p. 79).[6] She shows herself to be much attuned to the spirit world of West Africa as she describes the ways in which the spiritual customs and superstitions of Africans are not that much different from those of her fellow English. Her appreciation of these customs throughout this essay and her insistence on highlighting the similarities, rather than the differences, between their beliefs and the beliefs of the British is a special characteristic of women authors, including several of Kingsley's contemporary female travel writers.[7] Margaret Strobel claims, "In comparison with accounts by Victorian men, women's travel narratives incline less toward domination and more toward discovery" (1991, p. 36). The discovery was both about the outside world and its customs, as well as about themselves and their inner lives (ibid., pp. 36–37).

After beginning her essay with a ghost story from the southern coast of England that turns out to be a failed suicide attempt by a man and not an actual haunting, Kingsley shifts her observations to what she considers to be the real ghosts of West Africa. She calls her essay "a few rough notes" (1896, p. 81), and readily admits that in a "'land of the living that's thronged with the dead'" (p. 89), it is impossible to adequately describe each supernatural occurrence. However, her classification system for the spirits is more like a well-organized scientific study, providing numerous examples to illustrate how particular souls exist and function.[8] About the various African souls, Kingsley states, "For some time I thought four Families would do, each containing, of course, many genera and varieties, not to mention individual freaks, but now I have been obliged to enlarge the number of Families to nine" (p. 81). The four souls she discusses are: "the soul that survives," "the bush soul," "the dream soul," and "the shadow on the path" (p. 81). In what follows, Kingsley cleverly gives her readers European descriptions of African spirit manifestations, making these descriptions more accessible (and acceptable) to her audience. Though she discusses a way of life foreign to most readers of *The Cornhill*, her way of presenting these souls is in keeping with contemporary Victorian psychological studies and modes of thought about the human mind.

Kingsley personifies the bush soul as wild, usually appearing in the form of an animal. The bush soul often acts contrary to its human or "acts up" as a way of addressing a problem with its human: "If a man sickens it is because his bush soul is angry at being neglected" (p. 82). The witch doctor is then brought in to administer to the patient before it harms its human body.[9] Kingsley's descriptions would have been familiar to someone in Britain reading her essay because she describes this type of spirit in terms of a split personality that cannot be controlled. This was an issue that increasingly affected Victorian society throughout the latter half of the nineteenth century, as studies of schizophrenia and split personalities abounded both in medical journals and in popular literature of the day. As early as James Hogg's *The Private Memoirs and Confessions of a Justified Sinner* (1824), there were literary concerns over the idea of the double, or uncontrollable, part of the human mind. Closer to Kingsley's time, Robert Louis Stevenson's *Strange Case of Dr. Jekyll and Mr. Hyde* (1886) addressed the issues of what can happen when one's personality "splits" into two people. Kingsley says that the bush soul "gives great trouble," because it does not know that "by exposing itself to danger recklessly, it injures itself, and if you die it dies" (p. 82). This soul may make a respectable man act differently than usual, and even wildly at times: "that same man may have a sadly flighty, disreputable bush soul, which from its recklessness gets itself injured or killed, and causes you sickness or death" (p. 82). This soul may cause trouble to its human, but it also cannot live happily without its host: "When the man dies, the animal of the soul 'can no longer find a good place,' and goes mad, rushing wildly to and fro; if it sees a fire, it rushes into it; if it sees a lot of people, it rushes into them, until it gets itself killed, and when it is killed—'finish'" (p. 82).

The dream soul is not as wild as the bush soul, but bears a striking resemblance to the human subconscious, or what is studied in dream states. Kingsley calls this soul "the greatest nuisance a man possesses. It seems an utter idiot, and, as soon as you go to sleep, off it ganders, playing with other souls, making dreams" (p. 83). Once again, Kingsley sets up these African ideas and beliefs as similar to British ones, thereby making them easier for her audience to relate to. She even describes "ousted" dream souls and the "asylums" that witch doctors keep for these wandering spirits who have lost their original homes. The souls which replace the original souls are called "insisa" (p. 83), which are a lower class of soul, because they are a type of squatter in the human mind. These souls are usually found in people who die young, in twin children, or people who have not received a proper burial. Others are more troubling and involve people who "have blood stains on them" (pp. 83–84), suggesting criminal pasts. The blood on the human leads to a demonic possession of the insisa, who haunts its new-found human form:

> It is true they are very careful how they leave their new-found body, but the blood on them is very likely to attract all sorts of devils. Blood on a soul devils always smell out and go for, and then the unfortunate, innocent man who has housed one, gets epileptic fits, general convulsions, or the twitches, and has to go to great expense, and endure some rigorous treatment to get all the devils, and the carrion soul they have come after, cast out of him. (p. 84)

This "carrion soul" that the devils come for could be from some misdeed in the person's past which causes the possession or haunting. The witch doctor is called in again to perform a spiritual healing much like the Christian practice of exorcism. In *Travels in West Africa*, Kingsley also comments on the Africans' fear of ghosts, something they have in common with her British readership:

> They regard their god as the creator of man, plants, animals, and the earth, and they hold that having made them, he takes no further interest in the affair. But not so the crowd of spirits with which the universe is peopled, they take only too much interest and the Bantu wishes they would not and is perpetually saying so in his prayers, a large percentage whereof amounts to "Go away, we don't want you." "Come not into this house, this village, or its plantations." (1897b, pp. 442–443)

After briefly classifying the fourth type of soul, "the shadow on the path," which is the "photographic image" (1896, p. 84) unique to each human being, Kingsley begins a lengthy discussion of the soul's existence after its release from the human body. As in European cultures, Kingsley stresses the importance of proper burial in African culture in order for the soul to have rest. If the soul is not buried properly, it continues to haunt its former locale: "The soul does not leave its old haunts until it is buried in a suitable and proper manner, no matter how long a time may elapse before the ceremony is carried out by the relations" (p. 85). In the meantime, these souls can haunt family members, especially husbands who die before their wives: "what those poor women have to go through—those who are not killed for having bewitched it, or to be companions to it in the underworld, or representative of its earthly wealth—is beyond description all along the entire coast; but in every district the customs vary" (p. 86). However, some widows show strength against these ghostly husbands, something they were unable to show while their husbands were living. Kingsley notes that "the widow has a rare good stout stick given her, wherewith to whack her deceased lord's soul if it gets beyond bearing with during the first six weeks' mourning, during which time she keeps in the hut" (p. 86). Like other stories of persons who return to haunt the places most dear or most familiar to them, these souls remain near their former bodies or homes. Kingsley discusses "the habit of the soul to haunt its hut, or place where it left its body, until such time as it is buried, *i.e.* sent off to the spirit-world, either for re-incarnation [...] or for permanent residence" (p. 86). This description would have been familiar to any Victorian reader in Great Britain, where the tradition of haunted houses had persisted for well over a century, both in popular lore and fiction. Kingsley manages to bridge these geographically distant regions by describing a cross-cultural fear of ghosts that invade the supposed safe space of the domestic home: house or hut.

In other parts of the essay where spirits are gendered, female spectres are described as being more benevolent than their male counterparts. Kingsley mentions the "genus of devils," Sasahbomsum and Shramantin. As opposed to Sasahbomsum, who exhibits behavior similar to European vampires—he "kills and eats you" or "sucks your blood" (p. 89)—the female form, Shramantin, is a more nurturing spirit and distinct from most female revenants and femme fatales in contemporary British Gothic writings. Kingsley says of her: "the female form of this demon; she is not so bad, for she only detains her prisoners for three or four months in the forest, teaching them what herbs are good to eat, where the game come down to drink, and what the animals and plants say to each other" (p. 90). Kingsley is careful to spend time describing Shramantin as a spirit who is more interested in teaching and supporting life than in destroying. Thus, she presents a kindly spirit different from what most British would likely picture as a typical African "demon," which was generally linked to the African practice of "dark magic." In her portrayal of Shramantin, Kingsley presents her audience with a spirit who is nurturing rather than destructive, a native healing force that counters popular images of witch doctors, curses, and sacrifices.

In "Black Ghosts," Kingsley tries to present the African equivalent of heaven as a way of further showing the similarities between seemingly disparate cultures. In this other dimension, called "Srahmandazi," there are people, plants, animals, and even markets and villages, but, according to tradition, its temporal aspects are different from the world of the living, "and when the sun sets on this world it rises on Srahmandazi"

(p. 86). Kingsley attempts to bring her readers to a closer understanding of the nature of this other world by adding, "to all of the spirit-worlds of we poor human beings, when it comes to the final test—a day in this world of ours is worth a whole year over there; for, after all, these are only the shadows of things, their souls, in this spirit world" (p. 87). Kingsley is careful to make this description of the afterlife general enough to apply to either a Christian or African heaven, something that exists beyond human understanding, no matter whether that human is black or white, African or European. Taking this idea beyond a specific religion or ethnic region (Christian, fetish, African, European), the concept of a non-denominational "spirit world" allows an inclusiveness that supported Kingsley's socio-cultural views on the spiritual similarity of Africans and Europeans.

Some of the most telling social commentary comes at the end of the essay, when Kingsley addresses her readers directly and asks that they consider her examination of African spectral life, saying, "I hope that the readers of this incomplete sketch of the African's views concerning souls will not hastily write the African down an ass, but will remember the words of the greatest of ethnologists, E. B. Tylor, of Oxford" (p. 92). She then quotes Tylor's advice that learning about "savage" religions can help further mutual appreciation among cultures:

> Few who will give their minds to master the general principles of savage religion will ever again think it ridiculous, or the knowledge of it superfluous to the rest of mankind. Far from its beliefs and practices being a rubbish heap of miscellaneous forms, they are consistent and logical in so high a degree as to begin, as soon as even roughly classified, to display the principles of their formation and development, and these principles prove to be essentially rational, although working in a mental condition of intense and inveterate ignorance. (quoted in Kingsley 1896, p. 92)

As a way of reinforcing this view, Kingsley ends the essay with a comment about the similarity in cultures through the belief, and perhaps the basic human need, to believe in the existence of an afterlife, where we will all one day meet our loved ones again. She states that "the African idea of the continuity of the individualism of the soul is the same as our own" (p. 92) and quotes a passage from Tennyson's *In Memoriam* as an example of this similarity: "Eternal form shall still divide / The Eternal Soul from all beside, / And I shall know him when we meet."[10] These lines serve many purposes for Kingsley's social agenda. She understood "form" still divided Africans and Europeans but, in the afterlife, if all cultures will meet again, what lasts is the "Eternal Soul." It is this belief in the soul, whether it is African or European, which Kingsley wanted to present to her readers, and her essay provided an opportunity for the reading public in Britain to be introduced to spiritual beliefs, which, though labeled differently, were not so dissimilar from their own.

These same comparisons make up the content of Kingsley's 1899 address to the Society for Psychical Research, "The Forms of Apparitions in West Africa." Similar to the supernatural story that opens "Black Ghosts," Kingsley makes it clear to her audience at the beginning of the piece that she "has no concern" (1899, p. 331) with English or European ghosts. She also carefully establishes herself as a folklorist, instead of a paranormalist. Kingsley begins by describing what she believes to be possible medical causes behind the Africans' ghost-seeing, one of which she calls "a chronic state of malarial delirium," or what Victorians would have recognized as an "overheated" brain. The African's "undoubtedly more sensitive nervous system enables him to see things the duller-nerved Englishman does not" (p. 331). But Kingsley guards against contemporary views that Africans were hysterical or less intelligent with regard to their belief in a spirit world and their religious practice of fetish. In her insistence that Africans believe the material and spirit world to be one and the same, Kingsley is concerned to show that "this point of view is intricate, complex, and so on, but it is never for one single moment confused" (p. 333).

Kingsley's underlying social agenda is the most successful in her explanations of the different apparitions that West Africans see (or try to avoid seeing). In every description, she provides a European equivalent way of thinking about the role these ghosts serve in African society. The "over-god of gods" is compared to a great judge, who the Africans address the same way an Englishman would address a judge in court, a person "who had no personal knowledge of human affairs, but who could be depended on to be just if you could only get him to be interested and to understand" (p. 334). In a description of the African talking to an invisible spirit, Kingsley admits that she found the practice amusing before she learned to fully appreciate the cultural significance of these spirits and keeps her audience from assuming that this action is, again, the sign of a lesser intellect by using another analogy to explain the supernatural conversation in Western terms:

> By-and-bye—when I had been the silent spectator of several of these talks with the great god—the thing struck me as really very grand. There was the great man standing up alone, conscious of the weight of responsibility on him of the lives and happiness of his people, talking calmly, proudly, respectfully to the great god who he knew ruled the spirit world. It was like a great diplomat talking to another great diplomat of a foreign power, saying, "Let us keep our people from interfering with each other;" there was no whining or begging in it, and [...] the grandeur of the thing charmed me. (p. 334)

The second class of apparitions, and the African priest's involvement with them, Kingsley describes as a kind of Spiritualism, which would have been easily recognizable to any turn-of-the-century Victorian. She says that "the priests belonging to their various cults are always in ready touch with them,—on terms of easy familiarity. Sometimes the god takes possession of the priest or priestess, talking through him or her, but always with a strange voice" (p. 335).

The question of race is brought up in the essay, when Kingsley notes that many of the worst ghosts are white, but she explains this within the insulated world of West African local customs and stresses that this in no way has to do with antagonistic feelings toward Westerners: "I do not believe whiteness has anything to do with white men, for people who have no direct intercourse or experience of white men have white gods, and if you enquire if these white gods are like white men, you will be told, no, they are white like chalk, not like white flesh" (p. 336). Kingsley asserts that West Africans have no conception of race difference in making white gods evil because they are similar to white men; they have no motive to label by color, whether it is related to good or bad.

As in "Black Ghosts," Kingsley mentions Sasabonsum as she discusses that, in African as in European cultures, seeing evil ghosts is an ill omen. Kingsley describes these types of demons as "rulers of the witchcraft world; hated by priests and respectable house fathers from one end of West Africa to the other, and feared exceedingly" (p. 337). Sasabonsum is vampiric and preys on innocent Africans as he comes from "his underworld home to suck your blood at his leisure" (p. 337). She notes that there are several sorts of devils, as well as haunted houses, that plague Africans and Europeans alike: "When my friends came down to occupy these houses on the islands in the swamp for the fishing season, they had for the first week, until things were tidied up, a very lively time of it, and

I am bound to say that when things were tidied up and quite all right, from my host's point of view, the time, to one not brought up to that sort of thing, remained lively" (p. 340). In a later passage, she describes the fear of witchcraft and its consequences with a *Tam O'Shanter*-like example in which unsuspecting travelers encounter groups of women singing and dancing, only to discover after joining the festivities that the women are witches. These witches look for humans to eat and recall "one's early terrors of Fee-fo-fum vividly" (p. 338). There is also a story that bears a striking resemblance to the British changeling myth, in which African children are taken from parents by the "bibendi," spirits who take children to live in the supernatural realm for years at a time until the children manage to escape. Another story is akin to the popular tale "The Emperor's New Clothes" and involves Africans who make a bad bargain with the bibendi of the marketplace and, in return for better clothes, come home with nothing on at all.

Kingsley also briefly mentions how certain African ghosts are connected to anxieties dealing with homelessness and disease, social concerns that would have been recognizable to Kingsley's Victorian audience. One ghost, Tando the Hater, takes "the form of a weeping miserable orphan child" (p. 338), a spirit who spreads disease and death to anyone who takes the child in. Of course, in helping foster greater understanding between Africans and the British, Kingsley, in this instance, may well have been promoting greater social fears among her own countrymen. Her description of a ghost spreading disease harkens back to several haunted house stories of the mid-century that symbolized much the same fears about disease and the working classes.[11] Kingsley makes a similar connection in her description of malevolent ghosts that take the form of beggars, saying that "it makes the human being very careful how he deals with strangers" (p. 338).

Kingsley devotes the last portion of her address to defending the infamous practice of African fetish. She knew that this would be the most difficult comparison to make for her British audience, and it is here that she makes the most straightforward argument for the equality and sensibility of West African belief systems. Kingsley's enlightened view of fetish shows her to be more open-minded than many of her fellow nineteenth-century writers. For instance, Richard Burton's account of African fetish in *The Lake Regions of Central Africa* (1860) is representative of many contemporary derogatory descriptions of the belief system, descriptions that depict African superstition as childish and based on "inferior" intellect, qualities which, in turn, were used as an excuse for imperialist dominion over Africa and its indigenous people:

> The grand mysteries of life and death, to him unrevealed and unexplained, the want of a true interpretation of the admirable phenomena of creation, and the vagaries and misconceptions of his own degraded imagination, awaken in him ideas of horror, and people the invisible world with ghost and goblin, demon and spectrum, the incarnations, as it were, of his own childish fears. (vol. 2, p. 341)

Burton juxtaposes the African's beliefs as a lower form of superstition which cannot attain the same moral correctness of Christian religion, concluding, "By its essence, then, Fetissism is a rude and sensual superstition, the faith of abject fear, and of infant races that have not risen, and are, perhaps, incapable of rising to theism—the religion of love and the belief of the highest types of mankind" (ibid., pp. 343–344). Such base superstition, according to Burton, is a hallmark of "lesser" cultures: "Precisely similar to the African ghost-faith is the old Irish belief in Banshees, Pookas, and other evil entities; the corporeal frame of the dead forms other bodies, but the spirit hovers in the air, watching the destiny of friends, haunting houses, killing children, injuring cattle, and causing disease and destruction" (ibid., p. 344). The dominance of "evil entities" thus relegates these belief systems to a lesser form of worship that is directly opposed to Christianity. Burton surmises:

> A prey to base passions and melancholy godless fears, the Fetissist, who peoples with malevolent beings the invisible world, animates material nature with evil influences. The rites of his dark and deadly superstition are all intended to avert evils from himself, by transferring them to others: hence the witchcraft and magic which flow naturally from the system of demonology. (ibid., pp. 346–347)

Ulrike Brisson sees Kingsley's descriptions of fetish as a "political tool" which served "as a kind of mirror used to criticize British colonial policies, to question the missionary presence in West Africa, and, thus, to reify her own ideas on British rule along the West African coast" (2005, p. 328). Kingsley indeed recognizes the cultural biases inherent in the very word "fetish." In Kingsley's time, the meaning of fetish was the subject of much contention among anthropologists and ethnologists.

William Pietz states that, with its Portuguese origins, the word itself is "a cross-cultural situation formed by the ongoing encounter of value codes of radically different social orders" (1985, p. 11). Throughout her lectures and published writings, Kingsley insisted that the word be discussed as a type of religion, thus legitimizing the practice and putting it on the same level as European religious systems. According to Roger Luckhurst, her continual emphasis on the importance of fetish and her own experiences with African belief systems allowed her to show "how simple it was for mental sympathy to bring into intimate contact white and black" (2002, p. 173).[12] Kingsley compares the language of fetish to speaking any other language. It is no more alien than speaking French: "You all know up here people who have a great knowledge of French? Well, they always, when there is anything particular to be said, use a French phrase. I use a fetish phrase—that is all" (1899, p. 342). Kingsley therefore risks her own respectability and legitimacy as an ethnologist by admitting her appreciation of African fetish but, at the same time, defends the use of fetish by implicitly saying that if the person who the Society deemed worthy to be a guest speaker, the famous African cultural commentator, Mary Kingsley, can respect these practices, then they must not be that harmful. In her most daring critique, Kingsley defends fetish against claims that it is "a religion of terror," and turns the onus of misdeeds onto Europeans instead:

> Find me a more cheerful set of human beings in this wide world than the West Africans who believe in fetish; find me a region where crime for private greed is so rare as in West Africa [...] before you write down the men who do these things as fiends, I ask you to read any respectable book on European history, to face the Inquisition and the fires of Smithfield, and then to go and read your London Sunday newspapers. West Africa could not keep a Sunday newspaper going in crimes between man and man; its crimes are those arising from a simple direct absolute belief in a religion. From no region that I know can so truly go up the sad cry to God, *Doch, alles was dazu mich trieb, Gott, war so gut! ach! war so lieb!*[13] as from West Africa. (p. 342)

In this passage, Kingsley directly confronts her audience with their own inadequacies, moving from the historical crimes of religious intolerance, and England's own history of witch-burning, to finally laying the blame for modern intolerance at the Englishman's doorstep, in the pages of the Sunday newspaper.

Mary Kingsley has been called "a refugee from Victorian England" (Boehmer 1998, p. xxviii). Indeed, in a time when so many unmarried daughters devoted their lives to nursing aging parents, a familial duty that denied those women a chance to advance their own identities and opportunities, Kingsley created a new life for herself as she set out to find adventures that the average Englishwoman never imagined.[14] Yet, in her work as an ethnologist, she achieved something that perhaps she also never imagined during her years as a "spinster" daughter. In sympathetic works such as "Black Ghosts" and "The Forms of Apparitions in West Africa," she gave her reading public an opportunity to be introduced to cultures that they would not have otherwise known or appreciated. Through its ghosts, the customs of West Africa became much the same as those of Great Britain. Kingsley wanted her fellow countrymen and women to consider the question: If their dead shared emotional and psychological similarities, then why not the living? By focusing on spiritualistic and folkloric customs, Kingsley was able to transcend the corporeal bodies of Africans, making them more similar to Europeans through their belief in ghosts, hauntings, and other supernatural forces beyond the material world. This, in turn, supported her larger ongoing arguments about the similarity between Africans and the British. Her essays on the supernatural in West Africa go beyond racial divisions to show the universal human need to make sense of the mysteries of existence beyond death. Thus, these writings provide an important angle from which to view Kingsley's social crusade.[15] Read alongside her other political writings, they give us a more rounded sense of her ability to bridge the gulf in cultures, both living and dead.

Notes

1. Though Alison Blunt, in *Travel, Gender, and Imperialism: Mary Kingsley and West Africa* (1994), notes that Kingsley's motives regarding her travels changed over time, her overall political stance seemed to be one in favor of *laissez-faire* policies for West Africa (see especially Blunt, Chapter 3).
2. See Dorothy Middleton, *Victorian Lady Travellers*, pp. 173–174.
3. Several critics have discussed this and other passages in terms of Kingsley's gender strategy of presenting herself as a non-threatening female explorer. See Roger Luckhurst's section on Kingsley in *The Invention of Telepathy* (2002); Ulrike Brisson's "Fish and Fetish: Mary Kingsley's Studies of

Fetish in West Africa"; Lynette Turner's "Feminism, Femininity, and Ethnographic Authority," *Women: A Cultural Review* 2.3 (1991): 238–254; and Alison Blunt's "Mapping Authorship and Authority: Reading Mary Kingsley's Landscape Descriptions," in Alison Blunt and Gillian Rose (eds.), *Writing Women and Space: Colonial and Postcolonial Geographies* (The Guildford Press, 1994), 51–72.

4. According to Dea Birkett in *Mary Kingsley: Imperial Adventuress* (1992), Kingsley grew increasingly attached to Nathan, though he did not return her sentiments (see pp. 137–142).

5. Lawrence Davies notes that this was a particularly productive time for colonial fiction with Gothic leanings in *The Cornhill*. In addition to Mary Kingsley's "Black Ghosts," the magazine also published Bernard Capes's "The Moon-Stricken," C. J. Cutcliffe Hyne's "A Lottery Duel," and Andrew Lang's "The Black Dogs and the Thumbless Hand." Within the next year, the magazine would also publish John Arthur Barry's "'Missing,' A Story of the South Pacific," Joseph Conrad's "The Lagoon," Mary Kingsley's "Two African Days' Entertainments," and Andrew Lang's "Ghosts and Right Reason."

6. Alice Stopford Green commented on the importance of humor in Kingsley's writing, saying that her "critics" misjudge its intention: "These critics little knew how often in her burning desire to arrest the attention of a people comfortable and at ease—a people not plagued like other folk nor brought into trouble like other men—in her desire to catch their wandering ear she would find a story, lighten it up with her humour, and hope that even as they laughed they might unconsciously catch the meaning shut up in the tale" (1901, p. 15). One of the best examples of Kingsley's humor used for political purpose is her essay "The Development of Dodos," *National Review* 27 (March 1896): 66–79.

7. For more on Mary Kingsley's contemporaries, such as Gertrude Bell, Isabella Bird, Amelia B. Edwards, and Mary Gaunt, see Dea Birkett's *Spinsters Abroad: Victorian Lady Explorers* (Basil Blackwell, 1989) and *Off the Beaten Track: Three Centuries of Women Travellers* (National Portrait Gallery, 2004).

8. Kingsley was no stranger to scientific practices. Having learned scientific principles from her father, she continued this interest in her own life and travels by collecting species of fish and other natural specimens to bring back to England.

9. Kingsley spent time with a witch doctor during her travels and later lectured on the subject to the London Society of Medicine for Women. For more information on her public lectures, see Dorothy Middleton, *Victorian Lady Travellers* (1965), p. 153, and Katherine Frank, *A Voyager Out* (1986), pp. 214–222.

10. Section 47, lines 6–8.
11. The use of ghosts as a metaphor for disease goes back to the beginnings of British literature. As early as the fourteenth century, Welsh poet Jeuan Gethlin (d. 1349) described the Black Death in supernatural terms: "We see death coming into our midst like black smoke, a plague which cuts off the young, a rootless phantom which has no mercy for fair countenance" (quoted in John Kelly, *The Great Mortality* (Harper Collins, 2005), p. 227). The anxiety over unhealthy residences is a recurring theme in Victorian haunted house stories and is often related to class issues. Ghosts represented contagion and illness among the middle and working classes. Sickness, death, and hauntings were also the result of unhealthy, overcrowded housing for the poor in more populated areas of England. As Sharon Marcus notes in *Apartment Stories* (1999), "in many stories illness and death follow as consequences of seeing a ghost" (p. 125). Mary Elizabeth Braddon contributed to this type of supernatural fiction with "The Ghost's Name," published in the *Mistletoe Bough* (1891). In her story, the sinister ghost that kills everyone who inhabits one particular room turns out to be typhoid fever.
12. For a discussion of Mary Kingsley's cross-cultural sympathy with native African beliefs and her work as an ethnologist, see Luckhurst's section on "Mary Kingsley and the 'Capacity to Think in Black'," in *The Invention of Telepathy*.
13. Gretchen's lines from the first part of Goethe's *Faust*: "Yet, everything that drove me to this, God, was so good! oh! was so sweet!"
14. In an 1896 interview for *Young Woman* magazine, Kingsley commented on this social discrepancy: "It is a curious inconsistency that little account is taken of a woman if she sacrifices herself on the domestic hearth, while should she follow in the track of men—frequently a much easier course—and undertake public or scientific work, everybody cries 'How marvelous!'" (quoted in Frank 1986, p. 219).
15. Kingsley continued her critique of British colonial practices in several articles published from 1896 to 1900 that addressed everything from liquor trafficking to hut taxes. See, for instance, "The Hut Tax in Africa," published in the *Spectator* (19 March 1898), pp. 407–408, and "The Liquor Traffic with West Africa," in the *Fortnightly Review* (April 1898), pp. 537–560.

Bibliography

African Affairs (1963), "Mary Kingsley Centenary, 1862–1962," *African Affairs* 62.246 (January): 7.
Birkett, Dea (1989), *Spinsters Abroad: Victorian Lady Explorers*, Oxford and New York: Basil Blackwell.

——— (1992), *Mary Kingsley: Imperial Adventuress*, London: Macmillan.
Blunt, Alison (1994), *Travel, Gender and Imperialism: Mary Kingsley and West Africa*, New York and London: The Guilford Press.
Boehmer, Elleke (1998), "Introduction," in Elleke Boehmer (ed.), *Empire Writing: An Anthology of Colonial Literature, 1870–1918*, New York: Oxford University Press, pp. xv–xxxvi.
Brantlinger, Patrick (1988), *Rule of Darkness: British Literature and Imperialism, 1830–1914*, Ithaca and London: Cornell University Press.
Brisson, Ulrike (2005), "Fish and Fetish: Mary Kingsley's Studies of Fetish in West Africa," *Journal of Narrative Theory* 35.3 (Fall): 326–340.
Burton, Richard F. (1860), *The Lake Regions of Central Africa: A Picture of Exploration*, 2 vols., London: Longman, Green, Longman & Roberts.
Davies, Lawrence (2009), "'Don't You Think I Am a Lost Soul?': Conrad's Early Stories and the Magazines," *Conradiana* 41.1 (Spring): 7–28.
Frank, Katherine (1986), *A Voyager Out: The Life of Mary Kingsley*, Boston: Houghton Mifflin.
Green, Alice Stopford (1901), "Mary Kingsley," *Journal of the African Society* 1.1 (October): 1–16.
Kelly, John (2005), *The Great Mortality*, New York: Harper Collins.
Kingsley, Mary H. (1896), "Black Ghosts," *The Cornhill Magazine* (July): 79–92.
——— (1897a), "The Fetish View of the Human Soul," *Folklore* 8.2 (June): 138–151.
——— (1897b), *Travels in West Africa*, London: Macmillan & Company.
——— (1897c), "West Africa, from an Ethnologist's Point of View," *Transactions of the Liverpool Geographical Society*, pp. 58–73.
——— (1899), "The Forms of Apparitions in West Africa," *Proceedings of the Society for Psychical Research* 14/35: 331–342.
Lane, Christopher (2003), "Fantasies of 'Lady Pioneers,' Between Narrative and Theory," in Philip Holden and Richard J. Ruppel (eds.), *Imperial Desire: Dissident Sexualities and Colonial Literature*, Minneapolis: University of Minnesota Press, pp. 90–114.
Luckhurst, Roger (2002), *The Invention of Telepathy, 1870–1901*, Oxford and New York: Oxford University Press.
Marcus, Sharon (1999), *Apartment Stories: City and Home in Nineteenth-Century Paris and London*, London and Berkeley: University of California Press.
McEwan, Cheryl (2000), *Gender, Geography and Empire: Victorian Women Travellers in West Africa*, Aldershot and Burlington: Ashgate.
Middleton, Dorothy (1965), *Victorian Lady Travellers*, New York: E. P. Dutton.
Pietz, William (1985), "The Problem of the Fetish I," *RES: Anthropology and Aesthetics* 9: 5–17.

Procter, James, and Angela Smith (2007), "Gothic and Empire," in Catherine Spooner and Emma McEvoy (eds.), *The Routledge Companion to Gothic*, New York: Routledge, pp. 95–104.
Strobel, Margaret (1991), *European Women and the Second British Empire*, Bloomington: Indiana University Press.

CHAPTER 6

The African Stories of Margery Lawrence

Along with her contemporaries Elizabeth Bowen, Violet Hunt, May Sinclair, and Eleanor Scott, Margery Lawrence excelled in the genre of supernatural/weird fiction. Throughout the 1920s, her first decade as a professional writer, she published supernatural stories in popular magazines, and later collected these stories in three noteworthy volumes. The first two, *Nights of the Round Table* (1926) and its sequel *The Terraces of Night* (1932), framed the original stories using the traditional "round" of ghost stories told by various narrators in a social setting.[1] *The Terraces of Night* was followed by another collection of supernatural stories, *The Floating Café* (1936). A self-professed "ghost-hunter," Lawrence's interest in the supernatural and the occult continued throughout her life, and she published both novels and short stories until her death in 1969.[2] In her foreword to R. Thurston Hopkins's *Ghosts over England* (1953), Lawrence describes herself as an amateur ghost-hunter and mentions her participation "in a great many 'clearings' of haunted houses." According to Richard Dalby, she was a member of the Ghost Club, as well as being a regular participant at séances held by the Irish medium and parapsychologist Eileen Garrett (1998, p. xvii). Margery Lawrence's open-minded attitudes regarding the otherworldly complemented her progressive outlook in other areas of life. As a progressive, independent woman, she perfectly symbolized the liberated decade of the 1920s. Her first novel, *Miss Brandt, Adventuress* (1923) is about a high-society female jewel thief, and strong women characters appear throughout her fiction. She published "I Don't Want to Be A Mother" in *Cosmopolitan*

© The Author(s) 2018
M. Edmundson, *Women's Colonial Gothic Writing, 1850–1930*,
Palgrave Gothic, https://doi.org/10.1007/978-3-319-76917-2_6

in January 1929 and the publication of her novel *Bohemian Glass* (1928), about debauched young artists in London's Chelsea neighborhood, was delayed because of its risqué subject matter.[3] Her fiction often addresses contemporary issues such as women's need for financial independence and sexual liberation, as well as topics centered on race and empire.[4]

In her Colonial Gothic stories, Lawrence presents an enlightened view of the negative effects of imperialism, particularly as she describes the British presence in Africa as a cultural intrusion that leads to suffering for indigenous peoples and colonizers alike. This theme is at the heart of three stories Lawrence set on the African continent. "Death Valley" (1924) concerns colonialism in Rhodesia as the unseen, violent spirit that "lives" in a dwelling in the middle of the jungle comes to symbolize the lasting, haunted nature of the British presence in the region. "The Dogs of Pemba" (1926), set on an island off the coast of East Africa, similarly tackles the subject of British colonialism as a negative influence through its treatment of a colonial official who slowly degenerates into an animal. Finally, Lawrence ventures into Egypt with "The Curse of the Stillborn" (1925), as she complicates the contemporary popular fascination with Egypt and the so-called "Egyptomania" of the 1920s in her examination of how the British failure to appreciate indigenous culture (symbolized in the efforts of a naïve missionary couple) can lead to violence and trauma. By showing the detrimental effects of the colonial encounter, Lawrence provides a critical point of resistance against an imperialist agenda. The repercussions faced by the protagonists in each story when they encounter the supernatural is symbolic of the power of colonial regions—in terms of belief systems, cultural heritage, and physical environment—to disrupt and resist the smooth workings of empire. Instead of using the supposed dark side of imperialism as a means of reaffirming Britishness, particularly male Britishness, Lawrence chooses to foreground the personal and wider cultural dangers which come from misunderstanding and underestimating people in colonial regions, places where British imperialism ultimately becomes a destructive rather than redeeming force.

Recent studies have attempted to recover the relationship between interwar modernist writing and imperialism. Nigel Rigby claims that though previous critics have tried to distance modernist writing as "high art" which should not be considered in relation to popular writing on or from empire—writing that, in turn, has been relegated to the realms of escapist literature not worthy of scholarly attention—the two cannot be separated. For Rigby, "empire was simply a part of life in between-the-wars Britain, whatever one's social class, habits or politics, and that all writers were inevitably exposed to the wide range of imperial narrative being produced at the time" (2000, p. 225). In her study of British women writers of the 1930s, Jane Garrity likewise attempts to correct what she considers to be popular misconceptions about women's involvement with ideas of nation and empire. Imperialism continued to be a prominent force in the British cultural psyche throughout the 1920s (the zenith of empire) and into the 1930s, and, as Garrity notes, imperialist propaganda could be seen in many different areas of public life, from the Boy Scouts and Girl Guides and children's literature of the day, to celebrations such as Empire Day (on Queen Victoria's birthday) and the Empire Games, which began in 1924 (Garrity 2003, p. 14). However, the popular misconception that British world dominance had faded at the beginning of the First World War meant that "little attention has been paid to how British women modernists identify with, repudiate, and interrogate the legacy of empire" (ibid., p. 13). Though her emphasis on these modernist women authors is centered specifically on experimental novels, the lack of critical attention extends as well to women's supernatural and weird fiction from the interwar years, a genre in which authors frequently expressed doubts about the imperial mission. The unexplained forces, unpredictable violence, and increasing emphasis on horror that threatens well-meaning but naïve protagonists in the supernatural stories from this period is, in part, a critique of the nebulous, unpredictable nature of relations between Britain and its colonial territories.

The ghost story, in particular, lends itself very well to critiques of empire. The revenant's emphasis on coming back to haunt, its need to expose secrets and speak the unspoken, complements imperialism's continuous need to keep its own dark past from returning to terrorize the present. Likewise, within a Colonial Gothic text, the marginalized voices of empire are able—much like the figure of the ghost—to haunt the narrative. This haunting, in turn, is a form of speech that expresses otherwise unspeakable suffering and loss. Patrick Brantlinger has discussed the close connection of occultism with anxieties surrounding the peak of British imperial power, claiming that "no form of cultural expression reveals more clearly the contradictions within that climax than imperial Gothic" (1988, p. 228). In other words, a belief in the occult and Spiritualism, much like support of imperialism, provided a bulwark against the British public's declining faith in Christianity as well as a "declining faith in Britain's future" (ibid., p. 228).[5] Alternate realities helped to make sense of the uncertainty in the ever-changing modern "real" world. Both fiction about the occult/supernatural and fiction about empire are concerned with what lies beyond the margins of everyday life. According to Simon Hay, because "the only-marginally-visible is precisely the central concern of ghost stories in general," these stories are thus "insistently about Empire" (2011, p. 10). Arguing that empire is the dominant "anxiety" in such stories, Hay posits that "the social totality that structures the world of the ghost stories, the truth underlying the mere experiences of the lives of characters and readers—this social reality has included from the genre's beginnings absolutely the hard facts of empire" (ibid., p. 11). The intimate relationships and importance of personal encounters—whether natural ones between the living or supernatural ones between the living and the dead—that are the central concern of the ghost story are also at the heart of colonial narratives.

"Death Valley" originally appeared in the November 28, 1924, issue of *The Tatler* and was later collected in *Nights of the Round Table* (1926) as "The Soldier's Story."[6] Set in Rhodesia, the events center on Dennison, a former member of the Rhodesian Mounted Police, who narrates the story of his traumatic experience with an unseen supernatural force while hunting for ivory with a group of fellow British policemen in the Zambezi Valley. Under the official guise of a surveying expedition, the men are trying to find a cache of ivory that has been "smuggled away from the Government's clutches" (Lawrence 1998a [1924], p. 105). When Dennison's friend Hill is tasked with searching an interior section of the valley, the local African police members who form a small part of the search party warn the British to stay away. Mbwana, whom Dennison describes as brave and with "the heart of a lion" (p. 107), tells them that the place is known locally as "Death Valley," an area that is "no good for white man or black" (p. 107). When pressed by the others to explain further, Mbwana says that "once white folks lived there—now no good, only house left." He claims that there are "Witch things there [...] bad things" (p. 107). Bill Jenks, the leader of the party, does not take the warning seriously, instead thinking that the rumors may be used by smugglers to keep people away from the house, which they then use to hide the ivory. Hill and Mbwana leave the group and journey to the house. A short time later, Mbwana returns in a state of terror, telling

Jenks "that Hill was killed by a *devil*, some devil that lives in a hut of sorts they found down there." According to Mbwana, no one ever sees this "devil," but everyone knows that "it's a *white* devil" (p. 110).

Dennison becomes increasingly puzzled over his friend's mysterious death and accepts Jenks's suggestion that he go to the house to watch over the body until the doctor arrives and certifies Hill's death. When he first sees the house, he imagines a once happy colonial setting that is being slowly but steadily reclaimed by its jungle surroundings:

> A small log-house it was, and the stockade round it of wooden logs and sturdily made; the square garden space within it was pitifully overgrown, and but a riot now of jungle flowers and weeds and upspringing young green things flourishing lustily where once a pretty pair of hands—who knows?—may have planted and watered, sown and weeded, with pathetic industry. (p. 112)

When he ventures inside, this sense of the past lingers eerily into the present. He notices that "it seemed curiously unlike a deserted house; indeed, it looked as if the owner had but just walked out for a moment, leaving his goods about to await his return" (p. 113). Dennison's unease gradually grows as he sees the body of Hill slumped on the floor against a wall and realizes that his friend had fired five shots from his revolver before apparently dying of fright: "The pale mouth was frozen into a dreadful square of horror, and the eyes were blank and staring" (p. 114). Dennison notices that the bullet holes are positioned in a small group at the height of a man's heart on the opposite wall from Hill. He wonders "what had stood there smiling while Hill, mad with fear, pumped shot after shot pell mell into its heart, and sank?," then feels "a cold nasty little feeling" at his own heart when he questions why he describes the unknown enemy as "smiling" (p. 114). Dennison's dogs likewise begin to show unusual fear in the house as they avoid the area that Hill fired toward.

When Dennison realizes that he must spend the night alone in the house, the terror escalates when the latched door begins moving as if someone from outside is trying to come in. Dennison takes his eyes away from the door briefly but then realizes that the rusty bolt (a bolt which he says took him a while to move because of its age) has opened silently, seemingly by itself. Knowing that some invisible presence is now in the house with him, Dennison tries to flee but finds himself trapped inside:

now at my back the cold wind crept, and stroked icy fingers across my shivering neck; for a second I tried to face it out, but it was useless. Creeping, furtive, smiling, that bitter little wind eddied behind me till my sweat-soaked shirt froze on my back and my hair stirred beneath its stealthy caress; with a panic yell my nerve gave out, and I made one frantic dive for the doorway and freedom...*and I couldn't get through!* (p. 117)

The ghost remains powerful and destructive, and the haunting that Dennison feels is the lingering presence of this "white devil," a representative of empire who did unnamed, unspeakable things and who cannot (or will not) leave his colonial domain, the little house in the heart of the jungle. The ghost possesses the house and refuses to concede his place within Africa, thus becoming a continually disruptive and deadly force for black and white alike. The invisible barrier that holds Dennison within the house is the trapping of empire in microcosm, a supernatural force that surrounds and confines him, so he cannot escape or easily extricate himself from its grip. The negative force that appears as "nothing," is representative of a battle where the "enemy" cannot always be adequately observed or whose motives completely understood and dissected. Dennison recalls:

a blank impalpable wall, elastic, but mercilessly strong, and there was I, clean mad with rage and a terror that grew worse every second, fighting like a maniac to get through that invisible barrier! Digging my fingers into the chinks between the logs that made the door-lintel, I fought like mad, sweating, babbling with panic...I was too far gone to think of decent pluck or sanity, or anything but that I *must* somehow fight through, get past this thing, whatever it was, for in my blind fear I knew that every minute this Terror in the room behind was growing stronger, more sure of itself, and if I couldn't get through...God, what poor Hill had seen, eh? Before kindly death came... (p. 118)

As the fates of Hill and Dennison demonstrate, those who involve themselves with the dangerous inheritance of imperialism must be prepared to fight, but not everyone survives. The inexplicable nature of how some people manage to survive the inherent violence of empire when others do not is a major concern of the story. Even more significant, it is a white man who symbolizes the previous generations of destruction and is the cause of the continuing unrest. Lawrence subverts the traditional imperial Gothic emphasis that focuses on the ominous nature of the "dark" jungle and its equally unknowable inhabitants as being the source of white terror. In her story, one colonial white man is trapped within a colonial terror that is specifically made by another colonial white man. Lawrence's insistence on having a *white* devil, a degraded white British man, as the locus for evil in her story is likewise in direct opposition to an imperialist doctrine that for decades had striven to represent Africa and its people as dangerous, backward, and unenlightened. Patrick Brantlinger notes, "By the time of the Berlin Conference of 1884–85, which is often identified as the start of the Scramble for Africa, the British tended to see Africa as a center of evil, a part of the world possessed by a demonic darkness or barbarism, represented above all by slavery, human sacrifice, and cannibalism, which it was their duty to exorcise" (1988, p. 179). Before beginning his tale, Dennison tells the group gathered to listen that his "yarn has no ending nor any explanation [...] just plain horror" (Lawrence 1998a [1924], p. 105). This idea returns toward the end of the narrative when the British question the African men and find that "they either wouldn't or couldn't say anything" (p. 119). The only information gathered is that the house is known as the "Death Hut" and "there was a white devil that lived there" (p. 119). Amongst this piecemeal background on the house and its former occupant, Dennison says, "The most curious thing I heard was from a very old native who said that it was a white devil lived there that killed folks... but he said it was a devil that *smiled*" (p. 119). Even after death, this colonial "devil" still relishes his ability to inflict harm and fear on the living. He is the destructiveness of empire made manifest.

The theme of keeping silent about unpleasant things that lurk in the not-so-distant past returns yet again at the conclusion to Lawrence's story. When someone asks Dennison about the fate of the two dogs, he begins by saying "I didn't mean to tell you" but then reluctantly finishes his story (p. 119). When he returns to the house the following day, he finds the two dogs "stone dead" near the body of Hill. Yet, what is even more disturbing to Dennison is what he notices on closer inspection: "their eyes, bulging with terror, were fixed, like [Hill's], on the wall with the bullet holes! Dead of fright, like him...but the most horrible thing was that all three pairs of eyes [...] seemed to have been swept by a blasting flame that sucked, on the instant, all the colour from them, leaving them blank-white and staring, colourless" (p. 120). The last lines of Dennison's narrative, a narrative which he himself admits has "no proper ending at all" (p. 119), are ones of speculation as he concludes,

"I often wonder—sometimes at night particularly—what in hell they all saw. Don't you?" (p. 120). In Dennison's case, the notion of seeing/ not seeing a terrible thing is connected to the idea of being a witness. Hill and the dogs see the terrible "white devil" firsthand and are forever damaged by their encounter. Yet, those who only witness atrocities indirectly, as Dennison does, are left with doubts and questions. Just as his battle with the white man's revenant within the house is a representation of the ability of the imperialist mindset to lure and eventually trap men like Dennison with noble or ignoble desires for heroism, wealth, power, and prestige within a colonial setting, Margery Lawrence suggests these struggles ultimately end unsatisfactorily for all involved. Dennison's initial summation, that his tale "has no ending nor any explanation" and is "just plain horror" is a fitting description of the imperial experience itself, a venture that will invariably provide only disillusionment. Equally important, Lawrence refuses to lay the ghost at the story's end. Like the lingering effects of imperialism, he is still there, an unseen, but no less harmful destructive and unsettling presence.

"The Dogs of Pemba," originally published in the November 26, 1926, issue of *The Tatler* and later collected in *The Terraces of Night* (1932) as "The Traveller's Tale," continues the theme of colonial brutality and retribution.[7] The story begins with a warning, as the narrator Garnett, an older and more experienced colonial planter, tells a younger man heading to the East that "*no* white man really understands the native, nor what he can do" (Lawrence 1999 [1926], p. 146). Garnett then recalls his first trip to Africa as the assistant for Hugh Kinnersley, the British Commissioner of Pemba. Garnett is excited for the opportunity, which he sees as an adventure, but even before he reaches Pemba, he begins hearing hints that Kinnersley is unstable. Garnett notes that the conversation is always somehow "guarded" and people become interested in him as they would "a young man on his way to the scaffold" (p. 147). These narrative gaps serve to highlight the mysteriousness of Pemba and the potential danger for Garnett, but the lack of communication also points to a greater deficiency in discussion about the damaging aspects of imperialism. Just like the curse that hangs over Kinnersley, the unspoken truth of empire haunts this narrative.

Garnett's first impression of Pemba is directly influenced by race and cultural difference. Amongst the mud huts, he sees the colonial Customs House stand "a little apart," "whitewashed," and "of a slightly better class" than the surrounding native structures (p. 148). His impression of the indigenous people is equally divided along racial lines and the dichotomy of black/white and "dark" jungle/"light" civilization. His "sense of forlornness" heightens as he watches the inhabitants "disappear like slim shadows into the welcoming dusk of the trees, and realised afresh how utterly alien is the white man in the tropics, those dark, strange lands that only know and love their own dark people" (p. 148). His description of the commissioner's house is similar. Around the house, "the dark bush fenced us in with an impenetrable blackness," while inside "all was bright and homelike" (p. 150). Garnett's use of home*like* is significant; the dwelling is an artificial representation of a real home somewhere far away. The brightness that keeps away the darkness outside is also artificial and supplied by several oil lamps. The Kinnersleys reside only on the upper story, away from the "unhealthy" environment outside, and surround themselves with "mosquito-curtains." The dinner is "an excellent meal," but one which is likewise a product of its colonial surroundings. Along with sardines served with lime, there is curried chicken with chilies and coconut and pawpaw for dessert. In describing the comforting aspects of this place, Garnett unwittingly admits to the very unhomely qualities of a place that tries but fails to be completely British, a place that insists on looking inward towards familiarity rather than outward towards a "fenced in" existence amid "blackness."

The fragility of this refuge is later threatened by the sound of the "dogs of Pemba," which Garnett describes as the cry of a pariah dog or jackal combined with "a ghastly, quite indescribably *human* element" (p. 152). Garnett assigns an evil, predatory nature to this sound which encircles and invades the house, as it "died away into eerie quivering echoes that trailed and hovered away into the silent trees, reluctantly, like a lingering evil thing loth to leave go its hold!" (p. 152). He calls his first experience hearing the sound "a shattering thing," and indeed it is on many levels. The noise disrupts the peacefulness of the evening and serves to remind the British that their presence in the region is unwanted, while it also reinforces the potential danger Kinnersley is in due to his treatment of the local people. After hearing the sound, Garnett's confidence in his new situation is likewise shattered. As he is faced with the reality of the colonial encounter instead of his preliminary romanticized view of empire, he thinks to himself: "London seemed very far away; the Mysterious loomed very near—and now with the primitive world and its people at our door-sills, all my glib self-confidence fell away from me and left me feeling unspeakably naked and shivering and frightened, face to face with the Unknown…darkest Africa and her people" (p. 154). There is more fear in this statement than condescension. Garnett places the blame for his current situation squarely on himself and his naïveté, and knows that he is completely unprepared for what awaits him. Even more significantly, there is no dependence on a British sense of bravado—false or not—to help Garnett maintain his transcendency over the indigenous people around him. Faced with the "Mysterious" and "Unknown" power of Africa, London can be no help. The might of the British Empire proves illusory.

Garnett is equally disheartened when he meets Kinnersley, a rough, hard-drinking colonial official whose physical appearance reflects his increasingly dissolute attitude and behavior. Garnett notices that he had been healthy and good-looking in his younger days before coming to Pemba, but "had palpably gone to seed," with heavy jowls, blue-tinted bags under his eyes, and cheeks "streaked with the red of broken veins" (p. 148). Kinnersley is also restless and has an extremely bad temper which he directs at anyone around him, particularly his Pemban servants. When one of them accidentally drops Garnett's suitcase, Kinnersley "rushed off into a sickening torrent of abuse" and hits the man on his bare legs with a riding switch (p. 150). Fearing that Kinnersley will kill the man, Garnett steps between them.

Kinnersley's unpredictable temper is thrown into sharp contrast with the introduction of his young wife Joan, who is initially depicted as the stereotypical British colonial wife: "She was small and slight and pale, but her eyes were a lovely hazel, her voice low and pretty; altogether she was pretty—very pretty—in a fragile way, with curling hair that lay in damp rings on her white forehead" (p. 150). Yet, this outward fragility belies an intelligence and understanding of her position as a British colonial resident in Pemba. As the voice of reason, she constantly checks her husband's outbursts towards the inhabitants of the area, telling him that they "can't afford to" anger them. She likewise confides in Garnett that they "aren't popular with the natives on the island" (p. 151), telling him, "I've tried my best, but it's no use. They just do what we pay them for, but nothing further" (p. 152). Though she has been on the island for a shorter period than her husband, Joan's understanding of their situation as a colonial power in relation to the local people is much more balanced and nuanced. She tells Garnett, "these people of Pemba are the most strange and mysterious in the world. Aloof, secretive, unfriendly—not exactly hostile; at least, I understand they were not so at first; but they keep themselves utterly apart from everybody, even from other natives. They have their own customs, their own rigid caste rules, their own secret ceremonies" (p. 154). Though she, too, is caught up in the trappings of her place within a colonizing body, Joan recognizes that the people of Pemba are not "evil," but different. She understands that any hostility on the part of the people is to be blamed on her husband and, though she does not directly say so, she implies that he is responsible for his own downfall. Joan realizes that the danger her husband is in is due to his mistreatment of the local people, particularly the daughter of a tribal leader, a former mistress whom he cast off after Joan arrived in Pemba.

The curse that turns Kinnersley into a dog is befitting his savagery towards the Pembans. When Garnett first arrives, but before he is aware of the curse, he notices that Kinnersley snarls, drools, and pants. When he later enters his room at night after a conversation with Joan, Garnett becomes fully aware of the change. He sees Kinnersley "curled up on the bare floor, stripped to the waist, his great torso hairy as a beast's, most curiously hairy, his head tucked down towards his knees as a dog lies" (p. 156). Upon looking around the room, he sees "a half-gnawed lump of raw meat, scarred and torn with the savaging of the teeth that, still in a human face, were rapidly becoming animal" (p. 156). After being faced with this confirmation of Joan's fears regarding the change in her husband, Garnett again projects his fear of the unknown onto his surroundings. He becomes terrified as he imagines "that black mouth that lay so close to the little lonely house, waiting, it seemed to my excited fancy, to engulf it. That bush! That dark, sinister stretch of giant tree and stream and swampland, of strangling creeper and poison thorn, of beast and snake and reptile terrible and unknown; of people still more terrible, more unknown!" (p. 157). Just as Kinnersley, before and after the curse, lashes out at the people he does not understand, Garnett likewise blames the people and the environment of Pemba for having "sinister" intentions. Though Garnett admits that this projection was a product of an "excited fancy," he nonetheless is an embodiment of how fear and misunderstanding turns cultures against one another. Joan Kinnersley, however, provides a counterpoint to the unreasoning fear and self-preservation of Garnett and Kinnersley. She feels fear but turns that fear into personal resolve through a more enlightened sense of cultural understanding. Unlike Garnett and Kinnersley, she knows that the inhabitants of Pemba have a specific reason for what they are inflicting on her husband, and she admits that the reason is justified.

The violence that Kinnersley inflicted returns to make him the victim. Garnett admits that, given what the commissioner had done to the people of Pemba, his bestial appearance "must have been the very expression of his innermost self" (p. 158). He witnesses the tribal medicine man hit Kinnersley with a string of beads which contains the signet ring he gave to the Pemban woman, and, in a reversal of the dominant role Kinnersley has abused, he now "cowered upon the ground, scrabbling in the dirt with imploring hands, gibbering horrible incoherencies that [...] ran into more horrible guttural sounds that were not words at all—he had gone already too far back for human speech" (p. 158).[8] This is a symbolic inversion of what the Pemban people were to him: less than human, inarticulate, creatures to be beaten. Yet, there is a major difference that Lawrence seeks to show her readers and one that connects to a key passage earlier in the story. The Pembans have a more noble reason for the violence because they are seeking retribution for the wrong done to the woman, who "loved Kinnersley [...] despite his drunken brutalities" (p. 160). As Joan said, they were not hostile until Kinnersley arrived. On the other hand, Kinnersley's violence is senseless and meant for no other reason than to maintain fear and subservience among a colonized people.

Claire Charlotte McKechnie has noted that "the dog is fundamental to our understanding of how biological disorder, sickness, and degeneration function in the portrayal of monstrosity" (2013, p. 135). As man degenerates into a beast because of his actions in colonial regions, there is an implicit comment on the cultural and moral disorder that comes as a byproduct of empire as well. In "The Dogs of Pemba," this moral disorder extends to the climactic struggle between Kinnersley and Garnett. When the latter attempts to save Kinnersley, because, as he says, "Whatever the man had done, it stuck in my gorge to see a white man cringing before these jungle savages" (Lawrence 1999 [1926], p. 159), Kinnersley suddenly turns on him and attacks. As they wrestle on the ground, Kinnersley savagely bites Garnett until Joan appears with a revolver and shoots her husband. Garnett's misplaced sympathy for Kinnersley and his readiness to absolve him of any wrongdoing simply because he is white and therefore "better than" the colonized black people ultimately puts his own life in jeopardy. In other words, his insistence on upholding a faulty imperial ideal creates a greater disorder that leads potentially to more loss of life. Once again, Joan is the one who more thoroughly understands the situation and acts decisively to end it without becoming bogged down with sympathy that she knows her husband does not deserve. Garnett recalls:

> She had seen the end of the scene I had witnessed, and tells me she shrieked to me not to go down to meet Kinnersley—her quick woman's mind had leapt to the horrible truth before my blundering intuition had grasped it. She had shot to save me—and shot to kill, knowing instantly that for his own sake now it was better to kill quickly and kindly the raging wild thing that had once been Kinnersley, a man like other men. (p. 159)

Unlike many colonial women of the time, especially in male-authored fiction of the period, Joan is not shielded from the "unpleasant" aspects of the colonial encounter. She witnesses firsthand the violence her husband inflicts on the people, confronts the knowledge that he was unfaithful to their marriage, and manages his degeneration into a literal beast. She takes the definitive step to end Kinnersley's life and thereby end the "disorder" caused by her husband, something Garnett is unable to do. She thus rids both herself and the Pemban people of the real evil force that existed within the dark jungle: the British colonial official. Joan is also ultimately rewarded for her action. She saves Garnett, who she then marries, and returns to England.

As Cyndy Hendershot notes, "Gothic bodies disrupt stable notions of what it means to be human. They break down the demarcations between animal and human, death and life, and male and female" (1998, p. 9). In her examination of the function of empire and the animalistic in the work of H. G. Wells, Arthur Conan Doyle, and Joseph Conrad, Hendershot claims that "other [non-British] cultures exist only insofar as they help define British consciousness, that is, pose a threat to its stability" (ibid., p. 124). Likewise, the colonial setting, no matter where in the world it is located, is only important in its role as "a backdrop for examining the British male subject and his propensity for degeneration" (ibid., p. 124). Yet, there is another layer here beyond degeneration anxieties that exists in women's Colonial Gothic writing. Women writers tend to be less concerned with anxieties centered on diminished masculinity (male power and superiority) because of direct colonial contact with indigenous peoples. Rather, their writing frequently examines how the British harm themselves (both as individuals and as a wider culture) as well as the indigenous cultures with which they come into contact. In her Colonial Gothic stories, Margery Lawrence exhibits a more complex critique of empire because, as a woman, she can imagine something beyond the world of the imperial male. Written from the point of view of the feminine "Other" that so worried fin de siècle male writers such as Wells, Doyle, and Conrad, these stories present an alternative approach to descriptions of the imperial encounter, one that moves away from the often-centralized, "dominant" white male viewpoint.

The ultimate fates of the unnamed colonial in "Death Valley" and Kinnersley in "The Dogs of Pemba" complicate other male-authored imperial narratives that insist "on the maintenance of British masculine subjectivity as it encounters a fantasized imperial Other" (ibid., p. 149). Just as both male protagonists can be seen as more progressive reimaginings of Kurtz, the Pemban woman and Joan Kinnersley serve as counterpoints to the African woman and the Intended in Conrad's *Heart of Darkness*. Marlow variously sees the African as mysterious, unknowable, pathetic, and dangerous. His descriptions of the African mistress reflect this limited viewpoint and never allow her complete humanity. She is either "a wild and gorgeous apparition of a woman" or a wild savage, but never fully human:

> She was savage and superb, wild-eyed and magnificent; there was something ominous and stately in her deliberate progress [...] Her long shadow fell to the water's edge. Her face had a tragic and fierce aspect of wild sorrow and of dumb pain mingled with the fear of some struggling, half-shaped resolve. She stood looking at us without a stir and like the wilderness itself, with an air of brooding over an inscrutable purpose. (Conrad 2006 [1902], pp. 60–61)

He inscribes her actions with a meaning that best suits his own conclusions about the "dark human shapes" (ibid., p. 60) that inhabit the Congo. By imagining the indigenous people as "fierce," "wild," and "dumb," Marlow releases himself from any moral responsibility as an agent of empire. Instead of coming into closer contact with them as people, it is easier for Marlow to keep them at a distance. They remain ill-defined, mysterious "shapes" that have "inscrutable purpose[s]," rather than any acknowledged complexity of thought and feeling.

It is significant that Marlow likewise describes the Intended as a ghostly figure while he conflates both women with a supernatural force that has the power to disrupt and destroy: "I shall see her too, a tragic and familiar Shade resembling in this gesture another one, tragic also and bedecked with powerless charms, stretching bare brown arms over the glitter of the infernal stream, the stream of darkness" (ibid., p. 76). As Abena P. A. Busia notes, these women "are both essentially trapped where their men find them, as fixed points of conflicting desires [...] they have been pawn and prize" (1986, p. 361). Yet, equally important is the notion of the women as apparitions, a representation that seeks to minimize their potential vitality and, consequently, their ability to be active agents within a society that seeks their cultural and political insubstantiality. Connected to this sense of beyond-ness, each woman also represents death. When Marlow tells the Intended that Kurtz's last words were her name, he tells the lie that he always claimed was like death, but also tells the inner truth that he cannot outwardly admit—namely, that Kurtz's last words were her name; she is the horror. Likewise, Hendershot has discussed the Intended as "terrifying" to Marlow because she "like the other women 'behind' European imperialism, seeks willfully to destroy English manliness through her collaboration with African savagery and the jungle's dangerous climate" (1998, p. 161). For Marlow, there is no redeeming quality in these two women: "The Intended hence becomes *her*, the Darwinian feminine force Marlow has battled in the Congo and also must battle in Europe" (ibid., p. 162). In this sense, the feminine has the power to destroy the positive potential that exists in her male counterparts. Whether black or white, foreign or domestic, "she" is a destructive force that works against empire.

The importance of both the Pemban woman and Joan Kinnersley in driving the major events in "The Dogs of Pemba" also complicates what Hendershot calls the "paternalism of new imperialism," which relied on the "domestic feminine as support for masculine, active 'benevolence' in the reaches of the empire" (ibid., p. 157). From an even broader perspective, Chris Bongie claims that imperialist discourse at the turn of the twentieth century relied on a dominant male voice: "For the most part, turn-of-the-century colonial literature can be read as an attempt at coming to terms with the challenge of speaking paternalistically rather than despotically about the subjects of imperial rule" (1991, p. 39). Yet, the dominance of this paternal voice consistently crowded out other voices. Brantlinger notes that "in imperialist discourse the voices of the dominated are represented almost entirely by their silence or their alleged acquiescence" (1988, p. 174). Likewise, Busia comments on how this agenda has resulted in the marginalization of the woman in the context of the imperial world. The supposed "incoherence" of the African woman in *Heart of Darkness* is a crucial strategy to this cultural silencing. She claims, "her language cannot be heard, and it is this singular factor which has had bearing on the representation of black women in imperial discourse" (Busia 1986, p. 361). This idea extends to the portrayals of white women as well, both inside and outside the text. Busia suggests:

> We are used to discussing the imperialism of the colonial novel with respect to the colonized peoples, but this concentration on the black/white divide has led to a disguising of yet another fiction inscribed by these [male-authored] texts; that of the "subject" nature of females in general, white or black. The parallel and equally powerful discourse of imperialism over the female is an integral part of the structuring metaphors of these texts. (1986, p. 362)

For this reason, Margery Lawrence's critique of empire is an important and necessary counterpoint to male-authored versions of colonialism. On another level, the women in "The Dogs of Pemba," because they are created by a woman, find more autonomy and greater "voice" within their respective text; they become more coherent.

Margery Lawrence published "The Curse of the Stillborn," in *Hutchinson's Mystery-Story Magazine* in June 1925 and included it as "The Egyptologist's Story" in *Nights of the Round Table*,[9] only a few years after Howard Carter discovered King Tutankhamun's intact tomb in the Valley of the Kings in 1922, an event that set off worldwide interest in Egyptian history and culture.[10] Yet, tales of mummies and the "mysterious East" had been a part of Western literature throughout most of the previous century. Long associated with popular literature, this "Egyptian Gothic," as Roger Luckhurst terms it, runs from an emphasis on "fear, vengeance and persecutory paranoia" to more complex themes of "fascination, awe, allure, desire and even religious transcendence" (2012, p. 158). Using Bram Stoker's *The Jewel of Seven Stars* (1903) to highlight the progression of the classic mummy story into a more refined form of Egyptian Gothic, Luckhurst claims, "The Egyptian influence remains insidious, permeating modern bodies invisibly, from a twilight zone where infection, psychical suggestion, the exertion of magical will and radioactive particles coexist in the vanishing point between science and the occult" (2012, p. 175). These concerns thus surpass "the histrionic accusations of Pharos to a steady and silent permeation of a domestic space with unknowable Egyptian influences, in a plot in which the poles of margin and centre are reversed by a creeping pervasion" (ibid., p. 175). Likewise, Ailise Bulfin has asserted that the popular form of the Egyptian Gothic mummy story, and the "paranoia" surrounding Britain's tenuous hold over Egypt and the Suez Canal which these stories represented, reached "a far wider audience than just those with a close interest in Egyptian affairs" (2011, p. 438). With this idea of cultural influence in mind, these stories indirectly commented on the negative aspects of colonialism and the need for Britain to withdraw from the region (ibid., p. 438). Though Margery Lawrence's story is not referenced in Luckhurst's or Bulfin's studies, "The Curse of the Stillborn" provides an important instance in this socio-political progression of the Egyptian Gothic through its emphasis on a powerful, ancient supernatural force that has a distinct motive for its vengeance against colonial misrule. The critique of colonialism in the story is centered on a British missionary couple who prove more detrimental to the Egyptian people than helpful. In particular, Lawrence's characterization of Matilda Bond serves as a critical commentary on the intrusiveness of missionaries who try to alter local beliefs and customs to suit a strict Christian-colonial mission. Lawrence's opening description of Matilda (referred to as "Mrs. Bond") places her firmly within this tradition. She is "upright and heavily built, in uncompromisingly stiff white piqué, her thick waist well-belted, her weatherbeaten face surmounted by a pith helmet" (Lawrence 1998b [1925], p. 121). Her appearance makes her look "impregnably solid and British" (p. 121). Her attitude toward the Egyptian people at the beginning of the story is likewise impregnable. When Michael Frith, the narrator of the story, tries to urge Mrs. Bond to let Mefren, a young Egyptian mother who has given birth to a stillborn child, bury the child according to her own custom, she is dismissive, believing that "these people are ignorant, childish, superstitious" and thus do not know what is best (p. 121). Similar to the commissioner's house in "The Dogs of Pemba," the Bonds' physical placement within the Egyptian community is symbolic of their enforced dominance over the local people. The "little whitewashed church brooded over the tangle of mud huts like a white hen mothering a scattered handful of brown and alien chicks" (p. 122). Yet, Mrs. Bond proves an unyielding "mother" to her flock. When Takkari, the grandmother of the dead child, refuses Mrs. Bond's demands, claiming "Kistian bury no good," she decides to give the child a Christian burial despite the family's wishes (p. 122).

Lawrence's portrayal of Mrs. Bond contrasts with the more understanding, quieter nature of her husband, and Frith's commentary provides greater insight into the negative influence Mrs. Bond has over both the local people and her husband's work:

> His sympathies were entirely with Mefren and her dour, free-striding old nomad mother; why should they who were, at best, mere birds of passage, be obliged to conform to the hidebound ideas of this stupid Englishwoman? Left to himself "Peterkin," as the little chaplain was affectionately known, would have been a sympathetic, understanding father to these wayward children of his—it was the insistent domination of this well-meaning, sincerely religious, but supremely narrow-minded wife of his that drove him into insisting on the "Church's rights." (p. 123)

With Frith as her mouthpiece, Lawrence suggests that a less church-centric guidance and support as is represented in Peter Bond's attitude toward his missionary work would be much more beneficial than his wife's unyielding version of Christian "charity." Mrs. Bond's methods of dealing with the Egyptian people are also more dangerous and potentially more culturally disruptive because she is fundamentally naïve about the society around her. Again, Frith's narration gives readers a window into this mindset. He laments the fact that after three years among the Egyptians, Mrs. Bond is "no nearer comprehending them" (p. 121). When she insists on a Christian burial for the child, he warns her repeatedly to "let them have their own way" (p. 123). This warning is echoed by Takkari, who likewise warns Mrs. Bond that if she goes through with the burial, "your blood must be upon your own head" (p. 124). Mrs. Bond, however, can only recognize the burial as her supreme Christian duty and describes the struggle in equally affected terms. She tells Frith that she "wrought mightily with Mefren for the soul of her child, and at last [she] prevailed" (p. 124). Much like the imperial enterprise, Mrs. Bond can only see her duty as a form of British perseverance to be dominant to the point where the colonized culture is subjugated and ultimately silenced.

Yet, when Takkari gives her warning, her face is "pregnant with meaning" (p. 124), suggesting another form of gestation in the story and what "forms" from the uneasy joining of two cultures.[11] The story's supernatural element is another layer of illusion which blends with other unrealities, such as imperial misinformation about people who inhabited colonial regions. Critics have noted the detrimental effects that both explorers and missionaries had in the regions where they traveled. In discussing the wider implications of British societal views, Hendershot claims that British citizens "could learn 'authoritatively' about Africa only through misrepresentations" which then "structure the subject's perceptions of that geography and culture when they are physically encountered" (1998, p. 150). According to Brantlinger, these misconceptions were also forwarded by the missionaries themselves, who "were strongly tempted to exaggerate savagery and darkness to rationalize their presence in Africa [and] to explain the frustrations they experienced in making converts" (1988, p. 182). The necessity of the civilizing mission in colonial regions thus comforted the absolutist attitude of most Christian Victorians toward the end of the nineteenth century. In an otherwise rapidly changing world, this was a clear goal, one which, to their minds, had no moral gray areas. As Brantlinger says, "The world might contain many stages of social evolution and many seemingly bizarre customs and 'superstitions,' but there was only one civilization, one path to progress, one true religion" (ibid., p. 173).

In her attempt to follow what she sees as the one true cultural and religious path, Mrs. Bond is met with a force that destroys her self-righteousness. When the Bonds notice that a storm seems to be approaching their home, Mrs. Bond first meets the feeling of uneasiness with anger: "After the manner of many women, the inexplicable always had the effect of sharpening her temper; she hated any deviation from the ordinary as a cat hates getting wet" (Lawrence 1998b [1925], p. 126). Just as with her cultural "battle" with Takkari and Mefren over the burial of the baby, Mrs. Bond feels she must fight against that which she does not understand. But her encounter with the supernatural force that enters her home forces her to admit that there are other older—and perhaps stronger—powers in the world than her chosen religion. She tells her husband that she is "too good a Christian" to be fooled by Takkari's "jugglers' tricks" (p. 128). She desperately tries to keep her composure by resorting to Western customs. She pulls the curtains "to shut out the night and the wind and make ourselves cosy and sensible" (p. 129) and suggests that they play Patience. Yet, for all her effort, she cannot stop the supernatural force that takes "possession of the room" (p. 130). She becomes "like a cornered creature at bay" as the force reclaims what has been taken from it: "She knew now—she knew the Thing behind all this—in some way some streak of lightening clarity had told her—somewhere behind this awful manifestation moved Something that belonged to Egypt, that had demanded Its right of Its land, and had through her been denied it" (p. 130).

It is significant that after she admits the existence of the force, it then becomes even more real to Mrs. Bond through touch and sight. A "dry and cold and leathery" hand "with sharply pointed nails" (p. 130), touches her own hand and pursues her as she tries to escape: "It grew beside her swiftly in the darkness, indefinite, macabre, and of a terror unspeakable; a Thing swathed and clumsy and vague, shapeless, yet dreadfully, appallingly powerful, a blind Horror seeking vengeance" (p. 131). She then sees "bulbous eyes" through a gold mask that places its cheek on hers. The realness of the incident is confirmed by Frith, who finds the couple hysterical and notices a distinct smell in the room. He describes it as "bitumen and natron and dried spices and the intolerably ancient smell of the grave—the smell of the burial rites of old Egypt— stern, undying" (p. 131). The "undying" supernatural force returns to claim the child's soul that has been denied through the Christian burial that disregarded the ritualistic embalming process. Consequently, the "Ka" returns "in rage and anger at the neglect of the honours due to it [...] haunting the unfortunate being who had dared to do it this wrong" (p. 132). In a broader sense, this spirit is a symbolic soul of Mefren, Takkari, and the Egyptian people who have been denied the respect due to their ancient religion. Frith says that "Mrs. Bond forced her weak husband to pit his puny might against a great and ancient Force" (p. 132), and Lawrence makes it clear that the Christian religion of the Bonds is no match for the ancient Egyptian spirit who manages to overwhelm the power dynamics of the time. The touch of the Egyptian mask that leaves Mrs. Bond's face permanently "twisted" and "all wried sideways" (p. 133) is a mark that symbolizes the troubled connection of the two cultures, a closeness that both enlightens and destroys. Matilda Bond, who represents the often destructive intimacy of the colonial encounter, is permanently changed by her encounter with the unknown.

In her Colonial Gothic stories set in Africa, Margery Lawrence disrupts the positivist message of the British Empire. Specifically, she complicates the imperialist mission and its "official" promises of peace and prosperity by showing the darker motives of white colonizers, and how those motives ultimately harm both indigenous and British people within colonial regions. Her stories span British imperialism throughout the African continent, from Rhodesia to Pemba to Egypt. But no matter where she bases her critiques of colonialism, Lawrence consistently undercuts those who make up the backbone of empire—administrators, soldiers, missionaries, both male and female. By placing the blame for the failings of imperialism more squarely on British shoulders, Lawrence provides a more progressive reimagining of empire that complicates previous literary and historical accounts that, like the African policemen in "Death Valley," either would not or could not tell the whole truth about the British colonial presence and its haunting effects on the region.

Notes

1. The round of ghost stories was also used by Catherine Crowe in *Ghosts and Family Legends* (1859) and continued into the twentieth century in Gertrude Minnie Robins's (Mrs. Baillie Reynolds) *The Relations and What They Related* (1902).
2. Her later short story collections include *Strange Caravan* (1941) and *Master of Shadows* (1959). Lawrence also contributed to the psychic detective genre with her creation of Miles Pennoyer in *Number Seven, Queer Street* (1945). Her novels dealing with Spiritualism include *The Bridge of Wonder* (1939), *The Rent in the Veil* (1951), *The Yellow Triangle* (1965), *Bride of Darkness* (1967), and *A Residence Afresh* (1969).
3. Lawrence discusses the novel, based on her own experience as an art student in London, in the article, "Margery Lawrence's Book No Publisher Dares to Print," which appeared in *The American Weekly* on January 22, 1928. In the article, Lawrence also recalls previous adventures, including her romance with an Italian soldier who was killed in the First World War. While doing "war work" in Italy, Lawrence also recalls how she was arrested for being a suspected Romanian spy: "They were not so used to the 'mad English' in those days as they have since become, and probably they could not imagine why a very young girl should be careering over Italy by herself in the midst of a war" (p. 7). Later, she was arrested after she "contravened some of the conventions that fetter Italian women" (p. 7) and had to be rescued by the British Consul in Florence.
4. In addition to the stories discussed in this chapter, Lawrence examined race, empire, and the foreign through the use of the supernatural in "Floris and the Soldan's Daughter," originally published in *Hutchinson's Mystery-Story Magazine* in September 1925 and later in *Nights of the Round Table*; "Tinpot Landing," which was included in *The Terraces of Night*, as well as "The House of the Dancing Feet," originally published in *Sovereign Magazine* in December 1925; "The Mask of Sacrifice," originally published as "The Mask" in *The Tatler* in November 1923; and

"The Professor's Ring," which was published with the two latter stories in *The Floating Café*.
5. Brantlinger discusses the presence of this anxiety in the fantasy/supernatural works of H. Rider Haggard and Rudyard Kipling, who both turned to Spiritualism and the occult in their personal lives. Haggard, in particular, shared many of Margery Lawrence's views on the spirit world, reincarnation, dream states, premonitions, and the afterlife. In a 1923 diary entry, he wrote: "the individual human being is not a mere flash in the pan, seen for a moment and lost forever, but an enduring entity that has lived elsewhere and will continue to live, though for a while memory of the past is blotted out" (quoted in Cohen 1965, p. 122).
6. Lawrence was paid twenty guineas by *The Tatler* for the rights to publish the story. TL, 5 July 1924, Box 261, Folder 246.04, in the A. P. Watt Records #11036, Rare Book Literary and Historical Papers, The Wilson Library, University of North Carolina at Chapel Hill.
7. Lawrence was paid twenty-five guineas by *The Tatler* for the rights to publish the story (TL, 25 June 1926) and was later paid fifty dollars by New York's *The Danger Trail* magazine for the first U.S. publication rights (TL, 13 August 1926). Box 282, Folder 270.07, in the A. P. Watt Records #11036, Rare Book Literary and Historical Papers, The Wilson Library, University of North Carolina at Chapel Hill.
8. According to Elisabeth McMahon, the invisible world of witchcraft and spirits on Pemba, called *uchawi*, was "central to peoples' lives" and could "control people through fear" (2013, p. 170). European colonists typically labelled Pemban healers as "witchdoctors," aligning them with black magic rather than with healing powers (ibid., p. 175). Pembans who practiced witchcraft, like the man in Lawrence's story, were known as *mchawi*. Those who sacrificed relatives or who had several relatives die, gained more spiritual power and were known as *wachawi*. McMahon notes that the *wachawi* "had the ability to turn themselves into animals, especially dogs, and to fly [...] Many Europeans living on Pemba reported hearing 'packs of dogs' barking in the night, which all local people knew were the *wachawi* during their feasts" (ibid., p. 177).
9. Lawrence was paid fifteen guineas by *The Mystery Magazine* for the rights to publish the story. TL, 13 March 1925, Box 275, Folder 258.06, in the A. P. Watt Records #11036, Rare Book Literary and Historical Papers, The Wilson Library, University of North Carolina at Chapel Hill.
10. In the collection *Fifty Strangest Stories Ever Told* (1937), Lawrence recounted a dream she had while visiting Luxor:

> I dreamt that a brown hand was held out to me bearing on its palm a scarab of a very odd shade of deep purple-blue—and that the hand turned the scarab over and showed on the underside

an "A" engraved deeply into the stone. On waking I dismissed the dream as merely the result of ten days' crammed with tomb-studying, reading history and what not and went out for a final camel ride before packing to catch the night-train down to Cairo. On my arrival back at the hotel, Madame B met me in the hall, and told me that an Arab trader had just arrived [...] and would I like to see some of his things. Needless to say I jumped at the chance—and the first thing I saw, lying amongst a varied collection of scarabs, mummy-beads, carved figurines and the like, was the purple-blue scarab of my dream! I asked for its period, and the old man showed me on its back—the cartouche of Amenhotep the Second. And there was the "A" of my dream! (pp. 259–260)

Lawrence experienced other premonitions and supernatural occurrences throughout her life, several of which are described in her two contributions to *Fifty Strangest Stories*: "Queer Happenings" and "Queer Disappearances." She later wrote about several other encounters with the spirit world in *Ferry Over Jordan* (1944). For more on how the opening of King Tut's tomb captured public imagination in Britain, see Chapter 1, "King Tut and the Dead Earl," in Roger Luckhurst's *The Mummy's Curse* (2012).

11. The cultural conflict that is central to Lawrence's story was no doubt influenced by contemporary tensions between Egypt and Britain in the decades leading up to the formal end of British colonial rule in Egypt. Mervat Hatem notes that Egyptian women became increasingly active in the protest movement against British rule, especially during the Egyptian Revolution of 1919, and their involvement in public demonstrations led to the rise of feminism in Egypt during the 1920s (1992, p. 41). For more on Egyptian and British women's attitudes toward one another, see Hatem's chapter, "Through Each Other's Eyes: The Impact on the Colonial Encounter of the Images of Egyptian, Levantine-Egyptian, and European Women, 1862–1920," in Nupur Chandhuri and Margaret Strobel's *Western Women and Imperialism* (1992).

Bibliography

The American Weekly (1928), "Margery Lawrence's Book No Publisher Dares to Print" (22 January): 7.

Bongie, Chris (1991), *Exotic Memories: Literature, Colonialism, and the Fin de Siècle*, Stanford, CA: Stanford University Press.

Brantlinger, Patrick (1988), *Rule of Darkness: British Literature and Imperialism, 1830–1914*, Ithaca and London: Cornell University Press.

Bulfin, Ailise (2011), "The Fiction of Gothic Egypt and British Imperial Paranoia: The Curse of the Suez Canal," *English Literature in Transition, 1880–1920* 54.4: 411–443.

Busia, Abena P. A. (1986), "Miscegenation as Metonymy: Sexuality and Power in the Colonial Novel," *Ethnic and Racial Studies* 9.3 (July): 360–372.

Cohen, Morton (ed.) (1965), *Rudyard Kipling to Rider Haggard: The Record of a Friendship*, Rutherford, NJ: Fairleigh Dickinson University Press.

Conrad, Joseph (2006 [1902]), *Heart of Darkness*, 4th edn., Paul B. Armstrong (ed.), New York: W. W. Norton.

Dalby, Richard (1998), "Introduction," in Richard Dalby (ed.), *Nights of the Round Table*, Ashcroft, BC: Ash-Tree Press, pp. ix–xix.

Garrity, Jane (2003), *Stepdaughters of England: British Women Modernists and the National Imaginary*, Manchester: Manchester University Press.

Hatem, Mervat (1992), "Through Each Other's Eyes: The Impact on the Colonial Encounter of the Images of Egyptian, Levantine-Egyptian, and European Women, 1862–1920," in Nupur Chandhuri and Margaret Strobel (eds.), *Western Women and Imperialism*, Bloomington: Indiana University Press, pp. 35–58.

Hay, Simon (2011), *A History of the Modern British Ghost Story*, Basingstoke: Palgrave Macmillan.

Hendershot, Cyndy (1998), *The Animal Within: Masculinity and the Gothic*, Ann Arbor: University of Michigan Press.

Lawrence, Margery (1937), "Queer Happenings," *Fifty Strangest Stories Ever Told*, London: Odhams Press, pp. 257–260.

—— (1953), "Foreword," *Ghosts over England*, by R. Thurston Hopkins, London: Meridian Books.

—— (1998a [1924]), "Death Valley," in Richard Dalby (ed.), *Nights of the Round Table*, Ashcroft, BC: Ash-Tree Press, pp. 105–120.

—— (1998b [1925]), "The Curse of the Stillborn" in Richard Dalby (ed.), *Nights of the Round Table*, Ashcroft, BC: Ash-Tree Press, pp. 121–133.

—— (1999 [1926]), "The Dogs of Pemba," in Richard Dalby (ed.), *The Terraces of Night*, Ashcroft, BC: Ash-Tree Press, pp. 146–160.

Luckhurst, Roger (2012), *The Mummy's Curse: The True History of a Dark Fantasy*, Oxford and New York: Oxford University Press.

McKechnie, Claire Charlotte (2013), "Man's Best Fiend: Evolution, Rabies, and the Gothic Dog," *Nineteenth-Century Prose* 40.1: 115–140.

McMahon, Elisabeth (2013), *Slavery and Emancipation in Islamic East Africa: From Honor to Respectability*, Cambridge: Cambridge University Press.

Rigby, Nigel (2000), "'Not a Good Place for Deacons': The South Seas, Sexuality and Modernism in Sylvia Townsend Warner's *Mr Fortune's Maggot*," in Nigel Rigby and Howard J. Booth (eds.), *Modernism and Empire*, Manchester: Manchester University Press, pp. 224–248.

CHAPTER 7

Colonial Gothic Framework: Haunted Houses in the Anglo-Indian Ghost Stories of Bithia Mary Croker

One of the most famous Gothic conventions is the haunted house. Yet, there is still one group of dwellings that remains neglected by scholars: the Anglo-Indian residence. These haunted habitations, ranging from the quintessential residence of the British in India—the colonial bungalow— to grand palaces once occupied by the rajahs of India, add a whole new dimension to traditional haunted house stories set in Great Britain and North America. Frequently termed "uncomfortable" and "unhealthy," these colonial houses offer readers an implicit critique of British imperialism while also expanding the parameters of women's already significant contributions to the haunted house trope. One Anglo-Indian author who has essentially vanished from critical view is the Irish-born Bithia Mary Croker, a writer who created some of the most striking cultural commentaries on the British colonial presence in India. Her writing spans the years 1880–1920, the apex of the British Empire in India. In addition to increasing British awareness of the complex gender dynamics and role of women in British imperial society through her numerous best-selling novels, in several short story collections Croker also exposed the dangers and complexities of inter-cultural encounter that could come from colonialism. In narratives that are far more subversive than most of her more traditional romance novels, she uses ghosts and local superstitions to illustrate the nebulous relationships and the often fragile détente that existed between colonized and colonizer. It is in this area that we can make a connection with that other major literary genre to come out of

© The Author(s) 2018
M. Edmundson, *Women's Colonial Gothic Writing, 1850–1930*,
Palgrave Gothic, https://doi.org/10.1007/978-3-319-76917-2_7

empire, the imperial Gothic, whose scholars have also generally ignored Croker's work. In her stories, we see the British trying to maintain a hold on reality when faced with ghostly others, while at the same time struggling to uphold themselves as a superior ruling power when unexplained supernatural unrest threatens their sense of order and control. This chapter examines two of Croker's ghost stories and how each speaks to the cultural unrest of Anglo-India through the figure of the vengeful revenant. "If You See Her Face" and "The Red Bungalow" consider the effects of British/Indian tension that leads to violence and unrestful Indian spirits who ultimately triumph over their imperial rulers. These stories concern murders and other forms of violence caused as a direct result of the British presence in India, and haunted buildings with ties to both Indian history and British imperial history frequently structure this discordance by providing specific sites of trauma.

"If You See Her Face," is included in Croker's first collection of supernatural tales, *To Let* (1893).[1] In the story, Croker leaves behind the British memsahibs who populate the bulk of her Anglo-Indian work and enters into the debate over the social status of Indian women with her portrayal of the ghost of a nautch girl.[2] She was certainly not the first Anglo-Indian to tackle the often sensitive subject of Indian women in the nineteenth century, but she is one of the few Victorians who looked sympathetically on these women, seeing them as victims of male hegemony and, in the form of ghosts, as empowered women who use their learned skills against their oppressors. In many ways, Croker's story belongs with the British literature of the eighteenth and early-nineteenth centuries which described nautch girls in more favorable terms than their Victorian descendants. Numerous travelers and British officials characterize these dancing girls in positive terms, and "nautch balls" were popular (and morally-sanctioned) colonial pastimes for both men and women prior to the high point of British imperialism later in the century. One of the more well-known accounts is from the first volume of James Forbes's four-volume *Oriental Memoirs* (1813–1815). In a section on Indian entertainments, Forbes includes a complimentary description of these professional women:

> Many of the dancing-girls are extremely delicate in their persons, soft and regular in their features, with a form of perfect symmetry; and, although dedicated from infancy to this profession, they in general preserve a decency and modesty in their demeanor, which is more likely to allure, than the shameless effrontery of similar characters in other countries. Their dancers require great attention, from the dancer's feet being hung with

small bells, which act in concert with the music. Two girls usually perform at the same time; their steps are not so mazy or active as ours, but much more interesting; as the song, the music, and the motions of the dance, combine to express love, hope, jealousy, despair, and the passions so well known to lovers, and very easily to be understood by those who are ignorant of other languages. (1813, vol. 1, p. 81)

Not only does Forbes stress the professional nature of the dancing girls and the years of training required to become masters of their craft, but he also hints at the cross-cultural appeal of these women, who transcend territorial boundaries and languages with their expressive dances. Descriptions such as this would become nearly extinct by the latter half of the century.

Though the rise of Victorian morality in mid-century initiated a wider public concern for the lives of Indian women,[3] it did not include much sympathy for India's dancing girls or *devadasis*.[4] To most nineteenth-century Anglo-Indians, temple dancers, still commonly known as "nautch girls," were associated with prostitutes or other kept women. An article from William Browne Hockley's three-volume *The English in India* (1828), reprinted in the *Calcutta Review* under the title, "The English in India—Our Social Morality," openly condemns nautch girls as "professional courtesans […] associated with all that is impure" (p. 331) and questions the moral character of any British man or woman who attends nautch gatherings. And though they were not always directly associated with prostitutes, nautch-girl literature becomes increasingly anxious about their place and influence within Anglo-Indian culture. W. Trego Webb's "The Nautch Girl," from his collection, *Indian Lyrics* (1884), is an example of this tendency. Webb's favorable description of the girl's dancing in the first half of the poem gives way to an increasing fear of the girl's hypnotic power over men:

> As she winds in snaky wreathings to the droning of the hymns;
> Till the truth is lost in seeming,
> And our spirits fall a-dreaming,
> 'Neath the spell of rhythmic paces and the mist of woven limbs.
> (1884, lines 15–18)

These lines are followed by an equally anxious notion of the girl's inner thoughts. While she dances, "a passionate light […] Smote upon us from her dark eyes and the ripples of her hair" (ibid., lines 23–24).

Webb chooses the negative connotation of "smote" to suggest that the girl possesses a secret, hidden resentment of the men who surround her, and that her personal judgment on these gazers becomes a larger moral judgment on these men's complicity in her objectification.

Perhaps most disturbing to the British, these women represented several cultural contradictions and freedoms not associated with other Indian women. Unlike married Indian women, devadasis could own property and pass it down to their adopted daughters; they were free to be with multiple men and were very much "career women," making money from their learned skills. Because they did not marry, they were also free from *sati*[5] and the burdens of child rearing, as well as the physical labors of tending crops and performing other domestic chores.[6] They were, instead, educated in the art of dancing and seduction. According to John Shortt, the Surgeon-General Superintendent of Vaccination for Madras, in his article "The Bayadère; or, Dancing Girls of Southern India," which he presented to the Anthropological Society of London and later published in the Society's journal, nautch girls lived in "professional concubinage" (1870, p. 182), but were higher, socially, than prostitutes who did not dance professionally. Shortt outlines the training regimen of these nautch girls, which begins around age five and continues for three years. During this time, the girls practice for four hours each day, focusing on the six ways of using their bodies: eyes, facial features, breasts, hands, feet, and tumbling (ibid., p. 183). In a later description of specific dances, he pays special attention to the importance of the feet, the part of the body which Croker emphasizes on her supernatural nautch girl. Shortt's essay is certainly an anthropological product of its time, displaying casual prejudice against a Hindu culture that supports and maintains the devadasi tradition, with comments such as this all-inclusive slander, "Wherever the Hindu religion predominates, there immortality and debauchery run riot" (ibid., p. 194). But his essay does show sympathy for the nautch girls themselves, whom he regards as "poor unfortunate women" who are "victims of such a system," adding, "These poor creatures are more sinned against than sinning themselves" (ibid., p. 194). He concludes his essay by calling for increased educational opportunities for these girls as an escape from what he terms the "superstition and bigotry" of their families (ibid., p. 194).

"If You See Her Face" provides one of the more complex Croker revenants, mainly because the ghost in question is one of the nautch girls who was the subject of such continued cultural debate. The action of the story involves two British officials who, because of complications during their travels to Delhi, must spend the night at an abandoned Indian palace. The legend surrounding the palace tells of a rajah who once tortured and disfigured a beautiful nautch girl whose ghost supposedly still dances at the palace, and who causes the immediate death of any man who looks at her face. Croker's portrayal of her female Indian ghost is largely influenced by popular interest in Indian women during the last decades of the nineteenth century and the social complexities which she wanted to represent to the British reading public. Nancy Paxton notes:

> British and Anglo-Indian novelists more often present [dancing girls] as embodying unresolved conflicts concerning gender, sex, and romantic love. In other words, because the *devadasis* who appear in these later nineteenth-century novels are typically imagined as beautiful and sexual, sacred and taboo, mature free women who are not confined to the domestic space of the Indian zenana, they challenge many of the most important boundaries in colonial defenses of empire. (1999, p. 86)

I would argue that Croker complicates this idea, while also taking it a step further. In this story, she expands the gendered boundaries of empire beyond even Paxton's conception by introducing a supernatural element that reverses normative gendered readings of Indian women. Her ghostly temple dancer is both freed from domestic space and from the worldly space of the living. Her presence reminds the reader not of the socially free women written about by novelists, but of the objectification and abuse of the devadasi. One can read her as being confined in the recurring role of revenant—one who cannot find rest—but Croker's description allows for the opposite interpretation, that the dancer somehow finds a morbid pleasure in enacting her dance, changing it from a once objectified and oppressed act into a gesture of female power over the male (both Indian and British).

In the story, Gregson, as a "Burra-Burra sahib," represents the worst that imperialism has to offer. His status as a high-ranking government official means that he has the power to help those less fortunate Indians around him, but he instead uses his power to increase his own wealth and social standing, as the narrator states that he "liked to feel his own importance" (Croker 2000a [1893], p. 22). Croker characterizes him as the villain of the story with repeated references to his disrespect of Indians and poor treatment of those around him. He orders his Indian servants to do his will with "an imperious wave of his hand" (p. 21). Because he represents the interests of the seven-year-old Rajah of Oonomore, Gregson feels superior to the Indians who reside in the remote village where one of the Rajah's palaces is located. Croker uses Gregson's connection to Indian royalty to critique a larger male-dominated system of control and indifference that exists above and apart from the female section of society who are struggling to survive. When Gregson and his assistant, Percy Goring, arrive at the palace, the narrator contrasts the two worlds separated by the palace's gates:

> In front of [the palace] a large space was paved with blocks of white marble, which ran the whole length of the building, and it was surrounded by the most exquisite gardens, kept up in perfect order—doubtless by the taxes wrung from the wretched creatures outside its gates—a garden that was never entered by its proprietor or enjoyed by anyone from year's end to year's end, save the mallee's children and the monkeys. The monkeys ate the fruit, the roses and lilies bloomed unseen, the fountains dripped unheeded; it was a paradise for the doves and squirrels, like a garden in a fairy tale. [...] It was truly an oasis in the desert when one contrasted it with the bare, desolate, barren country that lay outside its walls. (p. 23)

In this passage, Croker calls into question an entire system of government that reinforces vastly unequal power relations to the advantage of both the Indian ruling classes and the British administration who support them. Rather than open the gates to his people, they, as part of the working classes and lower castes, are found too unworthy to benefit from the resources they help to maintain. They are "wretched creatures" who have less freedom than the monkeys and squirrels who freely take what they want. When we see Gregson's relentless dominance over the Indians in the village, and over the young and seemingly naïve Rajah, we begin to question who the real destructive force is in the story.[7] By characterizing Gregson in such a light, Croker manages to make the supernatural, deadly nautch girl the heroine of the story. She represents one of the locals, but, unlike the living inhabitants of the village, she is no longer confined to rigid social customs and class consciousness, and can take revenge on her oppressors from beyond the grave.

A recurring theme that runs throughout Croker's Anglo-Indian supernatural tales is the danger that comes from British men and women's failure to listen to the local inhabitants and to appreciate their understanding of the surrounding environment. This has to do not only with knowledge of the physical aspects of the landscape, but also the cultural knowledge of the customs, traditions, and superstitions from the past that still greatly influence the present. Assigned the role of hero in the story, Percy Goring represents a younger and less hardened British colonial presence than Gregson. In Goring, Croker is hinting at the possibility for the younger generation of Anglo-Indian officers and civil servants to reverse previous wrongs done to the Indian people. He represents a middle ground of cultural tolerance that Anglo-Indian officials and the wider British public needed to adopt. Goring is also less interested in the commercial gains of empire, instead preferring to spend his time hunting, dancing, and enjoying India as a place of adventure, not of conquest. In temperament, he is the opposite of Gregson. Goring is much more generous to the Indian people and recognizes the difficulties faced by the villagers, though he keeps these thoughts to himself. After he sees the village outside the palace, Goring immediately identifies the underlying problem in the management of the area, saying:

> It is a very poor district, and much too heavily assessed […] There is not even a pony in the place. The very Bunnia is in rags; the deer eat the crops, such as they are, since the deer are preserved, and there is no one now to shoot them. It is abominable! (p. 23)

Being a junior assistant, and therefore an underling himself, he is perhaps better able to recognize and describe the oppressive system that keeps these people poor. The contrast between Goring and Gregson is even more apparent when the two men enter the village. The locals initially see Gregson as a "great and all-powerful personage" (p. 22) who has the power to improve their situation by listening to their complaints. However, this hopefulness is quickly dimmed by Gregson's response:

> An aged beldame got in his way, and he struck her savagely with his stick. She shrank back with a sharp cry, and Goring, who was ever known as "a sahib with a soft heart," spoke to her and gave her a rupee—a real rupee; it was years since she had felt one! (p. 22)

Though Goring is warned that the woman has "the evil eye," he stays to listen to her and, in so doing, gets the information that will ultimately save his life, as she tells him, "I am a lone old woman; my kindred are dead—I have lived too long. I remember the former days—rich days; but bad days. Sahib, if you would be wise, go not to the palace Khana. [...] *If you see her face—you die!*" (p. 22, 23). Though Goring thinks to himself that the woman must be unbalanced, his generosity to her and his willingness to listen, elicit her generosity in return. On the other hand, Gregson's violence and indifference are met with the anger and curses of the crowd, who Croker uses to again bring attention to the sufferings of the Indians because of an inept system of colonial rule:

> You say we have land—true! [...] but what is land without crops? What is a remission of five per cent to wretches like us? It is but as a carraway seed in a camel's mouth! The wild beasts take our cattle and destroy our grain, and yet we must work and pay you, and starve! Would that the Rajah was a man grown! Would that *you* were dead! (p. 23)

This focus on the poverty of the villagers links to the mysterious nautch girl, who most likely came from the surrounding village. In his essay, Shortt mentions that many of these dancing girls came from poor families who sold their daughters to temples in order to support other members of the family: "I have no doubt but that advantage has been taken of the recent famine in various parts of Southern India, to send agents out to purchase girls to recruit the dancing girl and other prostituting classes" (1870, p. 187). This commodification continued once the girls were employed, as their services were sold to powerful, wealthy men outside the temple who paid according to the reputation and talent of each girl (ibid., p. 193).

The two men's respective fates in the story correlate to how each man chooses to react to his surroundings. Gregson's last moments before seeing the nautch girl are spent doing paperwork in the palace, thinking of nothing else except the business of empire. Goring, on the other hand, sits outside the palace, thinking of the mistreated people and about local stories he has been told. This sympathetic connection with his surroundings recalls stories and rumors about Khana's troubled history. Part of that history has to do with "crimes" and "hideous atrocities" (Croker 2000a, p. 24) that took place during the time of the grandfather of the young Rajah. This man, the "Tiger Rajah," who is aptly named for something indigenous and potentially dangerous, supposedly tortured a nautch girl. This story gives Goring the warning he needs to survive her apparition, while Gregson, who has no interest in local lore, is defenseless against the spectral presence.

The spectral girl uses her body and her training, a training which guaranteed commodification throughout her life, in order to take revenge on another oppressor. Both Goring and Gregson are entranced by her dancing, which Goring describes as a "poetry of motion" (p. 24). Croker also hints at the objectification of the girl by first allowing Goring to see only her disembodied feet. But this beauty turns deadly and, as Gregson walks out to where the girl's ghost is dancing, he sees her face and dies. This mixture of innocence and fatalness is described in Shorrt's essay in a different context:

> Some portions of the step resemble the hornpipe and jig, whilst they hop and dance from one leg to another, keeping time, now turning, now whirling, now capering, and now drooping, performing a coquettish pantomime with their antics, then affecting coyness, and dancing from the assembly, by suddenly turning away as if careless of their allurements, but returning to the attack with greater vigour and increased blandishments. (1870, p. 189)

His mention of an "attack" admits the power of the women to control and dominate the emotions of the crowd during these dances. In much the same way, Croker's nautch girl "attacks" with her dancing, but the result is not one of pleasure. Her attack, her individual act of revenge, extends outward to represent a moment when the powerless of India (especially the women represented by the nautch girl) fight back against both their Indian and British oppressors. Her action is the girl's and India's moment of retribution. The personification of the Indian subcontinent as female has been commented on by many scholars, but Indrani Sen's description of this connection between exotic/alluring country and femininity is particularly useful in a discussion of Croker's story about a supernatural femme fatale. As Sen notes, there are many undercurrents of anxiety over Indian femininity and the ability of Indian women to use their sexuality in order to control men (2002, pp. 58–60).[8] In her story, Croker reinterprets the notion of Indian women's power, extending their sexual influence into the realm of the supernatural.

No longer the prey of men like the Tiger Rajah, the girl uses her ghostly body to tempt other men, thereby becoming a huntress herself.[9] Like the tiger, she becomes an otherworldly symbol of a mysterious and terrible retributive power. In giving both the former rajah and the ghostly dancer qualities typically associated with the animal, Croker highlights both the destructive power which led to the rajah's violence and his attack on the girl, while at the same time suggesting the supernatural nautch girl's mysteriousness and the implacable, threatening role she plays in the story. In so doing, Croker gives the girl destructive capabilities equal to the former rajah. In this passage, Croker shows her knowledge of the tiger as a revered symbol for the Indian people, an animal representing both power and beauty. By possessing both these qualities in her supernatural form, the nautch girl is spiritually connected with the goddesses Durga and Jagadhatri, represented by the lion and tiger, respectively, and who both symbolize female force and energy. Both goddesses are associated with an invincible creative force, fierce yet beautiful, and also are associated with redemption—all qualities that the supernatural nautch girl embodies. Durga, as a goddess, represents a positive connotation of the supernatural, and popular belief held that if one saw her face, that person would live and thrive. Croker's treatment of this belief forwards the idea that, by causing the death of the evil or socially disruptive "enemies" of her people, the nautch girl, like Durga, brings greater well-being (or, at least the possibility of a better life) to her people. According to Shri A. Parthasarathy in *The Symbolism of Hindu Gods and Rituals* (1989), the goddess Durga is usually seen riding a lion and "holds a severed head in one hand and a lotus in another etc.—all these represent destruction of evil and protection of good" (p. 61). The nautch girl is also linked with the widespread belief that tigers were protectors and symbols of voluntary bodily sacrifice.[10] Though she died unwillingly, the girl nonetheless becomes more powerful in the afterlife and, as a ghost, serves as protector of her people by keeping the British forces at bay. After Gregson's fatal encounter, his Indian retainers readily admit, "Well, well, it was ever an evil place. […] It was the nautch-girl, without doubt" (Croker 2000a, p. 25). They tell Goring the same story that the old woman told him, showing that the villagers possess a former knowledge of her, which seemingly protects them. Croker is also deliberately ambiguous about who has fallen victim to the girl's stare. The comment, "More than one had seen her since, and perished thus" (p. 25), suggests that it is disruptive outsiders who do not carry the villagers' favor—symbolized in the warning they choose to impart to Goring but not to Gregson—who fall victim to the nautch girl. In this way, Croker allows the spectral body to find worth again in a visible, though not corporeal form, a body that is now used to harm and not to please, a form to wield power and not to yield to power.

Along with haunted palaces and their troubled pasts, the haunted Anglo-Indian bungalows that Croker describes can be considered a magnified representation of contemporary, historical fears centered on the colonial dwelling. Architectural scholars have addressed the contradictions inherent in the bungalow which created this cultural anxiety. In *Interiors of Empire* (2007), Robin D. Jones claims that the Anglo-Indian bungalow was intended as a refuge from India and Indian people, and states that "the intention of Europeans on inhabiting the colonial bungalow was [...] to reproduce a Westernized space and Western social practices. However, a combination of local factors [including how the bungalow was built] inflected the way in which they inhabited this dwelling, and disrupted their sense of home within the empire" (p. 27). It served as the most important domestic space during the British Raj and was meant to show British discipline, orderliness, and authority. However, the design itself worked against these principles. Due to the need for continuous ventilation, there was rarely an interior room and most rooms had doors opening directly onto the verandah. Because of this design, British families and their Indian servants frequently walked in the same areas, which made privacy very difficult. William J. Glover notes that this lack of privacy led to an increasing sense of displacement, as the bungalow became a social artifact that was "a source of both homely comfort and disquieting anxiety" (2012, p. 60). As early as the 1860s, the British themselves were voicing this sense of cultural discomfort. In 1862, Colesworthy Grant wrote in *Anglo-Indian Domestic Life*, "The exterior [of the bungalow] will, I doubt not, be sufficient to impress you with a feeling of absence from old England" (p. 7). In 1904, Herbert Compton expressed similar views in *Indian Life in Town and Country*, saying: "The Anglo-Indian's bungalow is as different from an English house in its external appearance and internal arrangement as is a temple from a church" (p. 212).

This feeling of unease within the colonial bungalow has led some scholars to describe the structure as a form of the "architectural uncanny." Most notably, Anthony Vidler says that these buildings give a sense of "estrangement," "alienation," and a "feeling of unease" (1999, pp. ix, 3). Vidler connects this feeling to the literary haunted house, a trope he calls both a "literary fantasy" and "architectural revival" (ibid., p. 17). He claims, "The house provided an especially favored site for uncanny disturbances: its apparent domesticity, its residue of family history and nostalgia, its role as the last and most intimate shelter of private comfort sharpened by contrast the terror of invasion by alien spirits" (ibid., p. 17). Especially after the 1857 Rebellion, these houses became architectural elements of the Indian landscape that held symbolic significance for both the British and Indians. Because of their violent pasts, these places were often thought to be haunted. Iris Portal, a member of a civil service family who lived in Meerut in the early twentieth century, remarked that many bungalows had plaques commemorating the violent deaths of their former inhabitants. She recalled:

> There was one bungalow near by where they had to take their beds out into the garden, not only for the heat but because things happened, like doors blowing open when there was no wind. Dogs would never stay in the house, and it was emphatically haunted. They all felt it and they all hated it, and that was one of the Mutiny bungalows with a plaque on it. (quoted in Macmillan 2007, p. 103)

Having lived in India and experienced this environment firsthand, Croker chose to transfer this cultural anxiety into fiction.

Croker's "The Red Bungalow," published in her final collection of short stories, *Odds and Ends* (1919), is one of the most disturbing haunted bungalow stories written by the author. It is comparable to Croker's earlier ghost stories, most notably "To Let" and "The Dâk Bungalow at Dakor." Yet, instead of only witnessing a past violent act like the protagonists in these two latter stories, the family in "The Red Bungalow" directly suffers from the malevolent spirit that inhabits the house.

The story is told by Liz Drummond, wife of a British Army colonel, who welcomes her cousin, Tom Fellowes, and his family to her station in Kulu. The family includes Tom's wife Netta and their two children: Guy, aged four, and Baba, aged two. Liz tries to convince Netta to take possession of another couple's bungalow once they return home, but Netta decides to rent the Red Bungalow. Although the house is spacious and well-planned, Liz describes the bungalow's odd presence in the station, saying, "for some unexplained reason, this particular bungalow had never counted; it was boycotted [...] *ignored*, as if, like some undesirable character, it had no place in the station's thoughts." Nonetheless, the house stands at a crossroads, "as if determined to obtrude upon public attention" (Croker 2000b [1919], p. 29). This description gives the bungalow a malicious, animated quality within the narrative. When Netta asks the agent why the rent is so low and why the house has remained empty for so long, he plays upon her ego, saying that it is "too majestic [...] for insignificant people" (p. 31). While Liz is alone in the house on this initial inspection, she hears "a long-drawn wailing cry" (p. 31) sweep through the house and becomes convinced that there is something wrong with the property, but Netta will not take her presentiments seriously. Liz's ayah later warns her about the rumors surrounding the bungalow and tells her not to let the "pretty little children" live there. She tells Liz that it is a "bad place," a "*bad* bungalow" (p. 33). Later, two more women warn Liz and Netta about the house. Mrs. Dodd tells them that local residents call it "the devil's house" and that "a terrible tragedy happened there long ago" (p. 34). Likewise, an older resident who is the wife of a government employee tells Liz that the problems are somehow connected with old mounds of brickwork on the bungalow's grounds where a palace or temple stood thousands of years ago, "when Kulu was a great native city" (p. 35). In this description, Indian history supersedes British history and hints at the fact that, although the present political autonomy of the Indians has lessened under British control, the power of ancient India and its supernatural energy has not diminished because of imperialism.

Initially, the Red Bungalow becomes the center of entertainments for the British in the station—badminton, dances, dinners, and play rehearsals—and everyone seems happy. Then the servants begin to leave and refuse to stay in the compound at night, claiming that "It" and a "Thing" occupies the bungalow and the grounds. However, Netta still does not listen to any warnings and claims that other women are only jealous of her for having such a nice home at such a cheap rent. While Liz and Netta are preparing for Baba's birthday party, they hear "a loud, frantic shriek, the shriek of extreme mortal terror" (p. 37) and when they rush into the children's nursery they see the following:

> There, huddled together, we discovered the two children on the table which stood in the middle of the apartment. Guy had evidently climbed up by a chair, and dragged his sister along with him. It was a beautiful afternoon, the sun streamed in upon them, and the room, as far as we could see, was empty. Yes, but not empty to the trembling little creatures on the table, for with wide, mad eyes they seemed to follow the motion of a something that was creeping round the room close to the wall, and I noticed that their gaze went up and down, as they accompanied its progress with starting pupils and gasping breaths. (p. 37)

This is an effective passage on many levels. Croker's decision not to describe this supernatural presence in the room with the women and children only magnifies the horror because it is left up to the reader's imagination. Also, the juxtaposition of the sunny, beautiful afternoon with this "thing" creeping around the room and the terrified children heightens the sense of wrongness. Guy can only yell "look, look, look!" but the women see nothing (p. 37). This is the colonial gaze taken to its deadly extreme. The supernatural entity has chosen to prey on the children alone, which allows Croker to consider colonial fears about the vulnerability of British children in India who were often victims of the harsh Indian climate.

After the incident, Guy dies of "brain fever" and Baba remains mute for the rest of her life. Netta takes her daughter back to England and all their possessions are sold. In this way, the Red Bungalow once again rejects any attempt to Anglicize it. Left empty once again, it becomes wild and inhabited with squirrels, scorpions, and white ants—the ghost reclaims the land for India. In a larger context, this is Croker's statement about what will eventually happen to British rule. The bungalow reflects empire itself. Like the house, British efforts may be "well-planned" but ultimately are not sustainable, will not be a lasting success.

In the Croker stories discussed in this chapter, and in many other Anglo-Indian supernatural tales of the time, there is a culture of silence that closes each story. Beyond the troubled image of supernatural retribution, readers are left to try to understand the silence of the characters who are involved in the events of the stories. In "If You See Her Face," Croker seems to agree with this view in her choice of ending: "Goring—*wise man*—said nothing" (p. 25, emphasis mine). On a symbolic level, Croker hints at the ongoing problem with not telling the whole story, suggesting that there is a danger in other people not knowing the details of these supernatural occurrences and thereby not learning valuable cultural lessons. It is dangerous to speak the truth—about what they witnessed, and about the uncomfortable truths of empire. In each story, there is the sense of a deeper anxiety causing the silence. Violent actions have consequences, and crimes can never truly be forgotten. Likewise, the past and present crimes of imperial domination also cannot be addressed directly. There is the feeling of anxiety in acknowledging the idea that Indians, such as the nautch girl and the unseen spirit who occupies the Red Bungalow, can come back, can assert their own power in the even more uncontrollable form of a spectre and, in so doing, upset the delicate balance of British power.

Both stories provide early examples of how Ken Gelder and Jane Jacobs describe the postcolonial ghost story, as one which is "often quite literally about 'the return of the repressed'—namely, the return of the 'truth' (or a 'truth effect') about colonization" (1998, p. 188). In these supernatural stories, Croker leaves her readers with an uneasy, oftentimes ambiguous ending representative of the characters' own uneasiness about their marginal position as outsiders in India. As Gelder and Jacobs point out, "To settle on a haunted site is to risk unsettlement" (ibid., p. 188), with a double meaning of the word "unsettlement." The inhabitants of these colonial haunted houses are displaced and unsettled. In writing about the ghosts who haunt abandoned palaces and bungalows, Croker makes an indirect, yet purposeful statement about the potential dangers of British colonization and imperialism, and the harm that such an occupation inflicts on both the living and the dead. In her stories, Indian revenants are far more powerful in the afterlife. They are freed from their subjugation, and the power dynamics that led to their control by the British are reversed.

These stories and the cultural anxieties that are reflected in their ghosts raise important questions. If the narrator tries to silence his or her knowledge, then how many others are equally complicit? How many people choose *not* to tell of such atrocities for fear of being implicated themselves? How many of these stories truly do go untold, fictionally or otherwise? Through her Anglo-Indian ghost stories, however, Croker attempts to solve this gap in communication. Even though her main characters often refuse to tell the story to others within the narrative, they do "tell" their stories from the perspective of a published piece of writing. Croker wanted her audience to acknowledge the tensions that arose because of colonialism, tensions which are represented in the rising of the ghosts that symbolize the unrest caused by imperialism. And although this may seem an odd way to try to reach the British reading public—through stories which most of her readership may not find believable—I would argue that Croker knew exactly what she was doing, and accomplished her aims better than most other Anglo-Indian storytellers of the period, including Kipling. Croker's stories are psychologically more complex than most other Anglo-Indian ghost stories of the time. Her female characters are rarely the sweet, docile heroines that populated Anglo-Indian romance novels of the day.[11] The British men who are typically represented as brave heroes defending the honor of their nation also frequently fall short of the heroic ideal that was celebrated in imperial romance and adventure fiction. And Indians who are stereotyped and over-simplified in many of the novels of the time become more complex and multi-dimensional in these ghost stories. Beyond the more well-known, often formulaic, adventure and romance fiction of the time, Croker gives us something more complex in her Anglo-Indian ghost stories, and the cultural warnings she offered to her contemporary readers still have relevance today.

Notes

1. Published by Chatto & Windus, *To Let* was widely popular and garnered critical praise. Contemporary reviewers noted Croker's ability to tell a realistic Indian story and to consistently entertain readers with her narrative technique. Croker followed *To Let* with *Village Tales and Jungle Tragedies* (1895), *In the Kingdom of Kerry* (1896), *Jason* (1899), *A State Secret* (1901), and *The Old Cantonment* (1905), with the first two collections containing the majority of her Anglo-Indian ghost stories. For this chapter, I have chosen to use Richard Dalby's edition of Croker's supernatural works.
2. The word "nautch" is the Anglicized version of the Hindi/Urdu word "nach," meaning "dance."
3. The *Calcutta Review* continually carried articles about the social status of Indian women, many of which condemned their limited freedoms, the practice of early marriage, and the tradition of sati. The opening lines of an 1869 *Calcutta Review* article on "Hindoo Female Celebrities" best sums up this interest: "Few subjects engage so much of the public attention at the present time as the condition of Hindoo females. It is discussed in the legislature, in public assemblies, and in domestic circles. It is the fertile theme of philanthropists, reformers, and public lecturers. Affecting, as it does, the great question of the regeneration of India, it has well-nigh become the absorbing topic of the day" (p. 54).
4. An exception to this tendency is Edward Solomon's *The Nautch Girl, or, The Rajah of Chutneypore*, a comic opera which opened at the Savoy Theatre in June 1891. The production ran for almost a year before touring the British colonies. It featured Leonore Snyder as the sympathetic nautch girl, "Hollee Beebee," who, after regaining her Brahmin status, embarks on a successful dancing tour of Europe. At the end of the opera, she returns to India and is reunited with her love, Indru, son of the rajah.
5. The Hindu religious practice of sati involved a recently widowed woman sacrificing herself (whether voluntarily or involuntarily) on her husband's funeral pyre. British missionaries campaigned against the practice, and sati was officially outlawed in India in 1829.

6. Although they were not well educated, there were exceptions to this rule. Some devadasis learned multiple languages, including English.
7. As an Irish woman transplanted to India, Croker had a broader understanding of the negative effects of colonialization and could thus create a villainous British government official perhaps more easily than her contemporary Anglo-Indian/English writers.
8. Sen goes on to connect educational reform for Indian women with this colonial anxiety over native female sexuality: "the thrust of this educational effort appears to have been to recast the much-maligned Indian female sensuality of the zenanas with its preoccupations with the body and bodily functions and with its rites on sex and sexuality" (2002, p. 65).
9. Croker may well have had in mind the Indian folktale, "The Brâhmin Girl That Married a Tiger," which was collected for the British reading public in *Tales of the Sun: Or, Folklore of Southern India* (1890), edited by Georgiana Kingscote and Pandit Natêsá Sástri and published in London and Calcutta.
10. For more information on the symbolism of the tiger in Indian and Asian tradition, see Jack Tresidder's entry in *The Complete Dictionary of Symbols* (2004). Tresidder's description of the tiger's symbolism, and his comparison of the animal to the lion, help to further highlight the deeper symbolic meaning of the nautch girl in Croker's story. Tresidder mentions that both animals represent "death and life, evil and evil's destruction" (p. 478). In the story, the nautch girl is a destroyer, but by causing the death of the corrupt and power-hungry Gregson, she is protecting her people.
11. These romances were popular throughout the Raj period and followed a basic narrative formula which typically included a young and naïve woman arriving in India from Britain, her struggle to survive and thrive, either physically or socially, in the new and strange land, and her eventual marriage to a heroic and respectable Anglo-Indian man.

Bibliography

Compton, Herbert (1904), *Indian Life in Town and Country*, New York: G.P. Putnam's Sons.

Croker, Bithia Mary (2000a [1893]), "If You See Her Face," in Richard Dalby (ed.), *"Number Ninety" and Other Ghost Stories*, Mountain Ash, Wales: Sarob Press, pp. 20–25.

——— (2000b [1919]), "The Red Bungalow," in Richard Dalby (ed.), *"Number Ninety" and Other Ghost Stories*, Mountain Ash, Wales: Sarob Press, pp. 26–38.

"The English in India—Our Social Morality" (1844), *Calcutta Review*: 290–336.

Forbes, James (1813), *Oriental Memoirs*, 4 vols., London: White, Cochrane, & Company.
Gelder, Ken, and Jane M. Jacobs (1998), *Uncanny Australia: Sacredness and Identity in a Postcolonial Nation*, Carlton, VIC: Melbourne University Press.
Glover, William J. (2012), "A Feeling of Absence from Old England: The Colonial Bungalow," in Kathy Mezei and Chiara Briganti (eds.), *The Domestic Space Reader*, Toronto: University of Toronto Press, pp. 59–64.
Grant, Colesworthy (1862), *Anglo-Indian Domestic Life*, Calcutta: Thacker, Spink.
"Hindoo Female Celebrities" (1869), *Calcutta Review* 48: 54–60.
Jones, Robin D. (2007), *Interiors of Empire: Objects, Space and Identity Within the Indian Subcontinent, c. 1800–1947*, Manchester: Manchester University Press.
Kingscote, Georgiana, and Pandit Natêsá Sástri (1890), "The Brâhmin Girl That Married a Tiger," in *Tales of the Sun: Or, Folklore of Southern India*, London and Calcutta: W.H. Allen, pp. 119–130.
Macmillan, Margaret (2007), *Women of the Raj: The Mothers, Wives, and Daughters of the British Empire in India*, New York: Random House.
Parthasarathy, Shri A. (1989), *The Symbolism of Hindu Gods and Rituals*, Bombay: Vedanta Life Institute.
Paxton, Nancy L. (1999), *Writing Under the Raj: Gender, Race, and Rape in the British Colonial Imagination, 1830–1947*, New Brunswick: Rutgers University Press.
Sen, Indrani (2002), *Woman and Empire: Representations in the Writings of British India (1858–1900)*, Hyderabad: Orient Longman.
Shortt, John (1870), "The Bayadère; or, Dancing Girls of Southern India," *Memoirs Read Before the Anthropological Society of London* 3: 182–194.
Solomon, Edward (1891), *The Nautch Girl, or, The Rajah of Chutneypore*, London: Chappell.
Tresidder, Jack (2004), "Tiger," in *The Complete Dictionary of Symbols*, San Francisco: Chronicle Books, p. 478.
Vidler, Anthony (1999), *The Architectural Uncanny: Essays in the Modern Unhomely*, Cambridge: MIT Press.
Webb, W. Trego (1884), "The Nautch Girl," in *Indian Lyrics*, Calcutta and London: Thacker.

CHAPTER 8

Animal Gothic in Alice Perrin's *East of Suez*

Throughout her more than forty years as a best-selling author, Alice Perrin created striking cultural commentaries on the British colonial presence in India. Though perhaps best-known today for her romance novels set in India, Perrin gained initial fame writing Anglo-Indian ghost stories that, like her contemporary Bithia Mary Croker, are more subversive than her longer fiction. Born in India in 1867, Perrin was the daughter of a Major-General in the Bengal Cavalry and great-granddaughter to a former director of the East India Company. She spent sixteen years in India as the wife of an engineer in the Public Works Department and, after her return to England upon her husband's retirement, Perrin's supernatural stories appeared in the collections *East of Suez* (1901), *Red Records* (1906), *Tales That Are Told* (1917), and *Rough Passages* (1926).

Upon the release of *East of Suez*, critics immediately began making comparisons between Perrin and Rudyard Kipling. *Punch* compared *East of Suez* to the best of Kipling's stories, saying: "The authoress gives us a collection of cleverly-written stories which […] for graphic description, sharp incisive sketches of character, and effective dramatic situation, are second only to the *Plain Tales* by Rudyard Kipling; while two or three of them run even the best of Kipling's uncommonly close" (1901, p. 296). Another reviewer of *East of Suez* praised Perrin's ability to maintain both the reader's suspense and an overall high quality of storytelling, remarking, "The author has caught the atmosphere of the East, and one feels it in her work […] Some of her stories show considerable power in the region

© The Author(s) 2018   157
M. Edmundson, *Women's Colonial Gothic Writing, 1850–1930*,
Palgrave Gothic, https://doi.org/10.1007/978-3-319-76917-2_8

of the weird, and the supernatural, and have that quality of horror which ensures their being read, and talked about" (quoted in Tremayne 1901).

Indeed, as this reviewer says, quite a few stories in the collection feature the "weird," the "supernatural," and the horrific. Yet, what is particularly interesting is the extent to which animals play a key role in Perrin's treatment of the Colonial Gothic. Of the fourteen stories that make up *East of Suez*, at least half feature animals as central plot devices. They include a man wandering into a river and being eaten by a crocodile, a terrified woman being thrown from an out-of-control elephant, a man being carried away by a tiger, another man being stalked and killed by a tiger, a baby being partially eaten by a rat, a dead body being eaten by a jackal, and a pregnant woman being literally scared into premature delivery after an encounter with a monitor lizard. These animals, in turn, either directly or indirectly cause the deaths of characters, and their presence highlights the failures of the perceived safe space of the domestic colonial home as well as the wild unpredictability of the Indian outdoors. These gruesome plots portray graphic descriptions of the negative consequences of the imperial mission, and to a greater extent than other fictional versions of empire. This chapter centers on three specific instances of "Animal Gothic" from "Caulfield's Crime," "A Man's Theory," and "The Biscobra." Each of these stories combines colonial anxiety, cultural tension between Indians and the British, violence, madness, and death in narratives that ultimately call into question the "civilizing mission" of empire while employing Gothic narratives as subversive comments on colonial power structures.

In recent years, there has been increased interest in the way animals functioned within the British colonial enterprise, as well as the many ways these animals found their way into fiction. Teresa Mangum claims, "Nowhere is the animal at once so ferocious and so admired as in the genre that has been called empire fiction, empire adventure fiction, and even imperial male romance" (2007, p. 165). Though Mangum's examination of colonial animals centers on the novels of Rider Haggard, her discussion is equally relevant to the imperial concerns and anxieties in Perrin's fiction. Beneath the fictional struggles between man and beast in colonial regions such as Africa and India (often symbolized through the act of hunting), there is something far more sinister and unsettling about the stability of the imperial mission. The role of predator and prey is constantly shifting and being called into question, and the "uncharted wilderness" often checks the "arrogance" of the British colonial explorer.

The colony as a place of conquest and dominion becomes instead "a world of unimaginable power, struggle, fury, and shocking death" (ibid., p. 166). For Mangum, this dynamic, when considered in popular fiction, signaled possible weaknesses within the imperial structure: "Venturing into territories that were not only hostile but sufficient unto themselves prompted genuine fear that Europeans were in the worst sense invaders—predators who, far worse than animals, actively chose to act in ways that (ironically) exposed their instinctive violence and domination through their relentless encroachments" (ibid., p. 170).

"Caulfield's Crime," which is the most frequently anthologized Alice Perrin story, focuses on the repercussions of violence against Indians. The story concerns an Englishman who has an intimate knowledge of India but misdirects his abilities by abusing his power, ending up the victim of a reincarnated Indian spirit who returns from the grave to seek revenge over a violent, needless death. In Perrin's story, the avid hunter and adventurer (normally viewed as the quintessential Englishman) goes from hero to villain as she creates the unlikable, brutish persona of Caulfield. Perrin does not hesitate to pass judgment on his character from the very beginning, suggesting that the act which makes up the major event in the story is, indeed, a "crime" committed by a British officer who has few, if any, redeeming qualities. The first appearance of "Caulfield's Crime" in the 1892 *Belgravia Annual* was substantially revised by Perrin before the story's appearance in *East of Suez*. In earlier versions, Caulfield's personality is described in more detail. In the opening paragraph of the periodical publication, the unnamed narrator describes Caulfield as "the worst-tempered fellow I ever met" (Perrin 1893, p. 598), and then continues to say that he is "vindictive" and "passionately violent" (p. 598).[1]

In the first lines of the revised story, Perrin tempers Caulfield's personality, describing him as "a sulky, bad-tempered individual who made no friends and was deservedly unpopular" (Perrin 2011b [1901], p. 125). Caulfield is also known for being a good shot and an excellent sportsman. From the opening paragraphs of the story, Perrin establishes Caulfield as another example of the popular image of the British imperial sportsman. As Harriet Ritvo says: "The connection between triumphing over a dangerous animal and subduing unwilling natives was direct and obvious, and the association of the big game hunter with the march of empire" was an established trope in contemporary sporting and adventure tales set in India and Africa (1987, p. 254). Thus, "the hunter emerged as both the ideal and the definitive type of the empire builder" (ibid., p. 254). This image of the hunter was largely based on imperialist attitudes which sought to raise the British over colonized peoples, making the act of hunting a "display of white dominance" (MacKenzie 1988, p. 7). Yet, Perrin complicates this idealized image of the heroic British male. To everyone's surprise, the usually solitary Caulfield invites the story's unnamed narrator, who is a junior officer, on a hunting expedition. On their way, they encounter an old Indian priest, and Caulfield commits an act of violence that prefigures his later, even more violent "crime." During this first encounter, the narrator immediately associates the fakir with an animal, saying, "The man's face was long and thin, and his pointed teeth glistened in the sunlight as he demanded money in a dismal monotone. Caulfield flung a pebble at him and told him roughly to be off" (Perrin 2011b [1901], p. 127). Caulfield then tells the narrator that the fakir "must have been a pariah dog in a former existence" to which the other man responds that the old man was more like a jackal and a "wild beast." In *Empire and the Animal Body* (2014), John Miller discusses how animals functioned in popular adventure fiction of the late nineteenth century, saying, "The representation of a resemblance between native and animal was a common trope of colonial discourse, forcefully asserting the supposed gulf between coloniser and colonised and opening a range of violent and repressive possibilities for colonial rulers as racial others are emptied of their human status" (p. 2). Though both Caulfield and the narrator soon forget the fakir, their dehumanizing comments about the man will literally come back to haunt them both.

The two men think no more of this encounter until they reach the place where the duck and snipe are plentiful and, as they prepare to shoot, they discover that the fakir has scared away the game. The men continue the hunt only to have the birds again scared away by the fakir. This time, without hesitating, Caulfield shoots and kills the Indian man. As they approach the body, the increasingly disturbed narrator notices that the fakir's face "seemed more beast-like than ever" and asks what they should do next. Caulfield responds by implying that silence is the only option, saying, "Killing a native is no joke in these days, and I should come out of it pretty badly" (Perrin 2011b [1901], p. 128). They both agree to cover up the murder by hiding the body and returning later with shovels to bury the man. When they return to the spot, they find a large, gray, one-eared jackal "lying on the fakir's body, grinning and snarling at being disturbed over his hideous meal" (p. 129).

Perrin's choice of a jackal reflects the cultural attitudes towards the animal within the colonial environment. William John Burchell's *Travels in the Interior of Southern Africa* (1824), describes the uncanny noise made by the jackals, while also giving them human-like qualities:

> Every night, the *jackals*, attracted perhaps by the smell of so much meat, approached us [...] The sound of their barking was peculiar, and might not inaptly be compared to that of *laughing*. It would not have been easy to shoot one, as they are real cowards, slinking away the moment they perceive any person coming towards them. (2: 285)

Likewise, Edward Turner Bennett's *The Tower Menagerie* (1829) describes the jackal in equally Gothic terms:

> They even break into the cemeteries of the dead, and tearing open the graves by means of their powerful claws, disinter the buried corpses, on which they glut that horrid propensity for feeding on carrion, which is at once the most striking and the most disgusting of their peculiarities. Their fondness for this polluted species of food tends of course not a little to increase the natural antipathy with which they are regarded by the natives of the countries in which they abound, and renders them objects of peculiar detestation and abhorrence. (p. 75)

In *The Descent of Man* (1871), Charles Darwin suggested that the jackal was less domesticated and therefore more immoral than the dog: "Our domestic dogs are descended from wolves and jackals, and though they may not have gained in cunning, and may have lost in wariness and suspicion, yet they have progressed in certain moral qualities, such as in affection, trust-worthiness, temper, and probably in general intelligence" (1: 50). John Lockwood Kipling, in *Beast and Man in India* (1892), further details the connection of the jackal with impending danger, saying, "The jackal's night-cry,—the wild chorus with which the band begins its hungry prowl, is of evil omen" and "it is believed that when the cry is raised near the house of a sick person, it is a sure presage of death" (p. 278). When Caulfield and the narrator attempt to drive the animal away from the body, the jackal refuses to move, and the narrator begins to experience a repetition of his earlier encounter with the fakir. Both men notice that the jackal's face looks like the fakir's, and Caulfield throws a clod of dirt at it to drive it away. The unwillingness of the animal to move and the way it stands its ground against the men is the beginning of the dead man's revenge, as John Miller says, "Savage animals [...] constitute [...] an emblematic otherness that embodies the point at which colonial authority loses its grip" (2014, p. 36).

Unlike Fleete in Kipling's "The Mark of the Beast" (1890), who ultimately survives his encounter with the leprous Silver Man, Caulfield suffers a far greater punishment after his encounter with the supernatural and does not escape the consequences of his aggression. The two men successfully bury the body, but as the story progresses it becomes clear that they cannot bury the secret of the crime. Caulfield claims that he is being followed by the same jackal and convinces himself "that the spirit of the murdered man had entered the animal and was bent on obtaining vengeance" (Perrin 2011b [1901], p. 131). Caulfield then suffers from some sort of "fit" followed by a prolonged, agonizing death. The narrator says:

> For twenty-four hours we stayed with Caulfield, watching the terrible struggles we were powerless to relieve, and which lasted till the end came. He was never able to speak after the first paroxysm, which had occurred before we arrived, so we could not learn from him whether he had been bitten or not [...] Yet there was no shadow of doubt that Caulfield's death was due to hydrophobia. (p. 131)

Perrin's decision to give Caulfield the symptoms caused by rabies is significant.[2] Claire Charlotte McKechnie has discussed the cultural import of the disease in the second half of the nineteenth century, saying that, from the 1870s, rabies "became a literary Gothic trope [...] because it was associated with the bodily pain of infection, the biting trope, and human-animal transformation" (2013, p. 115). The disease also represented an "invasion" as it "emerged from the wilderness to invade organized spaces in the same way that the disease infiltrated the human body." In this way, according to McKechnie, "rabies ideologically and symbolically characterized anxieties about attack and invasion in the corruption of racial and biological purity" (ibid., p. 124). The narrator looks at the dead man's "white face with its ghastly, hunted expression," which brings the narrative back to the look on the fakir's dead face, only this time the role of hunter and hunted has changed (Perrin 2011b [1901], p. 132). This makes Perrin's story an important example of what Peter Morey calls the cultural reversal in Colonial Gothic stories, where the usually "acting" English and the "acted upon" Indians "often change places" (2009, p. 30). At this point, the narrator remains doubtful of any actual haunting or reincarnation of the fakir into the jackal. Yet, as he prepares to leave, he "caught a glimpse of a mass of grey fur, two fiery yellow eyes, and bared, glistening teeth [...] I struck at it with my stick, but instead of running away it slipped past me and entered Caulfield's room. The light fell on the animal's head, and I saw that it had only one ear" (Perrin 2011b [1901], p. 132). He tries to warn the other men, but the doctor tells him, "This business has shaken your nerves, and your imagination is beginning to play you tricks" (p. 132). The story ends with the narrator returning to his bungalow, as he says, trying to persuade himself that the doctor was right. This silence on the part of a narrator recurs several times in *East of Suez*, as other characters choose not to speak of the weird or supernatural event they witnessed.

However, in "Caulfield's Crime," this silence is more complex. On one level, the narrator chooses to remain silent because, like the doctor implies, people will think he is going mad. On a more ominous level, the narrator must remain silent because he is complicit in covering up a murder. This enforced silence at the end of the story is Perrin's way of addressing the fact that numerous acts of violence do occur in the real world of British India and have lasting consequences that are never fully realized by the wider public. Yet, she chooses to enact supernatural retribution on Caulfield instead of letting him get away with his crime that he most likely would have gotten away with in the natural world; he causes suffering and suffers in return. Caulfield is himself silenced long before he dies and is not allowed to articulate the cause of his death. In his loss of speech, Caulfield becomes beast-like in a way that echoes his beastly actions against the fakir, actions which highlight contemporary British fears of degeneration and call into question the "civilizing mission" of empire.[3] As Kelly Hurley says, degeneration "emphasiz[es] the mutability and flux of human bodies and societies" (1997, p. 65). Because of this emphasis, it "is a 'gothic' discourse, and as such is a crucial imaginative and narrative source for the *fin-de-siècle* Gothic" (ibid., p. 65). She continues by saying that "The narrative of Darwinian evolution could be read as a supernaturalist or Gothic one: evolution theory described a bodily metamorphosis which [...] rendered the identity of the human body in a most basic sense—its distinctness from 'the brute beasts'—unstable" (ibid., p. 56). Likewise, Timothy Clark suggests that in literary texts distinctions between "human and non-human can be unstable," which leads to a sense of eerie similarity: "The animal, like the ghost or the good or evil spirit with which it is often associated, has been a manifestation of the uncanny" (2011, p. 185), something that can be "either an attractive disruption of species boundaries [...] or a disconcerting one" (ibid., p. 185). The "disconcerting" nature of the animal/human meeting, when underscored by violence, is also an unsettling one because it threatens to undermine basic beliefs in the British imperial hierarchy—or, as Teresa Mangum terms it "predatory hierarchy" (2007, p. 166)—the "natural" ascendency of the British over both the people and animals they supposedly ruled. The arbitrary nature of alliances, whether between humans or between animal and human, is reflected within the colonial environment. As Mangum asserts, "the impossibility of knowing friends from enemies...the sheer indecipherability of sudden violence, and the threat of being destroyed by one's own exposed animal 'savagery'" ultimately "undermine the confidence of characters and plots alike in Britishness and the codes of behavior it signifies" (ibid., p. 167).

The idea of "narrative" is relevant here and provides another key point of comparison between Perrin's story and Kipling's "Mark of the Beast." Both narrators censor their stories through voluntary silence. The end of Kipling's supernatural tale abounds with phrases such as: "I tried to say 'Hydrophobia' but the word wouldn't come," "[Fleete] could not answer us when we shouted at him," "Several other things happened also, but they cannot be put down here," "This part is not to be printed," and "No one will believe a rather unpleasant story" (1913 [1890], pp. 299, 303, 306). To acknowledge the supernatural, the perceived irrational and unexplainable, is to admit the power of Indian belief and custom. In this way, the supernatural triumphs over rational (i.e. Western) power structures and imperial laws. In "Caulfield's Crime," the narrator's decision to remain silent is vital to upholding imperial order. Or, as Peter Morey says, "to claim as fact a phenomenon beyond the bounds of possibility is to leave the safety of imperial discourse—where everything is known, measured and classified" (2009, p. 43).

The supposed reincarnation of the fakir provides yet another aspect that both heightens the narrative interest of the story while, at the same time, allowing Perrin to comment on the broader significations of the belief among Indians. Reincarnation had long been a subject of interest to the British public, an interest attested to in the numerous studies of the subject in several British and American publications. In his chapter on animals and the supernatural in *Beast and Man in India*, John Lockwood Kipling stated that "the ascription of souls and a share in a future state to animals is [...] the most truly supernatural aspect of Eastern notions with reference to them" (1904 [1892], p. 353). This "supernatural aspect" extended to human interactions with animals as well, as Kipling also notes the Indian belief that men and women could "assume at will the form of animals" (ibid., p. 358).[4] Given these supernatural abilities, the fakir gains even greater cultural and supernatural importance in the story. By assuming the body of the jackal, he not only is able to exact revenge on Caulfield but, in a spectral sense, is able to "come back" as a revenant who seeks to redeem his own victimization and death through the figure of the vengeful spirit housed in the body of the animal. In the body of a living wild animal, the fakir is also free to terrorize more British inhabitants, people presumably like Caulfield, who kill and victimize Indians and animals alike. In this sense, John Lockwood Kipling's claim, that "no matter how savagely he may be beaten," the jackal "will pick his sore body up when left to die, and slink away to resume a life of crime" (ibid., p. 280), gains even more significance. The fakir's spirit continues to live and have a memory of past wrongs. He cannot voice his mistreatment, which is itself an interesting counterpoint to the narrator's inability/refusal to also speak of the crime. Yet, the jackal remains a living symbol of the crime, and the forced transformation of the fakir from a man of peace to a vengeful being is directly caused by his contact with the British.

In "A Man's Theory," Perrin eschews the supernatural elements so integral to "Caulfield's Crime" in favor of more realistic Animal Gothic horror. Yet, the story maintains her continuing critique of how the larger mismanagement of empire is reflected in troubled domestic relations between a British Civil Servant and his new wife. These troubles reach their climax when the husband's habit of "knowing best" (Perrin 2011a [1901], p. 99) is turned against him when his attempt to regulate his wife's care of the couple's infant son has tragic consequences. The story begins with an extended description of the unlikeable John Orchard. Orchard represents the seemingly "perfect" Englishman, but Perrin makes it clear that he is flawed in his mindset because he is too self-assured and unyielding in his expectations of others. This flawed nature holds true in his role as an Indian Civil Servant and as a husband and father. His attitude toward his work is particularly troublesome because he assumes he knows more than he does, which Perrin makes clear to her readers in the story's opening paragraphs: "He passed first of his year into the Indian Civil Service, and apparently, knew more about the country and the natives before he went out than did many men with twenty years' experience of both" (p. 99). The inclusion of "apparently" is crucial to this description because it undercuts all his supposed talents. Orchard has book knowledge of India but no instincts or firsthand knowledge of the country or its people. Throughout her stories and novels, Perrin makes it abundantly clear to her readers that the only successful British administrator in India is one who understands, appreciates, and sympathizes with the complexities of Indian and Anglo-Indian culture. Her heroes are frequently flawed, but they are willing to admit their mistakes, something John Orchard is never willing to do.

Outwardly, Orchard does everything he is supposed to for an Anglo-Indian man in his position. Before his marriage, he attends the local club, gives dinner parties, and instructs the local British women on "the proper way to manage servants and order meals" (p. 100). When it comes time for marriage, Orchard first considers how it could improve his social standing, and clearly places his career over love: "He considered that a man with money of his own, and good prospects, might safely marry early in life without harming his career. It gave him more social standing, and established a home, provided that the girl was healthy, good-tempered and obedient" (p. 100). The micromanagement that makes him so unpopular among his civil service colleagues also becomes a part of his marriage to the "single-hearted, unselfish" Mary Forde, who has recently returned to India after her education in England (p. 100). Perrin's sarcastic treatment of Orchard's character is again clear in his planning for the wedding: "He chose her trousseau (he had excellent taste), he selected her ayah, he made all the arrangements for the ceremony, and allowed her no voice in any matter at all. She meekly acquiesced in everything, so certain was she always that John knew best, a theory that coincided entirely with John's ideas" (p. 101).

However, the harshness of the Indian environment soon shows the extent of John's erroneous behavior. When the hot season arrives, he rejects the doctor's advice to send his wife and newborn son to the cooler regions of the northern hills, a refusal that leads directly to the death of his child by the story's end. His refusal also signals the breakdown of the marriage, as Mary begins to recognize how "cruelly inexorable" (p. 101) her husband is and begins to fear for her child's health. She lies awake each night in the heat "gasping for breath" and "soothing the child, that cried and whined continuously with the irritation of prickly heat and mosquitoes" (p. 101). John insists that the child be raised according to strict British principles of discipline, not recognizing that standard British rules about children do not apply the same way in India. He tells Mary, "Get the child into good habits from the beginning […] and it will save an infinity of trouble afterwards, besides laying an excellent moral foundation for his future character. A child should never be allowed its own way in anything" (pp. 101, 102). Later, he advises that his infant son is "a self-willed little beggar, and he must be taught how to behave himself" and concludes that "children in England sleep all night through" (p. 102).

The tension between John's unwavering insistence on discipline, Mary and the baby's increasingly fragile health, and the increasing harshness of the weather all signal a narrative building to an impending breaking point: "The days and nights grew drier and hotter and more unendurable. Mrs Orchard became thinner and paler and unnaturally nervous. The sight of a rat in her bedroom one night sent her into hysterics, and it took all her husband's sternest rebukes to calm her down" (p. 102). As Mary's mental and physical condition deteriorates, the untamed environment intrudes into the home and allows her no relief. She must constantly battle both the harsh physical conditions that surround her as well as the unrelenting ministrations of her equally harsh husband who has once again refused to allow her to comfort her child:

> Mary lay back in her chair unwillingly, and sighed. The night was stifling, and crowds of motley insects were buzzing and beating round every lamp in the room, while the lizards licked them down wholesale. There was a dense haze of dust and heat in the air, and outside the stars were scarcely visible, while the harsh hum of crickets and the barking of weary dogs were the only sounds that cut through the thick, hot stillness. The cries from the bedroom increased gradually until baby was roaring lustily. (p. 103)

Mary's motherly instinct tells her something is wrong when the baby's cries change from "screams" to "a feeble wail" (p. 103), but John will not listen. His final words to her are both truer than he realizes and, at the same time, partly false, once again suggesting how flawed his advice really is. He tells Mary, "After to-night you will have no more bother with him. Now he has stopped. He's tired of making such a row and has gone to sleep" (p. 103).

The disastrous consequences of his orders only become evident to Orchard after it is too late, for both his marriage and his son. Mary leaves the room unnoticed and when John hears a crash from the bedroom and goes to investigate, the true horror of the situation is revealed:

> He fetched a lamp from the hall, and saw his wife lying on the floor by the cradle, a huddled, unconscious heap. He held the light aloft and peered into the little bed. The baby face was white and still, the tiny fists tightly clenched. From the child's neck a narrow red stream trickled across the sheet, and on the pillow, hesitating whether to go or stay, and with its head and paws dyed crimson, sat a large grey rat.[5] (pp. 103–104)

This is the end that Perrin leaves her readers. There is no chance of redemption for John Orchard. In addition to witnessing the aftermath of the tortured death of his infant son, Perrin also leaves her readers guessing about the ultimate fate of Mary. In her fragile condition, a complete recovery from such a shock seems unlikely and could possibly lead to her death. In any case, the marriage is ruined. In the opening paragraph, the narrator states that Mary's "affection" for John "changed to hatred" (p. 99). The ending also proves the illusory nature of John Orchard's sense of control. His ultimate failure in trying to construct a correct way of raising his child points to greater flaws within his role as colonial administrator. His assured demeanor and his insistence on being "right" in all instances involving both his work and his marriage blinds him to the "hatred" of those around him. Not only does this lead to a child's death and the failure of his marriage, but Perrin's prolonged examination of the disastrous consequences of "A Man's Theory" points to the greater danger of having such men forwarding even more far-reaching theories and schemes within the colonial administrative system. The man who has control over everything is undone by a small animal that would, in most other situations, be a mere nuisance. By his refusal to consider and sympathize with other viewpoints (symbolized in his relationship with Mary), this minor pest becomes something with the power to destroy. Perrin leaves her readers wondering what other aspects of Orchard's role as a British civil servant (an ironic title in his case) are going to ultimately cause similar damage, and how many more people (Indians and British alike) will be hurt through his insistence that he "knows best."

The last story in *East of Suez*, "The Biscobra," also centers on the possibility of reincarnation, but instead of a surly military man, the narrative focuses on Frank Krey and his young wife, Nell. "The Biscobra" concerns itself with the interior domestic space and its invasion by the surrounding natural environment. Even before the Kreys arrive at their temporary house, the landscape itself is described in Gothic terms and appears alien and uninviting to their newly-arrived British eyes. They pass "an evil-smelling village tank, almost covered with thick green slime," "the post office, an ugly little red brick edifice with iron bars in front of the windows," "a bare length of road devoid of trees," and finally, "a large fig tree with thick, whispering leaves which shaded a tiny temple containing a strange, many-limbed idol smeared with red paint, that made Mrs. Krey think of blood, and the Mutiny, and hideous tales of human sacrifice" (Perrin 2011c [1901], p. 166). This description is an instance of what Kelly Hurley terms "Gothic natural history," where "the anomalous is reframed as the normal. Inert matter takes on life, vegetable species become mobile, and both these as well as non-human animal species acquire sentience, no longer the exclusive property of humans. As 'the human' loses its particularity, it also begins to be evacuated of its meaningfulness" (Hurley 1997, p. 61).

As the Kreys move into the equally depressing indoor space of their temporary home at a dâk bungalow, Perrin shifts focus onto Nell Krey's fragile health and Frank Krey's guilt over bringing his wife to such an unforgiving climate. The long-unoccupied house, Nell discovers, is not quite so unoccupied:

> The thatched roof needed renewing, the walls, seemed to be composed of mud and white ants [...] Wasps had made their dwellings in corners, and sparrows had built in the fireplaces, owls of all sizes lived in a state of sleepy serenity along the beams of the verandah, and mysterious creatures ran to and fro with sharp, pattering feet over the loose, discoloured ceiling cloths [...] All this was a trial to Mrs. Krey [...] and she waged untiring war against these unwelcome occupants of her house, for she dreaded and hated "animals," as she called owls, ants, rats, spiders, snakes, or anything else she was afraid of. She always looked under her chair before she sat down, peered with a lamp into every nook and corner before she got into bed, and was continually on the watch for insect, reptile, bird or beast. (Perrin 2011c [1901], p. 167)

The boundary between colonized and uncolonized space is blurred by the presence of the wild animals within the house. This "domestic war" soon takes its toll on the pregnant Nell, who becomes increasingly homesick and depressed in her new surroundings. She begins to have premonitions that "something dreadful" is going to happen and tells Frank that one day soon one of the two will have to face life alone. She is even more startled when Beni, the Kreys' faithful Indian servant, becomes distressed over what he thinks is a biscobra living in the thatched ceiling. He calls it "an evil beast" with a sting deadlier than the bite of a cobra (p. 170).[6]

The description then turns to what seems to Nell like the slow steady invasion of animals closing in around her. Thinking the biscobra has moved, she frantically looks for it in the shadows on the floor, while owls sit on the rafters and several bats swoop down from the ceiling. The appearance of the biscobra is unexpected, as the narrator describes its entry into the room as both sudden and prolonged, "There was a slight scratching sound directly overhead, as of claws clinging to woodwork, a faint hiss, and the next moment flapping and turning in the air, the green, scaly body of a large biscobra fell heavily on to Mrs. Krey's shoulder, where it hung for one hideous second, and then dropped with a thud on to the stone verandah floor" (p. 171). Perrin immediately follows this incident with a brief paragraph that describes Mrs. Krey's premature labor and her subsequent death, along with that of her child. Distraught over these sudden losses, Frank Krey leaves the area, leaving the faithful Beni to tend the grave of mother and child. This is the point in the story where the narrative becomes even more unsettling.

After focusing on the inability of a woman like Nell Krey to survive in the Indian environment, Perrin turns her attention to the gradual mental unraveling of Frank Krey. Unable to accept Beni's belief that the young biscobra living in the grave is the reincarnated spirit of his dead child, Frank loses all touch with reality.[7] Like the protagonists in "Caulfield's Crime," he cannot admit any truth that threatens to undermine his tenuous position of control that prides itself on being above Indian spiritual belief. Krey's repressed grief at the loss of his wife and child leads to his violent breakdown, and, like Caulfield, he is unmanned by the end of the story. What seems so natural for Beni is inconceivable to Krey. The possibility of such an intimate connection with India, a British child's spirit living in the body of an Indian biscobra, is the last straw for Krey's sanity. He becomes another example of Homi Bhabha's examination of the cultural power of the hybrid, the dismantling of British imperialism by uncanny forces. The ambiguous hybrid represents a "paranoid threat" that is "uncontainable because it breaks down the symmetry and duality of self/other, inside/outside" (Bhabha 1994, p. 165). This idea is perfectly encapsulated by the biscobra, the child's spirit living within a native animal, and that animal living inside the grave of Nell Krey. The reincarnation of the child thus represents a kind of supernatural hybridity. Frank Krey's only response to this belief system is reactionary violence, much like the violence of Caulfield toward the fakir. As soon as he sees the biscobra emerge from the hole in the grave and begin to drink the milk Beni has left for it, Krey does not speak but, instead, utters "a cry of horror, rage and madness" just before he beats the creature to death with his walking stick. Beni is likewise left at a loss for words after witnessing this sudden act. He manages to yell out that Krey has "slain the soul" of his child before "a rattle in the old man's throat choked his utterance, and he fell forward on his face" (Perrin 2011c [1901], p. 175).

"The Biscobra" is possibly the most unsettling story in *East of Suez*, not only in its subject matter, but in the way in which Perrin tells the story and in the concluding image of India with which she leaves her readers:

> The next morning a half-caste clerk and his wife came to lay a painted metal wreath on the grave of a relative, and they found Beni's lifeless body lying by the crooked white cross. Near at hand was an overturned brass vessel and a dead biscobra with its head beaten off, and wandering about the cemetery was an Englishman, who laughed and danced foolishly when they spoke to him, and from whose eyes the light of understanding had gone for ever. (p. 175)

The two appearances of the "uncanny" biscobra are followed by the equally sudden collapse of both Nell and Frank Krey. The story ends with village locals finding a dead body, a mangled biscobra, and a raving lunatic in a nearby graveyard. Perrin's use of the word "understanding" is also important here. Frank Krey loses his chance at obtaining a deeper understanding of the Indian environment and is left in perpetual mental and cultural darkness in the end.

Several critics have discussed the subversive elements in supernatural fiction. For instance, Tzvetan Todorov states that "the social and the literary functions [of the supernatural] coincide: in both cases, we are concerned with a transgression of the law. Whether it is in social life or in narrative, the intervention of the supernatural element always constitutes a break in the system of pre-established rules" (1975, p. 166). Likewise,

Peter Morey has claimed, "Where a supernatural economy of power is shown to operate, knowledge, for the Anglo-Indian protagonist, ceases to be a mark of power. It becomes instead a general understanding or enlightenment as to the altered realities of his position as a victim of supernatural or unknowable phenomena. It becomes a source of instability and lack of power" (2009, p. 26). Through the figures of unsettled spirits and Gothic animals, who, in turn, unsettle and trouble the living, Perrin provides some of the more subversive critiques of imperialism in Indian fiction written during the height of the British Raj. In her supernatural stories, she subtly criticizes imperial policies that could not have been questioned openly without public censure. Her stories subversively draw attention to problems caused by the British in India and, unlike many of her contemporaries who focused on more traditional narratives that often exploited Indian stereotypes, Perrin holds the British accountable for their influence as colonizers. She uses the form of the short story to provide the reader with narrative shocks that could not be sustained in a lengthy novel. Short fiction allowed her to explore complicated racial and gender dynamics in a concise literary form. Perrin's uncanny stories disrupt the traditional Indian adventure romance and advance a more daring form of social critique. And, as we might not expect of literature from the high tide of empire, the British are rarely blameless for the troubles which befall them.

Notes

1. Readers learn that Caulfield has recently transferred to the cavalry regiment under mysterious circumstances. Regarding the two men's relationship, the narrator says that Caulfield was twenty years his senior, and that he considered him "a great friend" whom he visited frequently during his early days in the new regiment: "He never asked me to come, or pressed me to stay, and yet, in some inexplicable manner, I felt that my visits were not unwelcome to him" (1893, p. 599). These details make the "crime" less of a surprise but give a better explanation for the narrator's loyalty to Caulfield toward the end of the story.
2. George Fleming described contemporary fears associated with rabies in *Rabies and Hydrophobia* (1872):

    > Of all the maladies that are transmissible from the lower animals to man, there is perhaps not one which possesses so much interest, nor a knowledge of which is so important for the human species, as that which is popularly, though erroneously, designated *Hydrophobia*.

> It is even to be doubted whether any of the many diseases which afflict humanity, and are a source of dread [...] can equal this in the terror it inspires in the minds of those who are cognisant of its effects, or who chance to be exposed to the risk of its attack, as well as in the uniform fatality which terminates the distressing and hideous symptoms that characterise the disorder. (p. 1)

In her examination of the cultural and literary importance of dogs and rabies in late nineteenth-century Britain, Claire Charlotte McKechnie notes that Fleming's description relies on Gothic language and reflects popular fears about the transmission and spread of rabies. She continues by saying that these fears were grounded in cultural anxieties about the close evolutionary link between animals and humans and that the mysterious nature of the disease was "emblematic of nature out of control" (2013, p. 122).

3. McKechnie connects rabies to contemporary societal fears of madness, saying that because the disease caused encephalitis and severe mental imbalance, it "was associated with sin, corruption, and unholiness," with an article on June 27, 1881 in *The Times* calling the disease "evil" (2013, pp. 125, 139, n. 24).
4. In *Reincarnation: A Study of Forgotten Truth* (1888), E. D. Walker noted the interchangeability of animal/human characteristics which led to a belief in the transmigration of souls:

> The remarkable mental cleverness of the highest animals, the cunning of the fox, the tiger's fierceness, the serpent's meanness, the dog's fidelity, seem to be human traits in other forms, and the animal qualities are striking enough in many men for them to be fitly described as a fox, a hog, a snake, etc. The characteristics of animals are accurately termed in expressions first applied to mankind, and the community of disposition between the erect and the debased animal creation has furnished words for human qualities from the lower orders of life,—as leonine, canine, vulpine, etc. Briefly, "the rare humanity of some animals and the notorious animality of some men" first suggested the idea of interchanging their souls among the primitive peoples, and has nourished it ever since among the oldest portion of the race as a vulgar illustration of a vital reality. (pp. 278–279)

5. James Rodwell, in *The Rat: Its History and Destructive Character* (1858) describes several instances where babies and small children were left alone and killed or almost killed by being eaten alive by rats, which, he says, have "a carnivorous appetite for hot blood" (p. 23). One instance described by Rodwell is similar to Perrin's story:

> A poor working woman having occasion to go from home, put her infant child to bed. Upon her return, and opening the door of the apartment in which her infant lay, she saw three large rats jump from the bed, and, on looking in the direction of her child, she was terrified at perceiving that the bedclothes were stained with blood. She instantly removed the coverlet, when a shocking spectacle presented itself. The rats had mutilated the poor infant and destroyed its life, having eaten away the wall of the belly, and actually destroyed portions of the intestines. (1858, p. 54)

6. The belief that biscobras (or what we today might call monitor lizards) were dangerous was a wide held fear among Indians. In *Beast and Man in India*, John Lockwood Kipling described the prevalence of the creature in Anglo-Indian society:

> The large lizard, *varanus dracaena*, which is perfectly innocuous, like all Indian lizards, is called the bis-cobra by some [...] and is counted highly dangerous [...] In Southern India, where lizards are numerous and are perpetually falling from the thatched roofs, there is a marvellously elaborate code of omens drawn from the varying circumstances, the parts of the body, house utensils, etc., upon which they drop. Less attention seems to be paid to lizards in the North, but even there they say, "A lizard has fallen on you, go and bathe." (1904 [1892], pp. 317, 318)

Describing the creature's near-mythic qualities in Indian society, Edward Hamilton Aitken in *The Tribes on My Frontier* (1883) says:

> But of all the things in this earth that bite or sting, the palm belongs to the biscobra, a creature whose very name seems to indicate that it is twice as bad as the cobra. Though known by the terror of its name to natives and Europeans alike, it has never been described in the proceedings of any learned society, nor has it yet received a scientific name. In fact, it occupies much the same place in science as the sea-serpent, and accurate information regarding it is still a desideratum. (p. 205)

7. Both Beni and the fakir's protectiveness toward the non-human creatures in their respective stories is representative of the contemporary philosophical belief that Eastern cultures were more advanced in their treatment of animals than Western cultures. For instance, in *History of European Morals* (1869), William Edward Lecky, claims, "it must not be forgotten that the inculcation of humanity to animals on a wide scale is mainly the work of a recent and a secular age; that the Mohammedans and the Brahmins have in this sphere considerably surpassed the Christians" (2: 177). Though we

cannot be certain that Perrin had this added philosophical layer regarding humanity toward animals in mind when writing these stories, the fakir's saving of the snipe—though his actions may partly be influenced by his desire to repay Caulfield for his earlier insults—and Beni's efforts to nurture the young biscobra put both Indian men in a more favorable light when compared to the aggressive and unhinged British men who seek to kill both birds and biscobra for much less noble reasons.

Bibliography

Aitken, Edward Hamilton (1883), *The Tribes on My Frontier*, Calcutta: Thacker, Spink.
Bennett, Edward Turner (1829), *The Tower Menagerie*, London: Robert Jennings.
Bhabha, Homi K. (1994), *The Location of Culture*, London: Routledge.
Burchell, William John (1824), *Travels in the Interior of Southern Africa*, 2 vols., London: Longman.
Clark, Timothy (2011), *The Cambridge Introduction to Literature and the Environment*, Cambridge: Cambridge University Press.
Darwin, Charles (1871), *The Descent of Man*, 2 vols., London: John Murray.
Fleming, George (1872), *Rabies and Hydrophobia: Their History, Nature, Causes, Symptoms, and Prevention*, London: Chapman & Hall.
Hurley, Kelly (1997), *The Gothic Body: Sexuality, Materialism, and Degeneration at the Fin de Siècle*, Cambridge: Cambridge University Press.
Kipling, John Lockwood (1904 [1892]), *Beast and Man in India: A Popular Sketch of Indian Animals in Their Relations with the People*, London: Macmillan.
Kipling, Rudyard (1913 [1890]), "The Mark of the Beast," *Life's Handicap: Being Stories of Mine Own People*, New York: Doubleday, Page, & Company, pp. 290–306.
Lecky, William Edward (1890 [1869]), *History of European Morals*, 3rd edn., 2 vols., New York: Appleton.
MacKenzie, John M. (1988), *The Empire of Nature: Hunting, Conservation and British Imperialism*, Manchester: Manchester University Press.
Mangum, Teresa (2007), "Narrative Dominion or the Animals Write Back? Animal Genres in Literature and the Arts," in Kathleen Kete (ed.), *A Cultural History of Animals*, Vol. 5, Oxford and New York: Berg, pp. 153–173.
McKechnie, Claire Charlotte (2013), "Man's Best Fiend: Evolution, Rabies, and the Gothic Dog," *Nineteenth-Century Prose* 40.1: 115–140.
Miller, John (2014), *Empire and the Animal Body: Violence, Identity and Ecology in Victorian Adventure Fiction*, London: Anthem Press.

Morey, Peter (2009), *Fictions of India: Narrative and Power*, Edinburgh: Edinburgh University Press.

Perrin, Alice (1893), "Caulfield's Crime," *Living Age* (4 March): 598–606.

——— (2011a [1901]), "A Man's Theory," in Melissa Edmundson Makala (ed.), *East of Suez*, Brighton, UK: Victorian Secrets Publishing, pp. 99–104.

——— (2011b [1901]), "Caulfield's Crime," in Melissa Edmundson Makala (ed.), *East of Suez*, Brighton, UK: Victorian Secrets Publishing, pp. 125–132.

——— (2011c [1901]), "The Biscobra," in Melissa Edmundson Makala (ed.), *East of Suez*, Brighton, UK: Victorian Secrets Publishing, pp. 165–175.

Punch (1901), Rev. of *East of Suez*, 121 (23 October): 296.

Ritvo, Harriet (1987), *The Animal Estate: The English and Other Creatures in the Victorian Age*, Cambridge: Harvard University Press.

Rodwell, James (1858), *The Rat: Its History and Destructive Character*, London: Routledge.

Todorov, Tzvetan (1975), *The Fantastic: A Structural Approach to a Literary Genre*, Trans. Richard Howard, Ithaca, NY: Cornell University Press.

Tremayne, Harold (1901), Rev. of *East of Suez*, in Harold Tremayne, *Dross*, London: Anthony Treherne.

Walker, E. D. (1888), *Reincarnation: A Study of Forgotten Truth*, New York: John W. Lovell.

CHAPTER 9

The Past Will Not Stay Buried: Female Bodies and Colonial Crime in the Australian Ghost Stories of Mary Fortune

Mary Fortune has recently been rediscovered as one of the first detective story authors. She was an unconventional Victorian colonial woman, subverting many of the feminine norms which predominated throughout the nineteenth century. Fortune gained a literary reputation writing in the then exclusively male genre of crime fiction and lived independently by supporting herself by writing, although she was never paid an adequate amount for her published work. Under the pseudonym "W.W." and "Waif Wander," Fortune wrote a series of over 400 stories for the *Australian Journal* entitled "The Detective's Album," which were narrated by police detective Mark Sinclair, and ran from 1867 to 1908. During her life, she published only one book, also titled *The Detective's Album* (1871), which collected several stories from the *Australian Journal*.[1] Though Fortune has received renewed scholarly interest, there has been almost nothing written on the importance of her use of murdered female bodies and the ghosts which subsequently arise out of this violence. Examining these supernatural bodies in Fortune's work adds important new dimensions to the areas of Colonial Gothic and Female Gothic. As speaking bodies, these women return from their graves with the distinct purpose of righting the wrongs done to them and seeking justice against those who killed them, while unpredictable instances of extreme violence and the perceived vulnerability of women in Fortune's stories show the new British settlement in Australia to be "unsettled."

Building on the work of Lucy Sussex and Megan Brown, both of whom have discussed Fortune as a pioneering female crime writer, this chapter examines three Gothic stories by Fortune: "Mystery and Murder" (1866), "The Illumined Grave" (1867), and "The Old Shaft" (1886).[2] In the stories, Fortune's use of ghosts and macabre deaths goes beyond crime writing. These stories become a perfect balance of realism and fantasy as Fortune combines supernatural elements and unsettled spirits with the realistic details of murdered bodies and forensic evidence. Sinclair himself admits in "The Illumined Grave": "I was always slightly inclined to be superstitious, in spite of hard friction in the commonplace world." Though Fortune wrote about murders arising from the acquisition of gold and property, her ghost stories involving women show broader concerns about gender. The gravesite is prominent in each story and integral to solving the mystery. Uncovering the body uncovers a murder and an act of violence against a woman. The murders are also about controlling and possessing women or attempting to limit their movements, symbolized in the many unnatural, cramped positions in which these bodies are found. The violent deaths of these women—who are stabbed, beaten, tied to trees, and raped—are followed by equally violent quasi-burials where bodies are thrown into shallow graves, stuffed into suitcases, and thrown down abandoned mine shafts, supposedly hidden places that, like the human subconscious, refuse to remain hidden.

Though Mary Fortune is now thought of as a pioneering detective fiction writer, her emphasis on the darker elements of the human psyche and the unspoken desires that lead to the numerous murders in her stories is an important instance in the early development of an Australian Gothic tradition. A few years before Fortune began writing, Frederick Sinnett had declared the impossibility of such a tradition, remarking in his 1856 essay "The Fiction Fields of Australia":

> No Australian author can hope to extricate his hero or heroine, however pressing the emergency may be, by means of a spring panel and a subterranean passage, or such like relics of feudal barons, and refuges of modern novelists, and the offspring of their imagination. There may be plenty of dilapidated buildings, but not one, the dilapidation of which is sufficiently venerable by age, to tempt the wandering footsteps of the most arrant *parvenu* of a ghost that ever walked by night. It must be admitted that Mrs. Radcliffe's genius would be quite thrown away here; and we must reconcile ourselves to the conviction that the foundations of a second "Castle of Otranto" can hardly be laid in Australia during our time. (p. 98)

Yet, in recent years, increased scholarly attention to nineteenth-century colonial Australian writing has yielded a body of literature that reflects a unique combination of European Gothic elements (the Gothic of Mrs. Radcliffe which Sinnett mentions above) and a reimagining of the Gothic that formed as a direct result of colonial encounters in Australia. The seeds for this reworking of the Gothic began early, with Australia as the penal colony where Britain conveniently banished criminals and social deviants, shipping away those who were not fit to live in "respectable" society. As Gerry Turcotte suggests, this convict culture meant that Australia immediately became "a world of reversals, the dark subconscious of Britain," and consequently, "Gothic *par excellence*, the dungeon of the world" (2009, p. 278).

Fortune's stories foreground the Gothic concern of secrets being uncovered, along with bodies. In so doing, her fiction undercuts the promise of land and riches that entranced so many later emigrés and reveals a colony that, in the later nineteenth century, remains very much "unsettled." For Ken Gelder and Rachael Weaver, this is a key component to Australian Gothic: "The genre turns towards precisely those stories of death and brutality that might not otherwise be told in colonial Australia, playing out one of the Gothic's most fascinating structural logics, the return of the repressed: quite literally, as graves are dug up, sacred burial grounds uncovered, murder victims are returned from the dead, secrets are revealed and past horrors are experienced all over again" (2007, p. 9). The idea of recovering untold stories and reclaiming silenced voices extends to Fortune's role as a writer and her choice of subject. As Megan Brown asserts, her emphasis on the plight of immigrant women in colonial Australia "changes the subject and the perspective from the more common male version to the female one and provides an alternative version of colonial experience" (2014, p. 105).[3]

Mary Fortune's "Mystery and Murder" was published early in her career in the February 10, 1866, issue of the *Australian Journal* as Number VI of the series, "Memoirs of an Australian Police Officer." The narrator, Mark Sinclair, is a detective officer with the mounted police based in Hobart Town, Tasmania, and recalls the events from a distance of ten years. At the beginning of the story, he is visited by a Mr. Longmore, who wants Sinclair to investigate the mysterious appearance of a woman in his house. Longmore's description immediately foregrounds the traumatic past of the woman:

> The figure was a slight and not tall one, attired in a white robe, and there was a horrible expression of terror in the white features, whose deathlike pallor was increased by the contrast presented by the longest and heaviest black hair I ever saw, and which hung in a mass over her left breast, and reached down to her knees. Her dress was of some silken material, for I heard it rustling, and down over the whole of the front, and also upon the large, loose sleeves, it was absolutely clotted with blood. (Fortune 2007 [1866], p. 33)

Initially, he is more alarmed at the fact that the woman is able to gain entry into his house, which he says is heavily fortified and secured for his daughter's safety. Longmore's description also shows that the ghost, instead of causing terror, is terrorized herself. Yet, this woman "in spite of fastened doors and windows" (p. 33) visits him every night, standing at the foot of his bed and "impatiently" waving her hand for him to follow her.

Sinclair is skeptical and thinks to himself that "it was all fudge" (p. 35). He inwardly marvels "that any man in these days of enlightenment, and possessed of his full allowance of brains, should insist upon the *existence* of a *ghost*" (p. 37). Despite these feelings, he agrees to spend a night in the man's bedroom in order to see the ghost for himself and get to the bottom of the mystery—supernatural or not. In later stories, Sinclair will become more accustomed to these unexplained happenings, as Fortune continued to return to the supernatural in many of her crime stories. This early story is, then, a starting point for Sinclair's exploration of the afterlife and lays the groundwork for his future otherworldly encounters.

Before Sinclair begins his vigil in the room, Longmore confesses the whole story behind the presence of the woman and reveals her to be his wife, who abandoned her husband and daughter years before "with a most disgraceful and low rascal" (p. 36). Longmore is adamant that the ghost is his wife but differentiates between her living and dead selves. He now refers to her as "it," suggesting a phenomenon that goes beyond gender, saying, "It is not her *alive*" (p. 37), and tells Sinclair, "when you have seen *it* I think you will acknowledge that I *must* believe it is supernatural!" (p. 37). When Sinclair likewise sees the woman standing at the foot of the bed, she makes the same motion for him to follow her. Though "horror-stricken" at the woman's look of "agony and terror" (p. 38), Sinclair pursues her and as she reappears outside the house, he fires a shot in her direction. Stupefied by this "bullet-proof visitant of the night" (p. 39), Sinclair and Longmore search the area where she was last seen. Sinclair is influenced to dig in the area, although he again admits doubt, "What could possibly have suggested to me the idea of making a search *in* the ground there I am totally unable to explain" (pp. 39–40).

At this point in the narrative, the Gothic real supplants the Gothic supernatural. The natural, decomposing body that provides evidence of the woman's murder gains emphasis over the supernatural ghost of the woman who leads the men to her dead body. The two men find a case "four feet long by three wide, and perhaps two feet deep" (p. 40). Inside, they find the remains, which Sinclair describes in detail:

> The figure lay upon its right side, the knees slightly drawn up so as to enable it to fit in the case; [...] The long heavy black hair was loose, and, gathered at one side, lay scattered over the left shoulder; and upon the skirt of the blood-stained dress, and under the hair, where it lay clogged and clotted, remained still the handle of a Spanish knife, the blade of which had passed directly through the unfortunate woman's heart! Although the body lay upon its side, as the space was confined, the head was turned so that the face looked upward, with the glaring wide open eyes fastened in a look so full of fear and horror, that I can never forget it. (p. 41)

Again, the woman is referred to as "it," as if both her ghostly form and her dead body are something beyond a woman. Yet, the appearance and staring eyes defy this loss of personal identity as she conveys her suffering through both the ghost and the body. Though "Mystery and Murder" is somewhat simplistic in its narrative structure and characterization, the dead woman and her murder become the center of the story. Although no words are uttered by her, the woman's body speaks the crime which explains her continued absence from her home and family. Sinclair learns that the woman was filled with regret and was trying to return to her family when she was killed by her lover. As a ghost, the woman is able to return to the home one last time.

Fortune's "The Illumined Grave," which appeared in the October 12, 1867, issue of the *Australian Journal*, is even more disturbing in its description of a murdered woman. It depicts the inability of a wealthy landowner to adequately protect his daughter from harm, as well as an implied sexual assault that occurs before the woman is murdered. As in "Mystery and Murder," Sinclair becomes involved in the case because of the disappearance of a young woman, the beloved daughter of a Mr. Bruce. While discussing the case with his acquaintance, Mr. Manners, Sinclair learns of "a pale blue light" that repeatedly appears to Strong, a local shepherd. Strong describes the sight as "a shadowy female form distinctly visible between the floating light and the boulder—a form in a white robe covered with blood, and heavy black hair, dishevelled, and matted with gore" (Fortune 1994 [1867], p. 21). Like the appearance of the murdered woman in "Mystery and Murder," this vision immediately suggests a traumatic end and violent death of the victim. Yet, it is not the blue light that compels Manners to pursue the mystery because he knows that there are "scientific explanations of those luminous gaseous exhalations that have been seen floating over the graves in churchyards by night" (p. 22). Instead, it is the female form that leads him to continue to question the supernatural occurrence. The possibility of violence against a woman is enough to pique the men's interest as they are initially fascinated by the supernatural appearance.

Ken Gelder notes, "Fantasies of separation and dispossession in the bush are matched…by fantasies involving closeness or contact of one kind or another" (1994, p. xiv). In Fortune's stories, this contact is often traumatic and depends on Gothic descriptions of crime. Karen Halttunen has observed that "Gothic fiction in general showed a marked predilection for scenes of torture, sexual violation, and murder, and treated such subjects in a manner calculated to arouse maximum revulsion and disgust" (1998, p. 67). This same idea is used by Fortune in her description of the sexual violence imposed on the young woman before her murder. The possibility of sexual assault is suggested earlier in the story, when the young woman is described as someone not interested in her many suitors: "She favoured none of them however. She was intellectual, and devoted to reading; disliked general society, and indulged, during their occasional residence at Broadbraes, in lonely rides on horseback" (Fortune 1994 [1867], p. 22). This type of behavior infuriated her killer, Commings, a privileged colonial settler who determined to have the woman despite her repeated efforts to distance herself from him.

The woman's attractiveness likewise continues after death, as Strong becomes possessive of this female spirit and takes a morbid pride in being the first one to see her. He is "in a state of great excitement" with flushed face and bright eyes as he tells the men, "I believe a murder has been committed on that spot, and that the spirit of the departed is crying out for vengeance" (p. 24). When Sinclair conjectures that the woman is buried in the spot where the light is seen, Strong registers surprise and possibly a bit of disappointment as he realizes that the spirit was not visiting him, "I thought the spirit appeared to me always because—because—" (p. 24). Fortune suggests that the shepherd liked having the woman all to himself, and, though in a much less violent manner, he, too, tries to impose a "relationship" in which she has no interest. Strong's comment also suggests that she appears to him for a particular reason. After hearing Strong's account, the other men go in search of the ghost, as Sinclair himself admits a sense of excitement as they near the area where she is seen: "I felt a strange eagerness for the termination of our adventure. [...] I was always slightly inclined to be superstitious, in spite of hard friction in the commonplace world; and, in spite of common sense and reason, and all the remainder of the objective faculties, I had some faint hope of myself seeing the spectral form, hitherto only visible to the shepherd Strong" (p. 26). Yet, despite the fact that the men are excited at the opportunity to observe this woman's spectral body, it is the dead woman herself who controls when and how they view her. As with other crisis apparitions who appear as a sign of some wrong done, the ghost controls the scene because she has ulterior motives for being seen. It is only through her appearance that she can guide the men to her body and eventually to her murderer. In his study of the unconscious mind, Frederic Myers describes this supernatural phenomenon as particular to "cases of violent death" where there is "intention on the deceased person's part to show the condition in which his body is left" (1907, p. 237).

As the "death-light" appears before the group, the woman's ghost seemingly manages to physically bridge the world of the living and the dead as Sinclair feels the touch of icy cold fingers that burn his hand immediately before the men leave the area out of fright (Fortune 1994 [1867], p. 28). This "missive from the world of spirits" is an actual piece of paper with a message written by the dead woman: "'Seized by Richard Commings, Booyong; fastened to a tree and left. Search among Bald Hill granites.—Anna Bruce'" (p. 29). This hand later is revealed to belong to Strong, who found the letter in the area soon after Anna's death, and therefore is not of supernatural origin. However, Fortune refuses to "explain away" the ghost of the murdered woman. After receiving the note, Sinclair begins to suspect that a crime has been committed and a mystery needs to be solved. He states, "I had no doubt now that the unfortunate girl had been murdered, for the spot also mentioned in her note was the very one whereon appeared the mysterious light, and I felt certain that beneath it lay the body of the once fair Anna Bruce" (pp. 29–30).

As with "Mystery and Murder," the woman has had an incomplete burial. She is buried in loose, sandy soil, in "a shallow hole about eighteen inches deep" (p. 31). Manners observes, "She has been dragged by the shoulders into the grave, and her long black skirt folded up over her body" (p. 32). This "blood bedabbled and decaying" body is then described in detail:

> Alas! it was truly the face of a murdered one we gazed upon, for under the long golden tresses that swept over the sinking bosom, on the fading brow where their wealth rested, lay a deep wide gash, that severed the white bone, and penetrated to the very brain! I had never seen the girl in life, but my heart grew cold with horror, while at the same time it burned with rage for retribution; and I hastily covered up the face of the dead once more with her own skirt. (p. 32)

It seems clear from the story that the murderer would not have been identified if it had not been for the presence of the ghost, who is the only person who knows the absolute truth and serves as the only eyewitness. According to Maurizio Ascari, "In the absence of witnesses and clues, the victim himself was regarded as the first agent of detection" (2007, p. 20). In this way, the ghost brings disorder to the ordinary, while at the same time bringing order in the form of justice.[4] Ascari describes this type of crime story as reassuring to a nervous public, who could enjoy a good mystery while also being confident that the criminals would eventually be brought to justice: "The idea that murder carries the seeds of its own discovery and punishment was reassuring in a world where social control was inefficient and criminals had a good chance of getting away with their misdeeds" (ibid., p. 18). This was especially true in 1860s Australia, where social control and government infrastructure in the colony was still in its early stages. This sort of "divine detection" provided readers with a reassuring "infallible justice" that went beyond the skills of the detective or policeman (ibid., p. 65). In "The Illumined Grave," Anna's father admits his powerlessness when he tells Sinclair that though he suspects Commings, who is "a bad man" and whose "sins are branded in his face" (Fortune 1994 [1867], p. 26), he cannot prove the man's guilt. Likewise, before Sinclair arrives to arrest him for the murder of Anna Bruce, Commings is "lapped in fancied security" and "lounging idly in his sitting room, with the weekly paper before him" (p. 33). Fortune's choice of such a character as the story's villain is significant in that it reverses the typical portrayal of such outwardly upstanding colonial men in Australian crime fiction. Anne Maxwell, in her discussion of short stories by Marcus Clarke, Campbell McKellar, and Ernest Favenc, suggests that when these authors write about violent crimes committed by respectable men, they tend to describe such characters and "their resultant sufferings" with "sympathy."[5] Likewise, according to Maxwell, "the men telling the stories, far from judging and condemning, pity and protect those who commit these crimes while sparing little thought for their victims" (2015, p. 60). The use of the Gothic and style of narration in these tales thus "play[s] a definitive role in casting an ambiguous moral light over these more hidden aspects of Australian society" (ibid., p. 60). There are no such gray areas in Fortune's stories about the abuse and murder of women, however. Mark Sinclair, as detective and narrator, is much more sympathetic to Anna Bruce and seeks justice on her behalf, never doubting that her murderer deserves his full punishment. But it ultimately takes both the living and the dead—Sinclair and Anna Bruce—to bring about Commings's downfall.

The unsettled Gothic nature of Fortune's crime stories was heightened by a need for established order amidst very real social anxieties over the loss of control and a seemingly unattainable personal safety. Stephen Knight claims that the popularity of these crime stories and their detective narrators was based on the Australian people's need for order during the early days of colonization and the increased influx of people desperate to make money in the gold fields. Although fictional, these detectives and their ability to solve crimes and restore order from chaos allowed readers of the *Australian Journal* to temporarily experience a sense of order, albeit fictional. According to Knight, "The world realised in [J. S.] Borlase[6] and Fortune had well-developed ideals of social coherence and relational establishment among the spreading suburbs of Melbourne and the small towns of the ranges and plains, and in that context police were a crucial ally" (1994, p. 113). These detective stories thus reveal "the intricacies of crime control among the realistically perceived tensions and fragmentations of the early days of gold and crime, where police did the best they could for a self-aware community that placed no value in fantasies of heroism" (ibid., p. 121). Fortune extends the emphasis on stolen property and wealth by focusing on women who become victims and who cannot be protected by men, no matter how wealthy or socially connected they may be, or how secure their houses are. Although they are not the direct possessors of Australia's material wealth, they are still vulnerable to crime.

Fortune's "The Old Shaft", which appeared in the January 1886 edition of the *Australian Journal* and was part of the long-running "The Detective's Album" series, features another woman's murder and makeshift burial. In this story, however, the woman's dead body becomes even more crucial in bringing about vengeance on her murderer. The unsettled relationship of Moira and Con Clancy is established early in the story, and Fortune uses her narrative to question the idea that the home was a safe space for women and to draw attention to the problem of domestic abuse. According to Penny Russell, spousal abuse was a very real concern in colonial Australia, proving that "the domestic haven could become a hell for some women" (1993, p. 31). Domestic violence took the form of both physical and sexual abuse, but colonial women had few options for escaping such situations due to their financial reliance on men and their isolation in rural locations away from other people who could offer support and protection.[7] Fortune's contemporary, Louisa Lawson, in her essay "The Australian Bush-Woman" (1889), described the hopeless situations many women endured on a daily basis, women whose lives formed "a record of ill-usage": "She may be an isolated woman prey, alone in the wilds with a brutal husband, yet she does not complain; she suffers silently [...] Resource she has none, nor escape, nor redress [...] She is a slave, bound hand and foot to her daily life" (1997, p. 37). After this description, Lawson goes even further, suggesting that these cases of abuse often lead to death. She says:

> The wife is at the man's mercy. She must bear what ills he chooses to put upon her, and her helplessness is his hands only seems to educe the beast in him. There is a vast deal of the vilest treatment. Some are worked to death and some are bullied to death; but the women are so scattered and so reticent that the world hears nothing of it all. (ibid., p. 38)

In her own journalism, Fortune returned to this issue of violence against women and the tendency of abuse to end in a woman's death. In her autobiographical series for the *Australian Journal*, "Twenty-Six Years Ago; or, The Diggings from '55," Fortune describes in the January 1883 issue a firsthand account of a murder similar to the ones which she included in her detective fiction: "It was dreadful to know that, hidden only by the still calico, that awfully rigid form was lying within, and I found myself wondering if the red painted spots were still visible on the cheeks of the dead, or if the long curls were dabbled in the stream that cruel knife had drawn from her breast" (p. 284). Fortune describes the death of a woman attempting to leave her abusive husband. After being repeatedly beaten, the woman is found "stone dead, with every limb and feature stiffened into rigidity" (p. 284). She has "a bundle gripped to one side and a knife in her breast" (p. 284). One of the policemen comments, "Poor soul, she has been on the bolt, and he found it out" (p. 284), a suggestion which draws attention to the fact that women who tried to escape such abusive situations were frequently unsuccessful and put themselves in even greater danger by attempting to leave their husbands/partners. According to Lucy Sussex, Fortune based this event on the murder of Sarah Williams by her husband in November 1855 (1989, p. 49, n. 6). After witnessing this abuse firsthand during her time in the remote Australian goldfield towns, and later in the low-rent boarding houses of Melbourne, Mary Fortune set out in her fiction to give these silenced women a voice.

In Fortune's story, the continued threats of violence become real when Con violently kills Moira by beating her to death with an iron bar. As in the earlier Fortune stories, the woman's dying gaze is foregrounded and continues to haunt Con immediately following her death. Her ghost, initially seen only by Con, is described as "a face and form of fearful significance" (Fortune 1886, p. 251). The "terrible accusing eyes, with the glaze of death creeping over them" give Con a fear of his wife that he never felt while she was living, as her spectral form gains the ability to intimidate a man feared by everyone. In describing Con Clancy's fear, Fortune cleverly returns to the murder weapon, which Moira now symbolically holds over her killer, as the narrator says that "there was a premonition of his doom in the terror that held his heart as in a grip of iron" (p. 251). When Moira's long-absent father suspects her murder after seeing a vision of his daughter lying in the corner of the room where she was killed, he subsequently finds her mangled body in the bottom of a shallow old mining shaft. As with the women in the previous stories, Moira's face is "upturned" and looking directly at the person who finds her, as if the body is impatiently waiting to "speak" and tell the story of its murder:

> Moira lay in a crushed heap against the side of the shaft, her gay blue dress and shining ornaments making a terrible mockery of the livid face and death white bare neck. [...] Having succeeded in carrying all that was left of the once lovely Moira to the room, Kyle laid the helpless form on

the table and decently composed the crushed ball-dress around the stiffened limbs. [...] Her form had set cold and rigid into the contortion her death agony and unbroken fall had induced; and in spite of her father's attempts to compose her attire the appearance she presented was almost too terrible for description. (p. 253)

The key word here is "almost." As an experienced crime fiction writer, Fortune knew these kinds of gruesome descriptions would keep her readers interested. However, these descriptions serve a greater purpose in the narrative. The rigor mortis of the body signifies Moira's resistance to be "fixed" in the attempt to sanitize her death and make it less grotesque. Her horrible appearance must be looked upon by both the guilt-stricken father and the guilty husband. The body communicates its torment to the living.

Because of his own guilt at the failure to protect his daughter and his anger at Con, Moira's father places her body on a table and ties the drunk and heavily sleeping Con's hands and feet, so he must gaze on his deceased wife when he wakes. The description of the killer and victim again coming face-to-face is given even more significance by the state of Moira's body. The table is positioned "so that his eyes might, as soon as they opened, rest on the livid face, gaping mouth, and staring eyeballs of his dead wife. The arm his blow with the bar had broken as she attempted to ward off her death-blow hung nearest to him" (p. 253). Upon waking, Con thinks the ghost of his wife has returned and begins cursing her and beating the body. Yet, this time, his physical abuse has no effect, and Con later ends up falling down the abandoned shaft and breaking his neck. The final revenge that Moira's body has on Con brings significance to her statement earlier in the story, that her husband will "go too far someday if he doesn't mind, for Moira Kyle is not a girl to be put upon by any man" (p. 249).

The state of these women's bodies is in keeping with Karen Halttunen's description of the nineteenth-century public's increasing fascination with "body-horror" and its detailed descriptions of the murder victim's corpse (1998, p. 74). Halttunen has argued that post-1800 murder fiction "focused overwhelmingly on images of the body in pain and death" (1998, p. 73). She adds that this "body-horror" was meant "to arouse the reader's repugnance (and excitement) in the face of the physiological realities of violent death" (ibid., p. 73). By having female ghosts in her stories, Fortune moves beyond the voyeuristic tendencies of most nineteenth-century murder stories, as these dead bodies transform from silent victim to speaking witness. In this way, they take control of their bodies once again and, in their ghostly visitations, decide who will see them and how they will be seen. Each woman is a victim of a man's violent attempts to possess her body and restrict her movements, but autonomy is regained after death through a supernatural afterlife. The insistence on a subjectivity that lasts beyond the grave is a particular characteristic of Gothic death. As Andrew Smith states, Gothic "explores how death shapes the subject's sense of what it means to be a person" (2012, p. 168). He goes on to say that amidst concerns over the frailty of the body, there is also the belief that there is an "inner life" that "transcends" any such physical weakness of the living (ibid., p. 168). According to Halttunen, "Popular murder literature did not pander to the lower social orders so much as it addressed the 'lower' part of human nature as understood within Victorian moral psychology, a nature being restructured by the growing requirements of the civilizing process" (1998, p. 81). The crimes that populate Fortune's stories suggest that Australia still had much progress to make, as the colony was still ruled by baser human emotions of greed, lust, and violence rather than established laws designed to protect people from such emotions. The ghost as uncovered body is therefore a physical return of the repressed, represented in the murderers' attempts to keep their crimes a secret by hiding the bodies. This uncovering is an important instance of what both Halttunen and Smith have discussed as the psychological component in Gothic literature about violent death. For Halttunen, "horror literature contributed not only to the *discovery* of the unconscious, but to the actual *making* of the modern unconscious, into which all the desires and practices newly condemned by humanitarianism were to be relegated by repression" (ibid., pp. 82–83). Likewise, Smith explains the preoccupations of Victorian Gothic death as grounded in the ideas of Frederic Myers, who believed that the communicating spirit that exists after death (which often took the form of a ghost) was a fundamental part of the subliminal mind. For Myers, this subliminal ability was part of the evolutionary process in which humans attained greater intelligence and morality (Smith 2012, pp. 165–166). His definition of a ghost "as *a manifestation of persistent personal energy*" (Myers 1907, p. 215) also fits well with Mary Fortune's supernatural beings as spirits with purpose.[8]

In the context of Fortune's Australian stories, this idea of individual selfhood extends to the nation as well. Ken Gelder and Jane M. Jacobs have described this notion in postcolonial terms, stating, "When a nation engages with others—indigenous people, immigrants, separatists—a sense of national identity is both enabled and disabled. The presence of 'foreigners at home' can intensify a nation's investment in the idea of a national 'self' at the very moment at which such an idea is traumatically unsettled" (1998, pp. 25–26). Likewise, Stephen Knight has discussed the "lack of personal location" (2006, p. 19) in nineteenth-century Australian crime stories, and this idea also works well with the presence of the ghost as a wandering body which lacks a suitable location (in this case, a proper burial). The ideas of "home" are useful when discussing the significance of Gothic dead bodies and the spectres that emerge because of death. In much of Gothic literature, ghosts are forces without an actual dead body described in the text. Mary Fortune's ghosts are more closely linked to their bodies, and thus, to the crimes that led to death. This emphasis puts the body in the foreground and gives it greater significance, especially when read with the theories of Frederic Myers in mind and how his ideas connect to more modern notions of unsettlement. Indeed, Fortune's stories are useful early fictional examples of his theories. Myers discussed the "'colonial' character" (1907, p. 10) of human personality that transcends physical death. The body then becomes "home" and the soul or continuing consciousness (represented by the appearance of the ghost) is "colonial" and wanders in search of something.[9] In Fortune's Gothic crime stories, "home" as physical body and "home" as domestic space are both violated. Ken Gelder sees this troubled sense of home as an "insistent theme in Australian ghost stories of not-so-distant crimes that work to give a particular place an unsettling significance, still 'felt' by those who traverse or inhabit it" (1994, p. xviii).

Gelder and Jacobs's idea of "self" can be extended to female selfhood as well. In the stories discussed here, the women are victims, but they are also active revengers and true revenants. As ghosts, they are allowed power to ultimately take control of their situations and exact change in the form of retribution they could not achieve in life. Yet, Fortune increases the retributive capabilities of these ghosts while also foregrounding the Gothic in these stories. The spectral women ensure that the men who harmed them suffer more than merely a guilty verdict in court. Instead, the ghosts lead each man to a violent death of his own. In her article on Mary Fortune and the *Australian Journal*, Megan Brown notes that, unlike many other periodicals of the time, the journal advocated female autonomy. She says, "Forthright and independent female heroines were valorised from the very first issue, particularly through the crime and mystery writing which formed a significant proportion of contributions. In these fictions, female characters are allowed the freedom to take on active roles" (Brown 2007, p. 77). In the case of Fortune's criminal and mystery Gothic fiction, this idea can be extended to the dead as well. Although victims in life, these female ghosts are given the "freedom" to become active agents after their deaths.

Lucy Sussex has suggested, "It is tempting to speculate that had Fortune been able to reach the middle-class audience of novel readers, she might have enjoyed Braddon's success. Instead, she was condemned to the pages of a colonial popular fiction magazine, one which readily put hastily finished and barely edited material into print" (2010, p. 138). Yet, Mary Fortune's Gothic crime stories manage to transcend the ephemerality of such workaday print and add an important new dimension to discussions of the significance of the female ghost. Her supernatural stories expand our understanding of both Colonial Gothic and Female Gothic, and allow readers to remotely experience the anxiety of both place and gender. In these three representative stories, the denial of a proper burial causes the unsettled spirits to return. The speaking female ghost appears in order to lead the living to her body, evidence that will then lead to the discovery of the woman's murderer. In allowing these women this important "return," Fortune transforms these victimized women into fearful/fear-inducing women who appear and demand vengeance. As supernatural dead bodies, these women now control the male gaze and invite male attention on their own terms, something they were unable to control as beautiful, living bodies. In so doing, Fortune makes the Gothic statement that ultimate vengeance and power lies with the dead.

Notes

1. Fortune's other foray into the Gothic genre was "Clyzia the Dwarf," which was serialized in the *Australian Journal* from 1866 to 1867.
2. See Lucy Sussex, *The Fortunes of Mary Fortune* (Ringwood, VIC: Penguin, 1989), "The Fortunes of Mary: Authenticity, Notoriety and the Crime-Writing Life," *Women's Writing* 14.3 (December 2007): 449–459, and *Women Writers and Detectives in Nineteenth-Century Crime Fiction: The Mothers of the Mystery Genre* (Palgrave Macmillan,

2010). See Megan Brown, "'I Shall Tell Just Such Stories as I Please': Mary Fortune and the *Australian Journal*," *Australian Literary Studies* 23.2 (2007): 74–88, and "A Literary Fortune: Mary Fortune's Life in the Colonial Press," in Anne Collett and Louise D'Arcens (eds.), *The Unsociable Sociability of Women's Lifewriting* (Palgrave Macmillan, 2010), 128–147.

3. It should be noted here that Mary Fortune confined her writing to the experiences of white Europeans in the colony. Brown claims that she was "almost silent" about Aboriginal people "and on the rare occasions when indigenous communities or characters were included in the narrative she portrayed them as non-threatening in most situations and even at times preferable to Europeans" (2014, p. 109).

4. In addition to Ascari's *A Counter-History of Crime Fiction: Supernatural, Gothic, Sensational* (2007), see Stephen Knight's *Crime Fiction, 1800–2000: Detection, Death, Diversity* (Palgrave Macmillan, 2004), for a discussion of the connections between crime fiction and the Gothic.

5. It should be mentioned here that Ernest Favenc's story "Doomed," published in the *Australian Town and Country Journal* in April 1899, is an important instance of the Gothic being used to critique the colonial enterprise. In the story, five young settlers are responsible for the senseless killing of an Aboriginal woman and her child. The woman's ghost returns to haunt the men, as each dies a violent death.

6. James Skipp Borlase (1839–1902) and Mary Fortune collaborated on the first detective stories in the *Australian Journal*. He later revised and reprinted "Mystery and Murder" under his name in *The Night Fossickers* (1867), although, according to Lucy Sussex, computer analysis of the early detective stories conducted at the University of Newcastle proves Fortune was the author. For more details on these attribution issues, see Lucy Sussex and John Burrows, "Whodunit? Literary Forensics and the Crime Writing of James Skipp Borlase and Mary Fortune," *Bulletin of the Bibliographical Society of Australia and New Zealand* (1997): xxi, pp. 73–106. In her chapter on Fortune in *Women Writers and Detectives in Nineteenth-Century Crime Fiction* (2010), Sussex claims, "There are at least three literary thefts in *The Night Fossickers*, of which the most substantial is 'Mystery and Murder'" and also notes that Borlase was fired from the *Australian Journal* in 1866 after he plagiarized Walter Scott (p. 126). In his edited collection, *The Australian Short Story before Lawson* (1986), Cecil Hadgraft includes "Mystery and Murder" under Borlase's name, unknowingly undercutting his negative appraisal of Mary Fortune's writing in the introduction to the collection. The story is fully attributed to Fortune in Ken Gelder and Rachael Weaver's *The Anthology of Colonial Australian Gothic Fiction* (2007).

7. See Kay Saunders, "The Study of Domestic Violence in Colonial Queensland: Sources and Problems," *Historical Studies* 21.82 (1984): 68–84, as well as Robert Hogg's chapter, "A Hand Prepared to Be Red," in his *Men and Manliness on the Frontier: Queensland and British Columbia in the Mid-Nineteenth Century* (Palgrave Macmillan, 2012).
8. Mary Fortune's use of the social supernatural complicates Cecil Hadgraft's assertion that nineteenth-century Australian fiction did not produce many notable supernatural stories because the ghosts were "too literal." He claims that "a ghost remains a ghost, a supernatural scene is hardly more than a vision to be frightened or startled by. There is not much of the suggestion that can induce us to muse and to wonder for a moment whether there may be a world beyond mundane experience" (1986, p. 31).
9. This idea can be extended to Mary Fortune herself, who was born in Belfast, Ireland, moved to Montreal, Canada, with her father, and then emigrated again to Australia. Her adoption of the pseudonym, "Waif Wander," also hints at the nomadic, unsettled lifestyle she had while living in Australia. Written at roughly the same time as Susanna Moodie's memoir, Fortune's own autobiographical account of her anxiety upon arriving in a strange new land with a young child is remarkably similar to Moodie's, with one arriving in Canada and another leaving it. Looking back on her arrival in Australia in 1855, Fortune recalls: "I began to realise that I was on the borders of a new life. All the perils of the sea were over, and it lay an impassable barrier between me and the old happy Canadian life. What fate was to be for me and mine in this land of gold over which the shadows of night were slowly dropping? Could the question have then been answered, would I have stopped and retraced my steps?" (September 1882, p. 36).

Bibliography

Ascari, Maurizio (2007), *A Counter-History of Crime Fiction: Supernatural, Gothic, Sensational*, Basingstoke: Palgrave Macmillan.

Brown, Megan (2007), "'I Shall Tell Just Such Stories as I Please': Mary Fortune and the *Australian Journal*," *Australian Literary Studies* 23.2: 74–88.

——— (2014), "A Literary Fortune," in Maggie Tonkin, Mandy Treagus, Madeleine Seys, and Sharon Crozier-De Rosa (eds.), *Changing the Victorian Subject*, Adelaide: University of Adelaide Press, pp. 105–122.

Fortune, Mary [Waif Wander] (1882), "Twenty-Six Years Ago; Or, The Diggings from '55," *Australian Journal* 18 (September): 33–37.

——— (1883), "Twenty-Six Years Ago; Or, The Diggings from '55," *Australian Journal* 18 (January): 280–285.

——— (1886), "The Old Shaft," *Australian Journal* 21 (January): 248–254.

——— (1994 [1867]), "The Illumined Grave," in Ken Gelder (ed.), *The Oxford Book of Australian Ghost Stories*, Melbourne and Oxford: Oxford University Press, pp. 19–35.

——— (2007 [1866]), "Mystery and Murder," in Ken Gelder and Rachael Weaver (eds.), *The Anthology of Colonial Australian Gothic Fiction*, Carlton, VIC: Melbourne University Press, pp. 31–43.

Gelder, Ken (1994), "Introduction," in Ken Gelder (ed.), *The Oxford Book of Australian Ghost Stories*, Melbourne and Oxford: Oxford University Press, pp. ix–xviii.

Gelder, Ken, and Jane M. Jacobs (1998), *Uncanny Australia: Sacredness and Identity in a Postcolonial Nation*, Carlton, VIC: Melbourne University Press.

Gelder, Ken, and Rachael Weaver (2007), "The Colonial Australian Gothic," in Ken Gelder and Rachael Weaver (eds.), *The Anthology of Colonial Australian Gothic Fiction*, Carlton, VIC: Melbourne University Press, pp. 1–9.

Hadgraft, Cecil (1986), "Introduction," in Cecil Hadgraft (ed.), *The Australian Short Story before Lawson*, Melbourne and Oxford: University of Oxford Press, pp. 1–56.

Halttunen, Karen (1998), *Murder Most Foul: The Killer and the American Gothic Imagination*, Cambridge and London: Harvard University Press.

Knight, Stephen (1994), "The Vanishing Policeman: Patterns of Control in Australian Crime Fiction," in Ian Craven (ed.), *Australian Popular Culture*, Cambridge and New York: Cambridge University Press, pp. 109–122.

——— (2006), "Crimes Domestic and Crimes Colonial: The Role of Crime Fiction in Developing Postcolonial Consciousness," in Christine Matzke and Susanne Mühleisen (eds.), *Postcolonial Postmortems: Crime Fiction from a Transcultural Perspective*, Amsterdam and New York: Rodopi.

Lawson, Louisa (1997 [1889]), "The Australian Bush-Woman," in Imre Salusinszky (ed.), *The Oxford Book of Australian Essays*, Melbourne and Oxford: Oxford University Press, pp. 35–39.

Maxwell, Anne (2015), "'The Beast Within': Degeneration in *Dr Jekyll and Mr Hyde* and Three Australian Short Stories," *Australian Literary Studies* 30.3 (October): 47–61.

Myers, Frederic (1907), *Human Personality and Its Survival of Bodily Death*, New York and London: Longmans, Green, & Company.

Russell, Penny (1993), "In Search of Woman's Place: An Historical Survey of Gender and Space in Nineteenth-Century Australia," *Australasian Historical Archaeology* 11: 28–32.

Sinnett, Frederick (1856), "The Fiction Fields of Australia," *Journal of Australasia* 1 (November): 97–105, 199–208.

Smith, Andrew (2012), "Victorian Gothic Death," in Andrew Smith and William Hughes (eds.), *The Victorian Gothic*, Edinburgh: Edinburgh University Press.

Sussex, Lucy (ed.) (1989), *The Fortunes of Mary Fortune*, Ringwood, VIC: Penguin.

——— (2010), *Women Writers and Detectives in Nineteenth-Century Crime Fiction: The Mothers of the Mystery Genre*, Basingstoke, UK: Palgrave Macmillan.

Turcotte, Gerry (2009), "Australian Gothic," in Marie Mulvey-Roberts (ed.), *The Handbook to the Gothic*, 2nd edn., New York: New York University Press, pp. 277–287.

CHAPTER 10

Fear and Death in the Outback: Barbara Baynton's *Bush Studies*

Born in New South Wales in 1857, Barbara Baynton's literary output is relatively small. Apart from a few newspaper articles, she published two collections of short stories, *Bush Studies* (1902) and *Cobbers* (1917), and one short novel, *Human Toll* (1907).[1] Yet, in her lifetime, she built a reputation as one of Australia's most talented writers. Contemporary critics praised her ability to realistically describe life in remote settlements far from urban centers. *Bush Studies*, considered by many scholars to be Baynton's masterpiece, consists of six stories that describe the isolation and desperation of men and women alone in the Australian outback. Baynton's storytelling, which unflinchingly describes bush life as a "survival of the fittest" scenario, is often described as realist. However, this chapter attempts to complicate and expand this traditional representation of Baynton's work by examining the Gothic elements—revenge, sadism, murder, rape, and death—that are present throughout the book, but are most prominent in the two stories which bookend the collection. These elements begin with the first story, "A Dreamer," where an unmarried pregnant woman wanders through the wilderness as she tries to return to her childhood home. Yet, there is no redemption waiting for this woman, who admits that "the sweat of her body" cannot alleviate "the sin of her soul." This sense of desperation is also experienced by characters in the following stories, leading to the ultimate victimization of a helpless woman and her child in the controversial concluding tale, "The Chosen Vessel," with its indictment of corrupt morality and ineffectual

© The Author(s) 2018
M. Edmundson, *Women's Colonial Gothic Writing, 1850–1930*,
Palgrave Gothic, https://doi.org/10.1007/978-3-319-76917-2_10

religion, both of which lead to the downfall of men and women in these far-flung colonial settlements.

In many ways, Barbara Baynton lived what she wrote about in *Bush Studies*. Born in Scone, New South Wales, to Irish immigrants, Baynton and her siblings endured the physical and mental harshness of bush life from an early age. She was regularly beaten as an example to the other students at the state school she attended, and noticed that the "better dressed" and "more prosperous" children were treated differently by the teachers (Hackforth-Jones 1989, p. 12). To escape the tediousness of life at home, Baynton accepted a position as governess to the Frater family living in Liverpool Plains, New South Wales. During her stay with the family, Baynton stayed in a bedroom that was built off the back of the small schoolhouse constructed by the Fraters (ibid., p. 19). When she decided to marry one of the older Frater sons (against the wishes of the father), the couple moved even farther into the bush, near Coonamble. The area was scrubland and the newlyweds established themselves in a small house which consisted of a bedroom, kitchen, and living room. Alex Frater sought work as a shearer, which left his wife alone for extended periods of time (ibid., p. 25). By 1889, Alex had abandoned his wife and their three small children for a younger woman. For a time, Barbara was forced to sell bibles door-to-door until she found a position as a housekeeper in the Woollahra residence of Dr. Thomas Baynton.[2] In 1890, after being granted a divorce and custody of her children, Barbara married Thomas Baynton (Krimmer and Lawson 1980, p. xii). Finally achieving a steadier life with a more supportive (and financially stable) husband allowed Barbara the leisure time she needed to begin her writing career.

According to Penne Hackforth-Jones, Baynton's writing of *Bush Studies* was a cathartic experience:

> Barbara had no illusions about her experience. She saw the bush as she found it, unbearable in part, beautiful and haunting in others. She had come to terms with it while she had to, but she wasn't going to pretend it was a garden. The gardens in Sydney *were* gardens—the bush was a battleground [...] The selector, battling his way against the seasons, was being neatly written up as a figure of clod-hopping fun for the city reader, and it must have been with a real sense of vindication she sat down to "write the bush out of her." (1989, p. 59)

Indeed, the nightmare visions of the collection are Baynton's way of exorcizing the demons of her past and coming to terms with her own complicated relationship with the Australian bush.

Yet, Baynton's efforts to have her volume of Australian stories published proved frustrating.[3] In an address to the Writers' and Artists' Union at the Sydney Trades Hall in 1911, Baynton described her difficulty in finding a publisher. After failing to interest any Sydney publishers, Baynton tried her luck in London. When several major publishing houses also turned down her work, Baynton was on the verge of returning to Australia when a chance meeting with Edward Garnett led to her collection being published with Duckworths. For Baynton, a major obstacle to finding a suitable publisher was her choice of distinctly Australian subject matter. According to Norman Lilley, who reported on Baynton's speech, Baynton claimed that Australian stories were not in keeping with the "popular taste" of the time, which was dictated by British readers:

> Englishmen were not interested in Australia; they knew nothing about it, and did not want to learn. They regarded it as a land of strange contradictions, where the birds did not sing and the flowers had no smell, and the trees shed their bark instead of their leaves; and nothing could persuade them that eucalyptus was not our national scent. They might read about the adventures of an Englishman in Australia; but they declined to take any interest in the country itself. What the English didn't want to hear about they simply shut their ears to. (1911, p. 21)

Baynton concluded that writers of the time could not "score a popular success with serious matter" (quoted in ibid., p. 21). Lilley notes that Baynton considered the Australian-based story a detriment to commercial success among the British reading public compared to other fictional imaginings of colonial regions:

> If Australia possessed ancient castles and moated granges and plenty of dukes the English would want to hear about it; but as it was they didn't care a dump for it. India they would hear about as being more romantic [...] but not Australia. So Australian writers were warned not to turn down their bread and butter and seek fame on the other side because they had received a little praise here. Though she was ashamed to say that a great

part of the general public here seemed to think that you must have the English hall-mark, and that the Australian was of no value.[4] (ibid., p. 21)

After the publication of *Bush Studies* and its failure to catch the interest of readers, Baynton expressed her disappointment to Vance Palmer, saying that "English readers are only interested in a background they know...and Australia to them is more remote than Abysinnia" (Palmer 1958, p. 15). She also warned other Australian writers to stay away from England, telling them instead, "Stay at home where you can write about what you know for the people you know" (ibid., p. 15).

What Baynton's collection lacked in commercial success, it made up for in critical applause. Most reviewers read *Bush Studies* favorably, and this reception only increased in the years following its publication. An appreciation of June 15, 1929, by Nettie Palmer which appeared in the *Brisbane Courier* following Baynton's death called Baynton a "literary pioneer" whose small literary output always represented a true picture of the human condition. Palmer describes Baynton's writing as "vigorous and relentless," and claims that this ability to look at the darker side of people was a particular strength of her fiction: "Descending with her characters into loneliness, dust, and bitterness, Barbara Baynton somehow links them with the whole of humanity" (Palmer 1929, p. 21). Her work is usually compared favorably to the realist fiction of Henry Lawson, whom David McKee Wright described in 1918 as "the first articulate voice of the real Australia" (1918, p. viii). Writing almost twenty years after Baynton's death, Vance Palmer, who had also praised the quality of Lawson's work, admitted that the "tough, primitive life" that Baynton described in her fiction "cut more deeply into the bone than anything written by Lawson" (1958, p. 15). A longtime acquaintance of Baynton, Palmer recalls that in the "fashionable club[s]" of London, she "still seemed like a bushwoman; there was an atmosphere of abundance about her" (1958, p. 15).

Although *Bush Studies* was positively reviewed, there were exceptions, particularly from Australian newspapers who took issue with Baynton's unflinching portrait of settler life in the outback. A January 17, 1903, review in Sydney's conservative *Daily Telegraph* commended Baynton for the portrayal of her characters, making specific mention of the women in "The Chosen Vessel" and "A Dreamer." Preferring the term "phantasies" over "sketches," the reviewer gives Baynton credit for her knowledge of bush life but disagrees with her decision to foreground "the cruelty, the raw animalism, the witless gaucherie of men, and the loneliness, hardness, and sorrow of women." For the reviewer, the "utter brutalism, senseless and pitiless, of natures coarsened down from normal human level" that exists in each story gives an untrue picture of life in the bush (*Daily Telegraph* 1903, p. 6). Another reviewer in the January 10, 1903, issue of Adelaide's *Register* claimed that Baynton had "unmistakable power" as a writer but lacked "reticence." The review faults Baynton for the too graphic nature of her stories and is concerned that "the picture given to English people of bush life is a truly horrible one." Her fictional "monsters of shamelessness" and their crimes are "more suited to a modern Belgian, or an Elizabethan dramatist, than to an Australian woman novelist" (*Register* 1903, p. 8). A review which appeared in Grafton's *Clarence and Richmond Examiner* on March 14, 1903, went even further in its rebuke of Baynton's portrayal of bush life. Like the previous reviewer, there is a greater anxiety, apart from the content of the stories, over the book's publication in England. The reviewer says, "England imbibes its impression of Australian bush life from what it reads, and far-fetched absurdities [...] dupes English readers into believing that life in the Australian bush is a class of savagery entirely and peculiarly its own." The treatment of such topics is even more disturbing because the stories come "from the pen of a woman" (*Clarence and Richmond Examiner* 1903, p. 8).

A. A. Phillips was one of the first scholars to examine how Baynton challenged the "self-confident Australianism" of the 1890s (1971, p. 149). Kay Schaffer later noted the feminist qualities of this "revolt" in Baynton's stories, particularly how they complicate and disrupt a male-centered nationalist tradition in Australian literature. She suggests that woman as a historical figure in nineteenth-century Australia has often been "muted" and that the "idea of the feminine [...] has been noted as an absent presence in the metonymic relations of man to the land and to mateship, the bush, freedom and egalitarian democracy" (Schaffer 1988, p. 149). Opposed to this tendency to relegate women to the background in history and literature, Baynton focuses on female characters who "disturb and deflate masculine values" (Schaffer 1988, p. 149). This emphasis on women's experience set in remote regions combines with a focus on fear, isolation, and violence to create stories that remain memorable because they refuse to uphold the nationalistic spirit that predominated in a colonial Australia that was slowly forging a national identity and distancing itself from its mother country. Schaffer concludes, "Nowhere are the horrors of outback life more powerfully represented than in [Baynton's] short stories" (ibid., p. 148).

Baynton's experience as a three-fold outsider from the predominant social and literary worlds of Britain—as a colonial Australian woman coming from a working-class background—allowed her an appreciation of life's hardships that she transferred to great effect in her fiction. Lucy Frost has claimed that Baynton "wrote best when she was writing about people left out in the cold" (1983, p. 59). This view from the margins of society and the hardships she endured meant that Baynton was well-prepared to write about the darker side of life in the outback. A. A. Phillips sees her work as particularly suited to the Gothic mode. He calls both "A Dreamer" and "The Chosen Vessel" "stories of nightmare" that belong to the tradition of Algernon Blackwood and Richard Middleton. These stories "are concerned to arouse the emotions of pity and terror" and "belong [...] to a popular genre of the period, the tale which aims to make the reader's flesh creep" (Phillips 1971, p. 150). However, not forgetting Baynton's artistic insistence on the importance of authentic literature in favor of the popular escapist literature which she felt dominated literary tastes in Great Britain, Phillips recognizes that her stories are "driven by a need to free her own spirit from nightmare obsessions" (ibid., p. 150). The combination of the real and the unreal gives Baynton's short fiction its unique power:

> Barbara Baynton is an Australian writer, and she is true to the most persisting characteristic of that breed: she firmly roots her story in the soil of the actual. She creates the line of the story, its symbolic detail, from the pressure of nightmare impulse, it is true; but she creates the sort of things which do happen. Her episodes are the events of life-as-it-is. (ibid., p. 152)

The nightmarish quality of "A Dreamer," the opening story in *Bush Studies*, sets the tone for the stories that follow. It describes an unnamed woman's journey through a hostile bush landscape to her mother's house; unknown to the daughter, her mother has died shortly before her arrival. The story opens with a series of reversals that, according to Leigh Dale, stress the "perversity" of the woman's journey and its outcome: "women should make homes, not return to them as strangers; mothers and children should be together, not apart; homecoming should be joyful, not full of terror" (2011, pp. 370–371). These instances of perversion and unfulfillment also make the story a Gothic one. The unnamed young woman is an outcast trying to return to a home that can never be what it once was to her. Because of the amount of time spent away from her birthplace, she returns as a stranger to an alien landscape where she no longer belongs. The porter, who "knew every one in the district" (Baynton 1980a [1902], p. 4), does not recognize the woman, and she is compared to an "ownerless" dog at the railway station. The woman sees the dog "huddled, wet and shivering" and feels a sense of "kinship" (p. 4). There is also a more indistinct sense of unease that follows the woman as she starts on her three-mile walk through the bush to her mother's house. The woman tries to keep this feeling of unease away from her, but it becomes a shadow that haunts her. As she moves through the silent town, the only sound is made by the "night workers" who are building a coffin. The woman tries to "lose the sound" by quickening her pace (p. 5), but its significance will literally come back to haunt her.

The Australian landscape is a major part of the terror in Baynton's stories. Indeed, as A. A. Phillips puts it, "the sense of the crushing isolation of bush-life" that is such a theme in her work is "exclusively Australian" (1971, p. 157). These fears point to a larger anxiety over the Australian colonist's relationship with the outback, as the land itself "resists" the settler-invaders. There is always looming "a sense of spiritual darkness emanating from the land itself, a feeling of primeval cruelty fed by the sunlight which glares instead of glowing, by the grey of the bush which some obstinate Europeanism within us insists should be green" (ibid., p. 157). This sense of a Gothic quality in the bush landscape—as land which "resists"—has long been a part of the Australian colonial consciousness. Complicating Frederick Sinnett's earlier assertion that Australia, as a colony, was too "new" for any unique Gothic treatment in literature, and thus had to rely on a tradition "imported" from Europe, Marcus Clarke proclaimed a Gothic aspect inherent in Australia's landscape. In his Preface to the collected poems of Adam Lindsay Gordon, published in 1876, Clarke described his native surroundings:

> The Australian mountain forests are funereal, secret, stern. Their solitude is desolation. They seem to stifle, in their black gorges, a story of sullen despair [...] The savage winds shout among the rock clefts. From the melancholy gums strips of white bark hang and rustle. The very animal life of these frowning hills is either grotesque or ghostly. [...] From a corner of the silent forest rises a dismal chant, and around a fire dance natives

painted like skeletons. All is fear-inspiring and gloomy. No bright fancies are linked with the memories of the mountains. Hopeless explorers have named them out of their sufferings—Mount Misery, Mount Dreadful, Mount Despair. (1997 [1876], p. 33)

This landscape gave Australians what they were lacking in more "traditional" European Gothic settings. It also gave them a place of unsettlement from which to examine the disrupted hopes and dreams of the settlers who sought to live there, but who, in turn, were made into desperate shadows of some former self. As Baynton's story and Clarke's description make clear, there is no sylvan valley awaiting European colonists who are trying to find a peaceful "home" within this natural setting, only "defiant ferocity" and "bitterness" (Clarke 1997 [1876], p. 33).

Nowhere in *Bush Studies* is the natural landscape so outwardly hostile as in "A Dreamer," a story that serves as a fitting fictional imagining of what Clarke describes as the quintessentially hostile Australian environment. In Baynton's story, nature itself tries to disrupt the attempted return home in one of the most effective descriptions of an antagonistic bush landscape. The wind has "teeth," "shrieks," and is "angry" (Baynton 1980a [1902], p. 5), while the storm which slows her progression homeward "rages," with violent thunder (p. 6). In several instances, the woman undergoes a literal battle with the natural elements around her that Baynton describes with human-like qualities. She attempts to cross a flooded creek by holding on to willow branches, and "malignantly the wind fought her, driving her back, or snapping the brittle stems from her skinned hands" (p. 7). Even the trees she grew up among have turned against the woman and resist her return: "they lashed her unprotected face. Round and round her bare neck they coiled their stripped fingers. Her mother had planted these willows, and she herself had watched them grow. How could they be so hostile to her!" (p. 8). When she attempts to call for help, the "wind made a funnel of her mouth and throat, and a wave of muddy water choked her cry" (pp. 8–9). In this story, the bush landscape takes the place of the abusive men who inhabit several other stories in *Bush Studies*. Like the men who physically harm, verbally intimidate, and degrade the women around them, this woman must suffer in silence in the absence of her husband.

The suffering that the woman undergoes through her interactions with the environment mirrors her internal regret at being separated from her mother for so long. Although Baynton never gives any details regarding the relationship of the two women and what may have caused the daughter to stay away from home for so long, the woman herself sees her suffering during the return to her mother's house as a form of expiation: "Long ago she should have come to her old mother, and her heart gave a bound of savage rapture in thus giving the sweat of her body for the sin of her soul" (p. 8). Yet, though the woman believes that "there was atonement in these difficulties and dangers" (p. 7), her mother's death makes her journey fruitless. Baynton foregrounds this physical and psychical distance between the two by juxtaposing the woman's thoughts of forgiveness and "atonement" with her inner fears of continued separation. As she nears the house, the woman remembers that her mother used to wait with a lantern on the other side of the creek but, on this occasion, the mother is absent and "there was no light" (p. 7). This sense of separation is echoed when the woman sees the "Bendy Tree," a supposedly haunted landmark where "a runaway horse had crushed its drunken rider against the bent, distorted trunk" (p. 6). This site, which symbolizes violence and loss, serves to alarm the woman whose nerves are already on edge. On the verge of confronting her own loss, she imagines that the scene of death is very near. She thinks she sees the "horseman galloping furiously towards her," then "above the shriek of the wind, she thought she heard a cry, then crash came the thunder, drowning her call of warning" (pp. 6–7).

After nearly drowning, the woman reaches the side of the creek where her childhood home is located. She feels that "every horror was of the past and forgotten" (p. 9), but her horror is not "past" but ahead. Toward the end of the story, there are added layers of imagination and false hope. The daughter imagines her welcome home, where the mother, who was herself "a dreamer," will comfort her daughter and tell her that she only imagined hearing her mother's call in the night. Not knowing her mother is dead, this "call" from beyond the grave could have been very real, and for the daughter, only a nightmare awaits. When she enters the house to find strange women in it, the daughter is taken to her mother's room. On her short journey to the room, all the fears that assailed the woman throughout her exterior travels come back with full force. She "grew cold and her heart trembled," and she looks at the women with "numbing horror in her eyes" (p. 10). By leaving the knowledge of the mother's death until the last line of the story, we travel with the woman and feel her frustration of hopes. She cannot undo the past and will presumably be haunted by her decision not to visit sooner.

The notion of the daughter's inability to return to the home she once knew also provides a metaphor for how the Australia/Britain relationship functioned in the lives of those first transported to the colony against their will and, later, those who chose to settle in Australia. For many of these people, Britain was the true "home" they would never see again. In Baynton's story, because she omits key details about the true nature of the daughter's extended absence from home and mother, we are left with a lingering feeling of our own disorientation regarding these events and a sense of mystery that will never be fully explained. We enter the woman's nightmare and are left there.

"The Chosen Vessel" is the final story in *Bush Studies*, and it is, as a parting image, Baynton's most powerful indictment of the isolating effect of the bush landscape, and the predatory, hypocritical people who inhabit that landscape and prey on the vulnerability of others.[5] The unnamed woman's story begins and ends with fear and violence. In the opening passage, she is forced by her husband to separate a cow from a calf. When the woman runs from the cow, her "angry" husband calls her a "cur," and the narrator lets us know that "in many things he was worse than the cow" (Baynton 1980c [1902], p. 81). Indeed, whereas the cow's potential violence against the woman comes from her motherly instinct to protect her offspring, the husband's verbal (and most likely physical) abuse of his wife is petty and mean-spirited. When she admits to him that she fears the "swagmen" who pass by their house coming and going from "the dismal, drunken little township" (p. 82) when the husband is away working as a shearer, he responds with insults rather than concern: "when she had dared to speak of the dangers to which her loneliness exposed her, he had taunted and sneered at her. 'Needn't flatter yerself,' he had told her, 'nobody 'ud want ter run away with yew'" (p. 82). This lack of sympathy leads the woman to reject any thought of going to her husband when she feels she is in danger.

Left on her own for lengthy periods of time, the woman tries to take precautions, but these prove futile given the limited resources with which she must work. When one of the swagmen comes to her door, she immediately fears him, as Baynton's description of the baby's unreasoning desire for the mother's breasts parallels his own immoral sexual desire for her: "She feared more from the look of his eyes, and the gleam of his teeth, as he watched her newly awakened baby beat its impatient fists upon her covered breasts, than from the knife that was sheathed in the belt at his waist" (p. 82). The woman tries to pretend her husband is sick inside the house and barricades herself within the house as best she can, but her tools (weapons) are rudimentary. She shoves scissors in the back-door bolt, puts a table and stools in front of the door, and barricades the front door with the handle of a shovel. But this proves useless given the poor construction of her house, which has cracks in the floorboards and large pieces of siding that are supported by flimsy wedges. Her husband is unwilling to protect her; her house is unable to.

The swagman returns after dark, and the suspense of his slow, calculated assault on the house is juxtaposed with the steadily building terror of the defenseless woman trapped inside: "Still watching, she saw the shadow darken every crack along the wall. She knew by the sounds that the man was trying every standpoint that might help him see in; but how much he saw she could not tell [...] Stealthily the man crept about" (p. 83). Lying as still and quiet as she can, she is forced to endure the swagman's attempts to find the weak point that will allow him into the house: "He was trying every slab, and was very near to that with the wedge under it. Then she saw him find it; and heard the sound of the knife as bit by bit he began to cut away the wooden support [...] she knew that in another few minutes this man with the cruel eyes, lascivious mouth, and gleaming knife, would enter" (p. 84).

The fear of the "swagman" or tramp as one of the criminal types roving around the countryside was pervasive in nineteenth-century Australian society. In his essay "Crime in the Bush," published in the February 11, 1899, edition of the *Bulletin*, Henry Lawson linked the formation of these degraded men to a harsh landscape that breeds only desperation and despair:

> there are hundreds of out-of-the-way places in the nearer bush of Australia—hidden away in unheard-of "pockets" in the ranges: on barren creeks [...] up at the ends of long, dark gullies, and away out on God-forsaken [...] flats—where families live for generations in mental darkness almost inconceivable in this enlightened age and country [...] Some of these families are descended from a convict of the worst type on one side or the other, perhaps on both: and, if not born criminals, are trained in shady ways from childhood. Conceived and bred under the shadow of exile, hardship or "trouble," the sullen, brooding spirit which enwraps their lonely bush-buried homes will carry further their moral degradation. (1965 [1899], pp. 276–277)

The anxiety surrounding the prevalence of these "degraded" men also pointed to other fears centering on the vulnerability of women left alone in isolated bush locations. In her discussion of the first published version of the story, "The Tramp," Nina Philadelphoff-Puren contends that Baynton's narrative should be read as an important literary and historical text, a fictional story that intentionally involves itself in the very real debates about the rape of colonial white women during the 1880s and 1890s. Focusing on the gang rape of Mary Jane Hicks in September 1886, Philadelphoff-Puren recounts how the case divided Australian public opinion. J. F. Archibald, the editor of the *Bulletin* during the ten years leading up to the publication of Baynton's story in 1896, continuously vilified Hicks on the presumed grounds that she was a "fallen" woman, a prostitute who had encouraged her attack (Philadelphoff-Puren 2010, p. 3). This stance was illustrative of the disparaging attitude toward female victims held by many colonials at the time and which made prosecuting rape so difficult. According to Philadelphoff-Puren, "The demand for eyewitnesses and corroboration, and Victorian judgements about female character and respectability, meant that many women's complaints of rape were disqualified before being tried" (ibid., p. 11, n. 11). Aboriginal women were at an even greater disadvantage in the colony when they accused white men of rape.[6] When the last defendants were released from jail in November 1896, just a month before Baynton's story was published in the *Bulletin*, the paper proclaimed that the victim was not Mary Jane Hicks, but the "Goddess of Justice." In this version of events, Philadelphoff-Puren notes that "men's violence against an actual woman was written away, only to be replaced with suffering of an abstract figure of the feminine and the cruelly wronged figures of the defendants themselves" (ibid., p. 5). Amid this mindset, Baynton's story writes the woman back into the discourse regarding rape. Significantly, her presentation of a young wife and mother, left alone with no one to protect her, complicated the prevailing notion that most rape allegations were false because they involved the deviations of supposedly "fallen" or "loose" women who were conveniently labeled as prostitutes. In Baynton's story, this dynamic is reversed, as the woman is a victim of the other misogynistic extreme, one which sought to disempower women by constantly belittling their appearance and usefulness. In this sense, the woman is a victim of her husband's verbal abuse even before the action that begins the story. Because of her apparent lack of self-esteem and her isolation from other men, she cannot be accused of any kind of seductiveness.

Thinking the swagman is about to enter the house and hearing horse's hooves, the woman desperately tries to unlock the doors and flee from the house in order to seek help. Yet, the horseman does not stop and, as she runs, the woman finds herself being "caught" instead by the swagman. Though the man "offers terms" for her to stop screaming, she continues, and he grips her by the throat. In a more violent imagining of the terrified woman in "A Dreamer" who cannot scream because the wind muffles her voice, the woman's stifled scream can only verbalize "Murder," which the startled curlews repeat as they fly away (Baynton 1980c [1902], p. 85). Though Baynton does not describe the woman's murder in detail, she uses the image of a sheep murdered by a dingo to symbolize the gruesomeness of the crime, the defenseless innocence of the victim, and the animalistic mindset of her attacker. This victimization is tied to the recurring failure of women to be heard in *Bush Studies*. This "central theme," according to Leigh Dale, takes many forms, from "a woman's voice which cannot be heard" to "women's words which are stopped up, thrown back, misrecognized or mocked" (2011, p. 372). Dale likewise suggests that, through the emphasis on "woman, sheep, murder" in both "Billy Skywonkie" and "The Chosen Vessel," we can read the killing of the sheep in the former story as an indirect description of the woman's murder in "The Chosen Vessel" (ibid., p. 377). In "Billy Skywonkie," the sheep dies a violent death: "He bent and strained back a sheep's neck, drew the knife and steel from his belt, and skillfully danced an edge on the knife." The witness to this killing, herself a victimized woman, notices that "the sheep lay passive, with its head back, till its neck curved in a bow, and that the glitter of the knife was reflected in its eye" (Baynton 1980b [1902], p. 60). The sheep is passive, the woman struggles, but the result is the same. Both are treated as, and die like, animals.

Baynton utilizes this image of sheep and lamb, mother and child, to describe the woman's mutilated body and the living, traumatized child who is left along the creek. This is the third instance in the story where she has been left helpless by a man: by her husband, by Peter Hennessey (the man on horseback who failed to help the woman as she fled her home), and by the swagman. Her child, the "lamb," "had sucked the still warm breasts, and laid its little head on her bosom, and slept till the morn." When the morning arrives, "it looked at the swollen disfigured face," cries, and "would have crept away, but for the hand that still clutched its little gown" (Baynton 1980c [1902], p. 85). When the body is discovered by a boundary rider, the "crows were close, so close, to the mother's wide-open eyes," and he "was forced to cut its gown that the dead hand held" (p. 85).

The remaining section of the story serves as a further comment on the danger of objectifying women. Hennessey comes to realize that the terrified woman who he refused to save because of his own fear and superstition—a figure who becomes "a ghastly parody of the Virgin Mary" (Krimmer and Lawson 1980, p. xviii)—is now in reality a murder victim. Yet, in forcing his vision of the Virgin Mary onto the woman, because of his own guilt at disobeying his priest over his vote in the local election, he also forces her to become invisible as a real person. Because of his fear of judgment and in order to save himself, Hennessey flees the scene and leaves the woman to her fate. His complicity in her eventual murder is reinforced by the priest who exclaims, "you did not stop to save her!" (Baynton 1980c [1902], p. 87). There are many layers of blame in "The Chosen Vessel," beginning with the husband, who, because of his past actions, is responsible for what happens to his wife. Then, the swagman who sees the woman as an object to serve his animalistic desires. And, finally, Hennessey, who refuses to help save the woman. Each of these men also represent a distinct threat against the woman: the husband who degrades her, the swagman who rapes and murders her, and Hennessey, who projects his vision of a female idol (ideal) upon her which reduces her to an abstract symbol.[7] Indeed, Baynton shows the danger behind such an objectification. Neither role placed on women—either that of woman as "civilizer" of colonial Australia, or woman as civilizer of colonial Australian men—is ultimately beneficial in the lives of these women. In Baynton's story, the woman is thus, as Krimmer and Lawson say, an "anonymous" victim "besieged by hostile predatory forces" (1980, p. xx). They describe this powerlessness as the means by which Baynton heightens the fragile existence of her (mostly) female protagonists, saying, "Each story has an inexorable progress towards a dire conclusion—death, rape, rejection or some combination of these—and the progress itself is in the form of an ordeal which serves to heighten the victim's (and our) perception of the horror of his or her vulnerability" (Krimmer and Lawson 1980, p. xxv). As Julieanne Lamond notes, Baynton's narrative style also frustrates readers' "access" to the inner thoughts of her main characters. This distancing, in turn, serves to "unsettle the reader by refusing to normalize or explain the often terrible behavior of the characters." Instead, we are encouraged to see these characters as "witnesses to the violence of their society" (Lamond 2011, p. 388). By keeping us away from the inner thoughts of her characters, Baynton also forces readers to themselves be witnesses to the violence in her stories, interlopers, eavesdropping on moments of desperation and pain. This tendency to keep readers at an enforced distance, when read in light of the voyeuristic nature of Gothic writing, amplifies the horror present in the story. Like Peter Hennessey, readers become complicit in the woman's suffering because we only observe from a distance.

Baynton's choice to fully realize the woman's rape and murder in the story is even more daring when compared to other contemporary narratives. For instance, Evelyn Adams's story, "Cruel Fate," published in her collection *Tales of Three Colonies* (1903), describes a domestic tragedy that unfolds in similar ways to Baynton's narrative.[8] It begins with the happy newlyweds, Alice and Alan Blackwood, who decide to "live an Arcadian life" on a rural farm (Adams 1903, p. 188). Once a week, Alan travels to the market in Sydney to sell their produce, leaving Alice alone at the farm. During one of his absences, an unemployed "tramp" whom Alice describes as "a good-looking, well-set-up young fellow" arrives and asks for work (p. 192). After Alice offers him tea, the man "broke into sobs" and arouses her sympathy (p. 194). She suggests other places where he might look for work and then offers the use of her hayloft if he cannot find anywhere else to stay. When he returns to the farm at dusk, Alice gives him dinner and while she is alone in the house, begins to question her friendliness toward the stranger: "Who and what was he? Was he some escaped prisoner? Had she been wise in admitting him? The nearest neighbour was more than a mile off" (p. 196). As she steadily becomes more unnerved and wonders if the man is "prowling round the house, peeping in at windows and doors" (p. 196), Alice decides to sleep with a loaded revolver next to her. When Alan comes home earlier than expected and climbs through the bedroom window, Alice, in her terror, shoots him repeatedly thinking he is the tramp. Hearing the shots, the man appears at the window and holds a candle over the scene. The story ends with Alice falling upon Alan's dead body. Though Adams's story touches on colonial women's fear of being alone and unprotected, it also suggests that Alice's second-guessing of the man's honest nature leads directly to her husband's killing. In her terror over the tramp's intentions, Adams also seems to suggest that Alice, even though a good shot, might not be the best person to have a loaded weapon. Even the fact that the woman has the ability to defend herself lessens her portrayal as potential victim. The impending danger of the tramp's presence at the farm and the notion that he might attack Alice is ironically reversed by the end of the story and is replaced by Alice's terrified but aggressive act. He is the only one there to presumably help Alice after her tragic "mistake."

Even though Adams's story is not as socially daring as Baynton's narrative, it does point to the recurring critique of the unsettled nature of the colonial home. In "A Dreamer" and "The Chosen Vessel," Baynton is particularly concerned with addressing the elusiveness of a safe domestic space, the "failed home" of the Gothic, within an equally harsh landscape. In both stories, Baynton disrupts the traditional idea of home as a place where women are safe, comfortable, and able to maintain a greater control over their own actions and the actions of others. Home is no longer a refuge. In her study of the tenuous position of colonial women in nineteenth-century Australia, Penny Russell suggests that European women were frequently excluded "from a national mythology which emphasised masculinity" and had to rely on "a circumscribed form of femininity" that found its only "sense of 'place'" within the home (1993, p. 28). Yet, as Russell notes, women's autonomy within the home was largely illusory, given the fact that as soon as fathers and husbands came home, women were forced to "[surrender] their control" of the household (ibid., p. 31). White colonial women occupied a social middle ground within the imperial enterprise; they were both victims of male dominance and complicit as part of an invading culture. Though Baynton may not have had this added layer of cultural complexity in mind when she was writing *Bush Studies*, the domestic uncertainty in her stories highlights the troubled existence of colonial dwellings on land seized from Aboriginal people. Colonial houses became symbolic of the "success" of empire as Europeans brought their "civilizing" influence to the colony, but there was also a darker side to this expansion because the buildings represented continuing male restraint on the female, as well as imperial restraint on the indigenous inhabitants.[9]

Ken Gelder and Rachel Weaver have suggested that "the colonial Australian Gothic gives us a range of vivid, unsettling counter-narratives to the more familiar tales of colonial promise and optimism we are often asked to take for granted" (2007, p. 9). In her emphasis on fictional stories which highlight the very real failure of the colonial enterprise, Barbara Baynton crafted some of the most unflinching portraits of settler life and deserves recognition within the Australian Gothic tradition. Her Gothic is harsh and unforgiving. As Gerry Turcotte says, "her work makes clear that the Gothic need not be escapist, excessive or frivolous" (1998, p. 282). Indeed, in her examination of brutality, hopelessness, and isolation, Baynton prefigured more modern, even postmodern, appropriations of the Gothic mode. In undermining the heroic ideal of empire at the turn of the twentieth century, the stories that comprise *Bush Studies* gain even more significance as early testaments that give voice to the suffering experienced by colonial women, narratives which prefigure the Aboriginal writers who would later contribute their own voices to a more inclusive—and more painfully honest—history of the lasting consequences of European imperialism.[10]

Notes

1. *Cobbers* is essentially a reissuing of *Bush Studies*, containing all the stories from Baynton's previous collection and including only two new stories: "Toohey's Party" and "Trooper Jim Tasman," a story influenced by Australia's involvement in the First World War. According to Sally Krimmer and Alan Lawson, Baynton resided in London during the war (where she had lived since Thomas Baynton's death in 1904), and both her London home and her country home near Cambridge were used as "open houses" for soldiers (1980, p. xv). An interview with Baynton published in *Home* magazine in September 1920 mentions another novel titled "Wet Paint," "in which the bush, Sydney society and London scenes will appear," but no trace of this manuscript can currently be found (quoted in Krimmer and Lawson 1980, p. 328).
2. Although Baynton's experience as a housekeeper was a positive one, this period of her life also encouraged her continuing sympathies with the working classes. In June 1911, she published "Indignity of Domestic Service" in the *Sydney Morning Herald*.
3. Vance Palmer claims that Baynton's collection "had so many refusals that she thought of putting it in the fire" (1958, p. 15).
4. According to Lilley, Baynton gave America credit for being more open to Australian authors: "America, Mrs. Baynton said, showed more desire to hear about Australia than England, and an Australian writer would have a better chance of succeeding there. The American magazines would take what the English publishers rejected as 'peculiar'; and so the Americans encouraged clever writers" (1911, p. 21).
5. The story was originally published in the December 12, 1896, Christmas Edition of the *Bulletin* under the title "The Tramp." This original

version omits the Peter Hennessey section. The editor A. G. Stephens was responsible for these editorial revisions regarding title and content. Baynton originally suggested the alternative title "What the Curlews Cried." For the publication of *Bush Studies*, Baynton retitled the story and restored the section which describes Hennessey and his "mystical" vision. For the original *Bulletin* publication and the revised *Cobbers* (1917), Baynton included the last line, "But the dog was also guilty." For this chapter, I have chosen to use the Krimmer and Lawson edition, which is considered the most standard version of Baynton's work to date, and which, in turn, is based on the *Cobbers* edition. Krimmer and Lawson state that this later revised collection, corrected by Baynton herself, "represents the author's final intention" (1980, p. 2).

6. For a discussion of the difficulties faced by both Aboriginal and white rape victims, see Judith Allen, *Sex and Secrets: Crimes Involving Australian Women Since 1880* (Oxford University Press, 1990); David Philips's chapter, "Anatomy of a Rape Case, 1888: Sex, Race, Violence and Criminal Law in Victoria," in David Philips and Susanne Davies (eds.), *A Nation of Rogues?: Crime, Law and Punishment in Colonial Australia* (Melbourne University Press, 1994); Jill Bavin-Mizzi, *Ravished: Sexual Violence in Victorian Australia* (University of New South Wales Press, 1995); and Marilyn Lake's article "Frontier Feminism and the Marauding White Man," *Journal of Australian Studies* 49 (1996): 12–20.

7. If we read the story with the Mary Jane Hicks case in mind, and the *Bulletin*'s assertion that the "Goddess of Justice" herself was a victim, we have another feminine abstraction to add to this list.

8. "Evelyn Adams" was a pseudonym for a "Miss Perry." According to a notice in the November 17, 1904, edition of the *Evening Post*: "Miss Perry, who lived in Sydney, Adelaide, Hobart, and New Zealand, also in Honolulu, has recently brought out a novel entitled 'Tales of Three Colonies,' under the nom de plume 'Evelyn Adams'" (p. 5).

9. Russell notes that Aboriginal women were doubly "outcast" as they were forced to train as domestic servants within these houses (1993, p. 30).

10. It is important to note here that Aboriginal people have not historically benefitted from the Gothic mode. In his survey of the Australian Gothic, Gerry Turcotte notes that, while the genre helped certain colonial writers find a more distinctive Australian voice, the Gothic also served to silence Aboriginal people. Turcotte says, "It is not surprising that Aboriginal writers have tended not to use the Gothic mode since it has generally represented for them a disabling, rather than an enabling discourse" (1998, p. 285). Historically, Aboriginal people have been portrayed "as the monstrous figures haunting the Australian landscape, spectres more frightening than any European demon, because they represented a physical threat to settlers and to theories of enlightenment which believed in the civilising presence of Whites" (ibid., p. 285).

Bibliography

Adams, Evelyn [Miss Perry] (1903), "Cruel Fate," in *Tales of Three Colonies: Australia, Tasmania, Zealandia*, London: Henry J. Drane, pp. 185–199.

Baynton, Barbara (1980a [1902]), "A Dreamer," in Sally Krimmer and Alan Lawson (eds.), *Barbara Baynton*, St. Lucia: University of Queensland Press, pp. 4–10.

—— (1980b [1902]), "Billy Skywonkie," in Sally Krimmer and Alan Lawson (eds.), *Barbara Baynton*, St. Lucia: University of Queensland Press, pp. 46–60.

—— (1980c [1902]), "The Chosen Vessel," in Sally Krimmer and Alan Lawson (eds.), *Barbara Baynton*, St. Lucia: University of Queensland Press, pp. 81–88.

Clarence and Richmond Examiner (1903), Rev. of *Bush Studies* (March 14): 8.

Clarke, Marcus (1997 [1876]), "Adam Lindsay Gordon," in Imre Salusinszky (ed.), *The Oxford Book of Australian Essays*, Melbourne and Oxford: Oxford University Press, pp. 31–34.

Daily Telegraph (1903), Rev. of *Bush Studies* (January 17): 6.

Dale, Leigh (2011), "Rereading Barbara Baynton's *Bush Studies*," *Texas Studies in Literature and Language* 53.4 (Winter): 369–386.

Evening Post (1904), "Personal Notes from London" (November 17): 5.

Frost, Lucy (1983), "Barbara Baynton: An Affinity with Pain," in Shirley Walker (ed.), *Who Is She?* New York: St. Martin's Press, pp. 56–70.

Gelder, Ken, and Rachael Weaver (2007), "The Colonial Australian Gothic," in Ken Gelder and Rachael Weaver (eds.), *The Anthology of Colonial Australian Gothic Fiction*, Carlton, VIC: Melbourne University Press, pp. 1–9.

Hackforth-Jones, Penne (1989), *Barbara Baynton: Between Two Worlds*, Ringwood, VIC: Penguin Books.

Krimmer, Sally, and Alan Lawson (1980), "Introduction," in Sally Krimmer and Alan Lawson (eds.), *Barbara Baynton*, St. Lucia: University of Queensland Press, pp. ix–xxxiii.

Lamond, Julieanne (2011), "The Reflected Eye: Reading Race in Barbara Baynton's 'Billy Skywonkie'," *Texas Studies in Literature and Language* 53.4 (Winter): 387–400.

Lawson, Henry (1965 [1899]), "Crime in the Bush," *Southerly* 25.4: 264–275.

Lilley, Norman (1911), "England and the Australian Writer. Barbara Baynton's Experience," *The Worker* (July 6): 21.

"Mrs Barbara Baynton" (1980 [1920]), in Sally Krimmer and Alan Lawson (eds.), *Barbara Baynton*, St. Lucia: University of Queensland Press, pp. 326–328.

Palmer, Nettie (1929), "Barbara Baynton. A Literary Pioneer," *Brisbane Courier* (June 15): 21.

Palmer, Vance (1958), "Writers I Remember—Barbara Baynton," *Overland* 11 (Summer): 15–16.

Philadelphoff-Puren, Nina (2010), "Reading Rape in Colonial Australia: Barbara Baynton's 'The Tramp,' the *Bulletin* and Cultural Criticism," *JASAL Special Issue: Common Readers* 10: 1–14.

Phillips, A. A. (1971), "Barbara Baynton and the Dissidence of the Nineties," *The Australian Nationalists: Modern Critical Essays*, Melbourne and Oxford: Oxford University Press, pp. 149–158.

Register (1903), Rev. of *Bush Studies* (January 10): 8.

Russell, Penny (1993), "In Search of Woman's Place: An Historical Survey of Gender and Space in Nineteenth-Century Australia," *Australasian Historical Archaeology* 11: 28–32.

Schaffer, Kay (1988), *Women and the Bush: Forces of Desire in the Australian Cultural Tradition*, Cambridge: Cambridge University Press.

Turcotte, Gerry (1998), "Australian Gothic," in Marie Mulvey-Roberts (ed.), *The Handbook to Gothic Literature*, 2nd edn., Basingstoke: Macmillan, pp. 277–287.

Wright, David McKee (1918), "Preface," in *Selected Poems of Henry Lawson*, Sydney: Angus and Robertson, pp. vii–xiii.

CHAPTER 11

Katherine Mansfield and the Troubled Homes of Colonial New Zealand

In a 1922 letter to Sarah Gertrude Millin, Katherine Mansfield stated, "I am a 'Colonial.' I was born in New Zealand, I came to Europe to 'complete my education' and when my parents thought that tremendous task was over I went back to New Zealand. I hate it. It seemed to me a small petty world [...] And after a struggle I did get out of the nest finally and came to London, at eighteen, *never* to return, said my disgusted heart" (1996, vol. 5, p. 80) Yet, despite her desire to distance herself from her native country, Mansfield did "return" to the land of her birth in several short stories centered on the settler experience. Several of these stories can be read as part of a burgeoning Gothic tradition in New Zealand, an area of interest which has only recently begun to receive critical attention. As Timothy Jones notes, "the shape" of a Gothic tradition in New Zealand "is still being negotiated in both critical and popular discourse" (2013, p. 468). On one hand, Lydia Wevers has proclaimed that New Zealand has "almost no gothic" literature (2004, p. 116), while Misha Kavka has likewise asserted that "New Zealand as a colony lacks the history to produce a properly haunted house" (2006, p. 62). Yet, critics such as Gina Wisker, Erin Mercer, and Edmund G. C. King have sought to highlight colonial New Zealand's Gothic qualities. Katherine Mansfield's contribution is an important part of this burgeoning critical area and provides a critically important counterpoint to her positioning as a Modernist. Several of Mansfield's most Gothically inspired stories were published early in her career, suggesting that these themes and characters were a way of exorcising her own self-professed hatred for New Zealand after her relocation to London. One of Mansfield's most overtly haunted stories, "The House" (1912) describes one woman's desire for financial security and domestic happiness, only to have these dreams abruptly end when the woman dies at the door of her idealized home. Shortly before the publication of "The House," Mansfield published "The Woman at the Store" (1912) in John Middleton Murry's avant-garde magazine *Rhythm*, but only after Murry (her future husband) rejected Mansfield's initial submission and requested something darker. The story centers on the haunted, unforgiving landscape of a remote and unpopulated countryside inhabited by wayward settlers. This landscape has a devastating effect on the story's title character, a lonely woman whose physical and emotional isolation culminates in the murder of her husband in front of their neglected child. Another desperate woman is at the center of "Millie" (1913). In this story, a lonely and unfulfilled wife has conflicted feelings for a young suspected murderer who she finds injured and hiding on her husband's property. Although Millie initially sympathizes with the man and sees his situation as similar to her own loneliness and desperation, she ultimately becomes complicit in his eventual capture.

Far from being sites of safety, comfort, and settlement, these abandoned, ramshackle, and isolated colonial dwellings become places of dislocation and disillusionment, colonial reimaginings of the haunted houses which were such a stalwart of late eighteenth- and nineteenth-century British Gothic. This isolation and lack of community proves destructive to the women who must exist as colonial exiles at the farthest margins of empire. Amidst this land of immense space, Mansfield conveys the claustrophobic prison of one's own mind, a confinement caused by limited opportunities. In an ironic twist on the promise of property and personal freedom that appealed to so many early settlers, Mansfield suggests that this opportunity always comes at a cost. Instead of fulfilling dreams, colonial New Zealand takes more than it gives and becomes a place which turns women into uncanny doubles of themselves or, sometimes, even monsters.

Katherine Mansfield had a love–hate relationship with her native New Zealand, wanting to escape her colonial life to pursue a more intellectually fulfilling life in London, yet never feeling as if she fully belonged in English society either. In a March 1908 letter to her sister Vera Beauchamp, Mansfield wrote of the dissatisfaction with her life in New

Zealand and its limiting effect on her writing: "You know that, situated as I am—I shall never make all that I mean to make of my life [...] Now I do think that we are all sent into the world to develop ourselves to the very fullest extent [...] and here there is really no scope for development—no intellectual society—no hope of finding any. You know exactly what this life is like and what life means here" (1984, 1: 42). When Mansfield arrived in England, however, she was singled out by her colonial background. Writing in her journal in 1916, Mansfield recalls her time as a student at Queen's College when the principal asked if anyone "had been chased by a wild bull" (1954 [1927], p. 105). Mansfield raised her hand and was told, "I am afraid you do not count. You are a little savage from New Zealand" (ibid., p. 105). Though light-hearted in tone, Mansfield's inclusion of the comment reflects her anxiety over her colonial, outsider status while in college. Later in 1919, she wrote:

> The red geraniums have bought the garden over my head. They are there, established, back in the old home, every leaf and flower unpacked and in its place—and quite determined that no power on earth will ever move them again. Well, *that* I don't mind. But why should they make me feel a stranger? Why should they ask me every time I go near: "And what are *you* doing in a London garden?" They burn with arrogance and pride. And I am the little Colonial walking in the London garden patch—allowed to look, perhaps, but not to linger. If I lie on the grass they positively shout at me: "Look at her, lying on *our* grass, pretending she lives here, pretending this is her garden, and that tall back of the house, with the windows open and the coloured curtains lifting, is her house. She is a stranger—an alien. She is nothing but a little girl sitting on the Tinakori hills and dreaming: 'I went to London and married an Englishman, and we lived in a tall grave house with red geraniums and white daisies in the garden at the back.' *Impudence!*" (ibid., pp. 156–157)

Yet, for all her feelings of wanting to be accepted by the "mother country," Mansfield's upbringing in New Zealand gave her an outsider's perspective on typical "English" life and manners, which she often found stilted and cold. In 1909, she declared, "To escape England—it is my great desire. I loathe England" (ibid., p. 40). She later wrote in her journal:

> No, I don't want England. England is of no use to me. What do I mean by that? I mean there never has been—never will be—any rapprochement

between us, *never* […] I would not care if I never saw the English country again. Even in its flowering I feel deeply antagonistic to it, and I will never change. (ibid., pp. 158–159)

Mark Williams suggests that it is this very tension between the two locations that allowed Mansfield to write so effectively about New Zealand. He says, "Mansfield did not make herself a modernist by abandoning provincial New Zealand in favour of cosmopolitan Europe. What she needed was a means of distancing herself from the limitations of the colonial world while retaining the sharp focus of the massive collisions it contained." Her experience in a colonial environment traveled with her and eventually made its way into her fiction: "She carried her New Zealand with her to Europe, both the bourgeois New Zealand of her own family who frustrated and supported her and the wild New Zealand which seemed to her of interest because it was unformed, unruly, unsophisticated" (Williams 2000, pp. 256–257).

This sense of a split personality, as someone who loved her homeland but also needed to escape from it, served Mansfield especially well in the creation of her darker-themed stories set in New Zealand. The troubled domestic space and "failed homes" of "The House," "The Woman at the Store," and "Millie" are products of Mansfield's own internal feelings of displacement. In the introduction to her edited collection of Mansfield's stories, Elizabeth Bowen describes these feelings as a type of haunting, the ghost of her home country that followed Mansfield throughout her life. She says that New Zealand "took its toll of her in dreams, broodings, and often a torturous homesickness. [It] was to return to Katherine Mansfield, but not before she had travelled a long way" (Bowen 1956, p. xiv). Anna Snaith asserts, "Her fiction-making, in as much as it was always a negotiation of homelessness for Mansfield, articulated the unsettled position of exile that results from a creole perspective, without a stable claim over either colonial or metropolitan space" (2014, p. 113). Snaith's discussion represents more recent shifts in critical discussions of Mansfield's work and the importance of her hybrid British identity which found its way into her New Zealand stories. In the past, as Saikat Majumbar notes, the "raw colonial elements of her work [have been] seen as occupying a negligible and marginal portion of her oeuvre" (2013, p. 78). The importance of Mansfield's colonial viewpoint, reflected in her earlier work, was frequently overshadowed by her later writing and her role in helping to shape the modernist movement in British literature. Snaith states that, in Mansfield's New Zealand stories, we gain a unique viewpoint that is somewhere between center and margin. These stories, "written in London for avant-garde periodicals, portrayed a savage land that both delivered the exoticized portrait demanded of her, and depicted the impact of British colonial violence" (Snaith 2014, p. 20). The process of reclaiming Mansfield as a colonial writer points to increased interest in the connections between colonialism and modernism. For Elleke Boehmer and Steven Matthews, these two (heretofore separate) areas of scholarship directly inform one another in important cultural ways, suggesting that "the preoccupation with alienation and disoriented or displaced identity shared by the new colonial writers, related to and interacted with the breakdown in universal systems of understanding that preoccupied the metropolitan Modernists" (2011, p. 287). At the same time, colonialism helped to introduce viewpoints that, in turn, questioned the system itself: "The experience of colonial rule produced cultural and aesthetic processes that ultimately helped to trigger the delegitimation of that rule: the dissociation of subjectivity, the dislocation of western sensibility, the valorization of the fragment, the reification of the alien, and the fascinated glance at the stranger" (ibid., pp. 287–288).

Kate Krueger has discussed the ways in which the short fiction of Barbara Baynton and Katherine Mansfield represents "an alternative colonial viewpoint" to the traditional male representation of Antipodean women's lives, most notably the version presented in Henry Lawson's "The Drover's Wife" (1892). Instead of the triumphant wife who overcomes all odds in support of her husband and nation, Baynton and Mansfield describe the darker side to such a life in stories which challenge "narratives of resilience" and, thus, more fully and honestly "consider the costs of adopting such a role" (Krueger 2014, p. 143).[1] Baynton and Mansfield concern themselves with "local conditions" instead of "abstract imperial ideals" and, consequently, their fiction "creates the very avenues of revision that undercut overarching colonial rhetoric that had immense power in dictating the way people imagined the Antipodes and lived within them" (ibid., pp. 144, 145). In addition to theme, Krueger posits that Baynton and Mansfield's stories are culturally important because they come at a moment when colonialism was transitioning into concepts of nationhood. Both writers "record ambivalences and tensions within such social and national ideologies as they are being consolidated in the moment that settler colonial identities are transitioning into national ones" (ibid., p. 153). Their use of modernism set in colonial regions "give[s] the reader a sense of what is at stake in the representation of landscapes that have been imbued with the weight of their new nations' self-definition, especially in terms of the consequences of such ideologies on the minds and bodies of women" (ibid., p. 154).

Baynton and Mansfield's emphasis on the effects of such harsh colonial environments, and the violence and isolation that descends upon "the minds and bodies of women" also draws attention to how their writing utilizes anxieties that are at the heart of the Colonial Gothic. Both writers focus on characters who are, in one way or another, at the periphery of not only a British identity, but also at the margins of their respective colonial societies. They are interested in the displaced, the outsider, the Other, and the dehumanizing effects of the bush environment. Yet, unlike Baynton, Mansfield frequently explores the latent otherness, and even savagery, that lurks behind conceptions of colonial womanhood. The women in her New Zealand stories, particularly "The Woman at the Store" and "Millie," can be just as dangerous as men. Both stories rely on violence for narrative effect and both feature women who are turned into darker versions of their former selves through extended isolation and figurative imprisonment in dwellings that serve as equally uncanny versions of "home."[2] The troubled nature of the home and women's need to find safety and stability within such a site is also a major concern in the often overlooked Mansfield story, "The House." In this ghost story, the main character desperately seeks a home of her own and can only briefly find such a place after her untimely death. Though "The House" does not portray a woman as monstrous as the ones in "The Woman at the Store" and "Millie," it is just as concerned with how loss and want can force women into uncanny, strange, and even unnatural versions of themselves because of a forced separation from home and family.

The importance of recognizing this particular Gothic strain in Mansfield's work has been a relatively recent interest of scholars who wish to build and expand on her contributions to modernism and colonial writing. C. K. Stead describes "The Woman at the Store" as a combination of "the thriller and the social documentary," a "version of Katherine Mansfield's central preoccupation—female sexual involvement and the destruction she seems to feel goes inevitably with it" (1981, p. 33). Claire Tomalin has likewise commented on the darker themes behind "The Woman at the Store," calling it "a vivid and almost sinister evocation of the atmosphere of the sparsely inhabited wilderness, the poverty and ignorance of the people settled there, the 'savage spirit' of the place" (1988, pp. 95–96). Though he does not focus directly on the Gothic, Bruce Harding, in his discussion of "Ole Underwood," "The Woman at the Store," and "Millie," examines these stories of betrayal and murder as fictional explorations of "the psychological states of the socially dispossessed" (1988, p. 122). More recently, Janet Wilson has noticed the spectral elements in Mansfield's later work but tries to distance these elements from the Gothic, claiming that the "subtle interplay between the ghostly and supernatural in bringing the family back to life in her art," in stories such as "At the Bay," "distinguishes Mansfield's work from the alienating spectrality of the Gothic" (2013, p. 34). Though this may be true of the later stories, this idea does not hold up quite as well in Mansfield's earlier colonial stories, particularly how she uses the Gothic mode to comment on the alienation of the settler. Gina Wisker explores Mansfield's use of "an unsettling domestic Gothic" and examines how Mansfield's utilization of the Gothic involves "gender-influenced constructions" which "fundamentally question and undermine taken-for-granted versions of cultural, gendered and social hierarchies and versions of the normal or real, including domestic security and family identities and relationships" (2012, p. 24). Likewise, Erin Mercer has focused on the Colonial Gothic elements of "The Woman at the Store," with its "shocking violence" and "threatening landscape" (2014, pp. 87, 91). By drawing attention to Mansfield's use of the Gothic—and, even more importantly, the Colonial Gothic—in her early stories set in New Zealand, we can begin to recognize how these stories provide an important commentary on how colonial life leads to an incomplete, haunted existence, symbolized through poverty and isolation, that turns women into spectral figures and monsters, unsettled ghosts of their former selves.[3]

Mansfield's "The House," published in the November 28, 1912, issue of *Hearth and Home*, describes one woman's brief possession of the home of her dreams just after her death. The woman can only experience a perfect life with her husband and son in the home as a ghost, as the story foregrounds a sense of momentary happiness that can only happen in the afterlife when the woman's spirit can "live" what the living woman could not. The story begins with the protagonist, Marion, as she tries to escape from a rain storm by taking cover on the porch of a stone house with a sign "To be Let or Sold"

(Mansfield 2012a [1912], p. 304). The house seems somewhat familiar to Marion and, by the end of the story, we learn that she is very near death when she arrives at the house. Mansfield gives readers hints at the woman's fragile condition. As she stands on the porch, she "was suddenly and unaccountably tired […] the wind seemed to take all your breath—and so cold, to eat into your bones" (p. 305). Her veil, which will become her death shroud, sticks to her face. Janet Wilson has suggested that "the opening or closing of the veil offers glimpses of the female subject at moments of crisis" (2014, p. 205). This use of the veil, according to Wilson, connects to the ghostliness of Mansfield's later stories, and her emphasis on vision and seeing/not seeing clearly: "Veiling and unveiling are aligned with the imagery of mist, which in falling and rising provides glimpses of an occluded reality. Indeed, because it is associated with a dimension of the unknown that offers intermittent, flickering moments of visibility, the veil that obscures and reveals, like the mirror and mask, can be linked to the spectral quality of her last stories" (ibid., p. 206). Yet, this emphasis on "occluded reality" and "moments of visibility" is equally important in "The House." Marion's veil is significant in that it represents the "veil" between the two spheres of life and death, and Marion's noticing of it clinging to her face immediately before her death foreshadows her ghostly vision from beyond the veil. She looks at the lamp on the ceiling and, though it looks familiar, she is "too tired to remember" (Mansfield 2012a [1912], p. 305). She leans her head against the wall of the house and dies there alone.

What follows is Marion's desire for domestic happiness played out in a spectral world. It contains a combination of contentment that is constantly undercut with creeping feelings of unease, loss, and incompleteness, as Marion feels she both belongs in the house and yet is a stranger to it. The interior reflects the wealth and security that Marion desires for herself and her family. On entering the "fascinating hall," which is full of warmth and firelight, her eyes are drawn to the pictures, pottery, "old oak settles," "their 'Bruges' brass," and "the standard rose-tree in its green tub" (p. 305). Amidst this comfortable domestic space, Marion feels a strong attachment to her husband John, but it is an attachment that has a sad note, hinting at the dead woman's inability to see her husband again and, likewise, the couple's inability to live the life she experiences in her ghostly dream vision. John tells her that he feels she has been gone "for a thousand years." He ironically says that when he sees Marion "in the mirror" he knows "that this is no dream, that through the years, I have but to look to find you, always there" (p. 306). Like the veil, the mirror also has symbolic meaning. Janet Wilson has noted that Mansfield often emphasized the "distorting, truth-telling, and doubling properties of the mirror," and it often functions in her stories to call attention to "moment[s] of psychological perception" (2014, p. 211). In "The House," John sees a version of Marion which does not exist; it is only a reflection. This vision again accentuates the unreality of Marion's existence as a ghost in the house. Marion seems to sense the fragility of this imagined, ghostly life—which is itself just a reflection—telling John that her "body aches for this, its resting place—for the pillow of your heart" (Mansfield 2012a [1912], p. 307). Yet, her desire is at the same time for a "resting place," a place to call home.

The sense of Marion's unfulfilled desire to have a comfortable home—and her loss of the life she does have—is symbolized in the story by Mansfield's use of ellipses whenever Marion's son and her role as a mother is (almost) mentioned. When Marion and John stop outside their son's nursery, the fear of her (un)reality comes over her: "Each time he mentioned the … each time she felt he was going to speak of their … she had a terrible, suffocating sensation of fear. If that should prove untrue, if that should prove its dream origin—and at the thought something within her cried out and trembled" (p. 308). In her possession of this house, Marion recognizes the fragility of her connection to the space and to the people in it. It is this desperate desire to belong that makes the house so peaceful to Marion. She tells John, "Oh, it is the sense of 'home' which is so precious to me—it is the wonderful sense of peace—of the rooms sanctified—of the quiet permanence—it is that which is so precious after—" (p. 309). Again, Marion cannot give voice to something she knows is unreal in her current state. Her expression remains incomplete. Yet, the fragility of this spectral home is compounded by the fact that this truly is a "dream" for Marion because what she experiences in the house as a ghost never existed in her life as a living woman.

The life Marion desires is just as ghostly as she herself is. It cannot be seen or felt. Marion's "home" was only ever a figment of her imagination and a projection of unfulfilled desire. This feeling of displacement and the need to settle within a home of her own likewise haunted Katherine Mansfield throughout her short life and repeatedly found its way into her fiction.[4] As Clare Hanson states, "When Mansfield writes of homesickness it is not easy to determine exactly where 'home' might be. Home is a shifting and unstable space which is rendered problematic by Mansfield's multiple cultural identities" (2011, p. 119). She was both colonial and British, but being both, she could never lay complete claim to just one place or identity. The "little colonial" who migrated to Europe was always somewhere between the land of her birth and the land which sustained her as an artist and published writer. This meant a constant sense of displacement which Mansfield described in a May 1915 letter to John Middleton Murry, saying:

> Why haven't I got a real "home," a real life—Why haven't I got a chinese nurse with green trousers and two babies who rush at me and clasp my knees—Im not a girl—Im a woman. I *want* things. Shall I ever have them? [...] and all this love and joy that fights for outlet—and all this life drying up, like milk, in an old breast. Oh, I want life—I want friends and people and a house. (1984, 1: 177)

For Mansfield, the idea of "home" and "house" symbolizes a more complete life that provides her with both material possessions and a family. Her detailed description of this imagined life is remarkably similar to Marion's own fantasy creation of the home she, like the author, will never realize. For Janet Wilson, the haunted nature of enforced distance and incompleteness in Mansfield's writing comes from her own "dualistic positioning" and "her habitation of multiple, layered states of being, magnified by her various allegiances to, and estrangements from, her New Zealand white settler and English migrant identities" (2013, p. 29). This identity, in turn, led to the "ghostly emanations from the past and phantasmagoric presences [which] are constituent of the divided and ruptured condition of colonialism" (ibid., p. 29). With this troubled "national identity" in mind, Hanson suggests that "home is thus *unheimlich* from the beginning in Mansfield's writing, undone by a colonial context in which its 'made-up' quality is foregrounded and it is disclosed as a copy without an original" (2011, p. 119). "The House" is particularly relevant here as a haunted house, and Marion's spectral vision of her life within that "made-up" house, is also a copy. Her vision of a happy life filled with material goods and a loving, happy family has no "original" in the living world; it is dispossessed and is only an empty, abandoned house.

The transitory nature of this idyllic home is seemingly forever closed to Marion by the story's end, making the narrative all the more tragic. When she hears her husband calling to her—as a group of people are trying to locate her after she goes missing—Marion tries to stop the call from the other side, wanting to remain in her perfect spectral world. Yet, when she rushes out onto the porch, the door shuts behind her, leaving her, again, cold and alone: "She pulled the heavy door open—wind and rain rushed in upon her—out into the porch she stepped—and the door banged to behind her. It was dark and cold ... and ... silent ... cold" (Mansfield 2012a [1912], p. 310). Calling attention to Freud's ideas of the double as both the return of the repressed self as well as a form of the alienated, dispossessed self, Hanson notes that the double in Mansfield's stories is another symbol of boundaries between the animate/inanimate, inside/outside, subject/object (2011, p. 122). As a spectral double of the dead woman, Marion's spirit, as she experiences momentary contentment within the home, gives voice to a need she cannot fully articulate in the living world. Her ghost thus represents what she can never have as a living woman. The two men who find Marion's body on the porch emphasize just how much the house represents Marion's unfulfilled dreams for a home of her own. One tells the other that he remembers Marion and her husband coming to look at the house, talking of "fixin' up nurseries and rose-trees and turkeys carpets" (Mansfield 2012a [1912], p. 311). He recalls, too, that Marion was especially taken with the lamp on the porch, an object that was a part of her last thoughts before her death. During the visit, Marion confides to the man, "We ain't got enough money to furnish a cottage [...] we're just dreamin' true" (p. 311). As Gerri Kimber has noted, in Mansfield's fiction, "money equals independence" (2014, p. 48), and without that financial support, Marion must exist in a dream world in both life and death. However, Marion's final placement outside the house after the door slams behind her gives the story an even darker tone, as the man's comments also stress Marion's lack of ownership of the house. She could not afford the house as a living woman, but even as a dead woman who tried to claim a piece of it in her last moments, she is still viewed as a kind of squatter: "people ain't got no right to go around dyin' as if they owned the 'ole plice. It'll be called 'aunted now" (Mansfield 2012a [1912], p. 311). As woman and ghost, Marion is left outside, in the dark and cold, forever trying to inhabit a home she can never have, can never completely possess.

"The Woman at the Store" appeared in the Spring 1912 issue of *Rhythm*. It features another unsettled property that represents a woman's failed dreams and continuing loneliness. Yet, this woman does not suffer

Marion's life after death. Instead, she is relegated to a living death after being forced to live a life of poverty and isolation that eventually leads to the murder of her husband and the continued mistreatment of her young daughter. In the opening paragraph, the unnamed female narrator and her two companions, Hin and Jo, are met with an unforgiving landscape that prefigures the harshness of the woman they will soon meet. The heat is "terrible," the wind "slithered along the road," and the dust "was like a dry-skin itching for growth on [their] bodies." The distance is like a sea, with "wave after wave of tussock grass […] and manuka bushes covered with thick spider webs" (Mansfield 2012b [1912], p. 268).[5] Based on Hin's memory of the place, the travelers expect "a fine store" with a creek running nearby, plentiful whisky, and, much to Jo's delight, a woman "with blue eyes and yellow hair, who'll promise you something else before she shakes hands with you" (p. 269). Before her marriage to the storekeeper, this woman was a barmaid, "as pretty as a wax doll," who "knew one hundred and twenty-five different ways of kissing" (p. 272).

Yet, when they reach the store, they find a woman who is the uncanny dark double to the one of their imagination. This version is founded very much on reality and the woman's efforts to survive on her own. The narrator notices that "her eyes were blue, and what hair she had was yellow, but ugly […] Looking at her, you felt there was nothing but sticks and wires under that pinafore—her front teeth were knocked out, she had red pulpy hands" and wears a pair of dirty boots (p. 270). This image reflects the rough life the woman has been forced to live and the transformation she underwent to survive. The idea that she is made of "sticks and wires" emphasizes her lack of femininity, as well as Hin's later comment that "she isn't the same woman" (p. 272).

Like the woman, the "whare" the store is in reveals the place to be another uncanny double for a "proper" English dwelling. Erin Mercer notes, "In European Gothic, the crumbling edifices of the past—castles, abbeys, crypts—provide the sites in which hauntings, strange events and violence occur" (2014, p. 89). In colonial regions such as Australia and New Zealand, there had to be other equivalents, and authors who utilized the Gothic in their fiction had to "locate the macabre and occult in the natural landscape" (Mercer 2014, p. 89). For Mansfield in "The Woman at the Store," both the landscape and the whare replicate and reimagine the European Gothic environment. As a former Māori house, the building itself symbolizes the forced physical and cultural displacement of the Māori after Europeans arrived in New Zealand and reflects the failed nature of European settlement given the deplorable state of the woman, her "home," and her family. The walls of the building are "plastered with old pages of English periodicals," and the absurd, uncanny nature of the place is heightened by the image of Queen Victoria's Jubilee from one of the "most recent" numbers. However, this feeble attempt at decoration and homeliness is besieged by outside forces: "Flies buzzed in circles round the ceiling, and treacle papers and bundles of dried clover were pinned to the window curtains" (Mansfield 2012b [1912], p. 270). This atmosphere, both within and without, infects the narrator with a sense of unease: "There is no twilight to our New Zealand days, but a curious half-hour when everything appears grotesque—it frightens—as though the savage spirit of the country walked abroad and sneered at what it saw. Sitting alone in the hideous room I grew afraid" (p. 271). In the story, this "savage spirit" is palpable. It literally roams the land and takes possession of the woman at the store. The lack of "twilight" likewise makes New Zealand a colonial region that represents an otherness that is very different from England. Additionally, the woman and her daughter represent an otherness that is the direct result of their failed colonial enterprise. Between the narrator, Hin, and Jo, the woman is variously labelled "a hungry bird" (p. 270), "mad," and an "old bitch" (p. 271). Jo, in his attempt to seduce the woman, calls her "female flesh" and insists that "she'll look better by night light," while Hin remembers her as a sexualized "wax doll" (p. 272). The woman, in her turn, blames her husband for her current state. After the group gets "slowly drunk," she tells them, "It's six years since I was married, and four miscarriages." She tells her husband that, if they were closer to a town, she would have him "lynched for child murder." Her suffering through four failed pregnancies is yet another example of how nothing good or productive can result in her current condition. She also blames her husband for her "broken" spirit and "spoiled" looks (p. 273).

The child is also "broken" and "spoiled" by her upbringing. The woman tells the narrator that she had no milk to nurse her daughter until a month after she was born. This means that the child starts her life stunted, as well as being another example of the woman's hardened, unfeminine nature. The girl is described as a "mean, undersized brat, with whitish hair, and weak eyes" (p. 272). Pamela Dunbar suggests that the child's strange appearance "becomes a signifier for the unnaturalness of the settlers' very presence in the colony" (1997, p. 46). This unnatural whiteness is also seen earlier in the story when the travelers are covered in the white dust of the pumice fields, and the narrator notices that Hin is "white as a clown" (quoted in ibid., p. 46). This unnatural coloring means the "new settler's white skin is envisaged in the tale, not as a mark of inherent racial superiority but as buffoon's mask or pathological state" (ibid., p. 46). Both instances, according to Dunbar, subvert "old-world belief in the superiority of the colonist by playing with the notion of whiteness as either mask or disease" (ibid., p. 47). The child also suffers physical and verbal abuse from her unloving mother and can only express her feelings by drawing on scraps of butter paper. The narrator calls these drawings "extraordinary and repulsively vulgar." She concludes that they are the "creations of a lunatic" and that "the kid's mind was diseased" (Mansfield 2012b [1912], p. 274). Yet, these drawings are the only way the child has of "speaking" her trauma. The narrator and Hin only learn of the woman's shooting and subsequent burying of her husband because the girl draws them a picture. The event is obviously ingrained in the girl's mind, and she represents future generations of other children in similar colonial regions who will be the damaged products of such unforgiving environments.

The woman's placement in the isolated store means that she has no recourse to help or support, legal or otherwise. The woman admits, "he left me too much alone. When the coach stopped coming, sometimes he'd go away days, sometimes he'd go away weeks, and leave me ter look after the store" (p. 274).[6] Her question of "wot for" remains unanswered because there is no satisfactory answer for a colonial system that allows such neglect to happen. Not being able to "keep" her husband, she decides to shoot him and bury him outside the building, an act that ensures his permanent placement near the home. Doreen D'Cruz and John C. Ross claim, "Female isolation thus serves as the crucible for arousing an existential self-awareness that militates against her sexual oppression as a woman" (2011, p. 29). The isolation that besieges the woman is destructive, but it is also necessary for the woman's survival. To survive, she must adapt, even if that adaptation must be in the form of an inhumane, violent "monster." The woman cannot obtain or keep this power if she stays an attractive, wifely and motherly woman. She only has power as a monster who lives on the periphery, a social deviant who defies cultural norms. The presentation of this type of woman also complicates contemporary notions that British colonials degenerated or "went native" due to close contact with indigenous people. Kate Krueger asserts that Mansfield "undercuts these assumptions, indicating that sexuality and deviancy are triggered by the built environment; and this has serious ramifications for the social spaces she occupies" (2014, p. 182). Lydia Wevers sees this "deviancy" as a type of decline, as the isolated woman—and it is significant that we never learn her name—goes from "woman" to "unwoman" (1993, p. 44). This transformation is a moral as well as a physical degeneration, yet, in the context of Mansfield's story, the woman was seemingly always an object. She goes from the objectified "woman" (a sexualized wax doll) to "unwoman," an unfeminine survivor who is a victim of her isolation and subsequent abandonment. Likewise, Alison Rudd notes that the story "illustrates a link between a remote landscape and psychological disturbance caused by the effects of isolation" (2010, p. 145). In "The Woman at the Store," the woman's savagery is caused by a failed colonial system and husband, both of which effectively abandon the woman in their disregard for her physical and emotional well-being.

Published in the June 1913 issue of *Blue Review*, "Millie" is another examination of the effects of isolation and a woman's choice between two lives. While the title character's husband and a few other men go in search of the supposed killer of a neighbor, Millie sits alone dwelling on her incomplete life. Like "The House" and "The Woman at the Store," this life is largely comprised of material objects that have an uncanny, distant feel to them, as if they are imposters that do not belong where they are. This mirrors Millie's own feeling of not belonging and a boredom that leads to an emotional desperation that she can barely admit to herself. As she "stare[s] at herself in the fly-specked mirror," she feels as if "[s]he could have had a good cry—just for nothing" (Mansfield 2012c [1913], p. 327). There are two pictures in her room that work as doubles of one another. One is titled "Garden Party at Windsor Castle," which shows a quintessentially English scene: "In the foreground emerald lawns planted with immense oak trees, and in their grateful shade, a muddle of ladies and gentlemen and parasols and little tables. The background was filled with the towers of Windsor Castle, flying three Union Jacks, and in the middle of the picture the old Queen" (p. 327). Millie wonders to herself "if it really looked like that," calling attention to her physical and metaphorical distance from the "home" country, as the picture provides a window into a land she will never actually see. The picture of the garden party is juxtaposed with a picture of Millie and her family, a gathering that, in its attempt to be English, becomes the spectral opposite or uncanny double of the "genuine" English scene: "She was sitting down in a basket chair, in her cream cashmere and satin ribbons, and Sid, standing with one hand on her shoulder, looking at her bouquet. And behind them there were some fern trees, and a waterfall, and Mount Cook in the distance, covered with snow" (p. 327). The artificial Englishness of the New Zealand couple is subverted by the native environment that surrounds them. Significantly, Mount Cook looms in the background as the ever-present symbol of British settlement. Just by its name alone, the mountain symbolizes British invasion/settlement of New Zealand and the forced displacement of the Māori. It was named by Captain John Lort Stokes in 1851 in honor of Captain James Cook, who circumnavigated New Zealand in 1770. As a site of cultural contention, the mountain's name was finally amended in 1998 to include its original Māori name, Aoraki. Yet, its dual identity as Aoraki/Mount Cook still points to issues of imperial claims on the region and the lasting influence of colonialism. This inclusion of the image in Millie and Sid's wedding picture also suggests her own "possession" by her husband (symbolized by the hand he places on her shoulder) and a sense of unsettlement which arises from her "lesser" status.

Immediately after looking at the picture, Millie wonders why the couple never had children, partially admitting that something is missing in her life, and if not children—she claims to have "never missed them" (p. 327)—then some kind of purpose. Pamela Dunbar notes that this lack of children hints at wider issues of displacement in the narrative: "Translated to a strange land she is unable either to bond with it or to commit herself to it—something the birth of a child might have implied" (1997, p. 56). The pointlessness of her life is further stressed as she "sat, quiet, thinking of nothing at all [...] 'Tick-tick' went the kitchen clock, the ashes clinked in the grate, and the venetian blind knocked against the kitchen window" (Mansfield 2012c [1913], p. 328). Faced with this relentless parade of nothingness, Millie suddenly feels "frightened" (p. 328). She seemingly hears someone outside and worries that it might be Harrison, the man accused of the murder, but this feeling also serves as a convenient cover that allows her to deflect her fear about the life she is trapped in onto something else outside herself.

Yet, this feeling returns after Millie sees the young man accused of the murder, who is wounded and helpless. The narrator says, "A strange dreadful feeling gripped Millie Evans' bosom—some seed that had never flourished there, unfolded, and struck deep roots and burst into painful leaf" (p. 328). Faced with something as meaningful as saving the life of the helpless man, Millie suddenly realizes how lonely she truly is as the feelings she has repressed surface and come to light. Millie vows, "They won't ketch 'im. Not if I can 'elp it. Men is all beasts. I don't care wot 'e's done, or wot 'e 'asn't done. See 'im through, Millie Evans. 'E's nothink but a sick kid" (p. 329). However, this promise that she tries to make to both herself and to Harrison is broken by the end of the story. When the men return from searching for Harrison, Millie continues to side with the runaway, telling herself, "I don' care anythink about justice an' all the rot they've bin spouting to-night" (p. 330). This thought is described by the narrator as a "savage" one, yet Millie's true savage nature comes to the forefront when Harrison is detected by a dog and tries to escape on one of Sid's horses:

> And at the sight of Harrison in the distance, and the three men hot after, a strange mad joy smothered everything else. She rushed into the road—she laughed and shrieked and danced in the dust, jigging the lantern. "A—ah! Arter 'im, Sid! A—a—a—h! ketch 'im, Willie. Go it! Go it! A—ah, Sid! Shoot 'im down. Shoot 'im!" (p. 330)

Bruce Harding notices a "slightly mocking tone" in Millie's outburst at the end of the story, which he describes as "a species of macabre comic satire heavily laced with scorn" (1988, p. 132). In this reading, Millie's words become "an unforgettable plea for those qualities of compassion which are habitually crushed and swallowed up by the exclusivity of affection within the marital tie in an aggressive masculine world" (ibid., p. 132). Her last words, then, are a bitter indictment of the dominant power structure and her own search for identity within that structure. Her words reflect the anger she cannot give voice to, either to her own husband or to society at large. Her decision to "follow" her husband, just as the dog in the story instinctively follows its master, means that she continues to be a prisoner but is also complicit in her own imprisonment. Millie's reaction recalls her comment about men being "all beasts" while she is nursing Harrison. Like the dog, she blindly obeys the men around her and is out for blood. In this sense, she becomes a re-emergence of the "savage spirit of the country."

In many ways, however, Millie is worse than the woman at the store. Harrison does nothing to Millie, and she immediately recognizes him to be not much more than a boy and in his current injured state, weak and powerless. Her cheering for his capture at the end of the story could be a displaced vindictive need to make men suffer in any capacity. Her kinder nature is, in turn, "smothered" in order for Millie to keep her sanity and to allow her to continue to exist in the incomplete, stunted life she leads. At this defining moment, Millie is revealed to have too much of the colonial "savage" in her; she has become like the men whom she earlier called "all beasts." In her isolation, Millie develops an alternative form of self just as the women protagonists in "The House" and "The Woman at the Store." D'Cruz and Ross see this transformation in spectral terms, noting that the monstrous "female double is the spectre of what society or chance had repressed in the woman" (2011, p. 31). In turn, the woman's forced isolation "releases repressed facets of the self that have been denied any sort of social articulacy. It is only in the imaginary of the isolated female that the repressed can take on some sort of shadowy identity before it is vanquished by the definitions that belong to the social consensus" (ibid., p. 31). These alternative selves are also products of the women's respective environments, landscapes which affect them in not only physical, but also spiritual and emotional ways as well.

The harshness of the landscape that encircles these women contributes to their transformation. For D'Cruz and Ross, this landscape "is framed with reference to the challenges it poses to colonial settlement and to its resistance to assimilation within the imaginary of the expatriate European colonial" (2011, p. 2). The idea of an imagined homeland is crucial to understanding the sense of displacement that pervades—haunts—these stories. For Mansfield, home was always somewhere else, meaning it was essentially nowhere. This had to do with her feeling of betweenness and hybridity as not quite English/not quite New Zealander. As Robin Hyde puts it, "People say K.M. ran away from New Zealand, but if you could see and understand her exact environs, you might sympathize with the belief that she ran away from a sham England, unsuccessfully transplanted to New Zealand soil, and utterly unable to adapt itself to the real New Zealand" (1991 [1938], p. 355).

In her journal in 1908, Katherine Mansfield described the limits society places on women as a type of haunting: "Here then is a little summary of what I need—power, wealth and freedom. It is the hopelessly insipid doctrine that love is the only thing in the world, taught, hammered into women, from generation to generation, which hampers us so cruelly. We must get rid of that bogey—and then, then comes the opportunity of happiness and freedom" (1954 [1927], p. 37). This need to get to the essence of life and its deeper meanings remains a hallmark of Mansfield's writing. In looking within, Mansfield also casts her view outward, towards a greater understanding of human experience. Elizabeth Bowen claimed, "Katherine Mansfield was not a rebel, she was an innovator. Born into the English traditions of prose narrative, she neither revolted against these nor broke with them—simply, she passed beyond them" (1956, p. xii). By examining her stories set in colonial New Zealand, we can recognize another way in which Mansfield moved beyond the literature of her day. In these stories of isolated, unfulfilled women, Mansfield sought to raise awareness of that cultural and financial "bogey" which haunted herself, and, in turn, her fictional women. And, in recognizing this ghost, through her writing she began the process of exorcizing it.

Notes

1. Jane Stafford and Mark Williams have also noted Mansfield's debt to Barbara Baynton's *Bush Studies*, claiming that it is "difficult to believe that stories like 'The Woman at the Store,' 'Ole Underwood' or 'Millie' could have been written without some knowledge of the colonial writing style represented by Lawson and Baynton" (2006, p. 154).
2. In his study of nineteenth-century New Zealand Gothic, Edmund G. C. King identifies two specific strands of Colonial Gothic. "Ethnographic gothic" deals with "ostensibly 'horrific' aspects of pre-European Māori culture," while "settler gothic" is concerned "with the sense of bodily and mental displacement that often accompanied the colonial experience." King notes that both types of Gothic "provided writers with a way of responding to a colonial landscape marked by all-too-obvious sites of prior possessions and dispossessions" (2010, p. 36).
3. "Millie" is included along with Edward Tregear's "Te Whetu Plains" (1919) and an excerpt from William Satchell's *The Toll of the Bush* (1905) in the "Colonial Gothic" section of Jane Stafford and Mark Williams's *Auckland University Press Anthology of New Zealand Literature* (2012).
4. In addition to the stories discussed in this chapter, Mansfield's "Old Tar" (1913) examines the idea of "home" as something remote and impossible. The story also foregrounds settler guilt, as the land which is passed down from father to son is effectively stolen from the Māori—for a "suit of clothes an' a lookin'-glass" (Mansfield 2012d [1913], p. 341)—an act which figures both the "white house" and white settlement as haunted by past misdeeds. The story ends with Old Tar exclaiming, "Oh, Lord, wot

'ave I done—wot 'ave I done, Lord?," while his feet "seemed to freeze into the cold grass of the hill, and dark thoughts flew across his mind, like clouds, never quiet, never breaking" (p. 344).

5. Mansfield's descriptions of the New Zealand landscape are influenced by her time spent in the wilderness. During her Urewera camping trip in 1907, Mansfield wrote in her journal:

> And always through the bush this hushed sound of water running on brown pebbles. It seems to breathe the full deep bygone essence of it all. A fairy fountain of green moss. Then rounding a corner we pass several little *whares* deserted and grey. They look very old and desolate, almost haunted. On one door there is a horse collar and a torn and scribbled notice. Flowers in the garden, one clump of golden broom, one clump of yellow iris. Not even a dog greets us. All the *whares* look out upon the river and the valley and the bush-gloried hills. (1954 [1927], pp. 28–29)

For more on Mansfield's impressions of this region of the North Island, see Anna Plumridge's edition of *The Urewera Notebook by Katherine Mansfield* (Edinburgh University Press, 2015).

6. Bruce Harding notes the similarities between the husband in Mansfield's story and the "thoughtless" and "boorish" husband in Baynton's "The Chosen Vessel" (1988, p. 122).

BIBLIOGRAPHY

Boehmer, Elleke, and Steven Matthews (2011), "Modernism and Colonialism," in Michael Levenson (ed.), *The Cambridge Companion to Modernism*, 2nd edn., Cambridge: Cambridge University Press, pp. 284–300.

Bowen, Elizabeth (1956), "Introduction," in Elizabeth Bowen (ed.), *Stories by Katherine Mansfield*, New York: Vintage, pp. v–xxiv.

D'Cruz, Doreen, and John C. Ross (2011), *The Lonely and the Alone: The Poetics of Isolation in New Zealand Fiction*, Amsterdam: Rodopi.

Dunbar, Pamela (1997), *Radical Mansfield: Double Discourse in Katherine Mansfield's Short Stories*, New York: St. Martin's Press.

Hanson, Clare (2011), "Katherine Mansfield's Uncanniness," in Gerri Kimber and Janet Wilson (eds.), *Celebrating Katherine Mansfield: A Centenary Volume of Essays*, Basingstoke: Palgrave Macmillan, pp. 115–130.

Harding, Bruce (1988), "Mansfield, Misogyny and Murder: 'Ole Underwood,' 'The Woman at the Store' and 'Millie' Revisited," *Journal of New Zealand Literature* 6: 119–136.

Hyde, Robin (1991 [1938]), "The Singers of Loneliness," in Gillian Boddy and Jacqueline Matthews (eds.), *Disputed Ground: Robin Hyde, Journalist*, Wellington: Victoria University Press, pp. 347–358.

Jones, Timothy (2013), "New Zealand Gothic," in William Hughes, David Punter, and Andrew Smith (eds.), *Encyclopedia of the Gothic*, Oxford: Blackwell, pp. 468–471.

Kavka, Misha (2006), "Out of the Kitchen Sink," in Misha Kavka, Jennifer Lawn, and Mary Paul (eds.), *Gothic NZ: The Darker Side of Kiwi Culture*, Dunedin: Otago University Press, pp. 57–65.

Kimber, Gerri (2014), *Katherine Mansfield and the Art of the Short Story*, Basingstoke: Palgrave Macmillan.

King, Edmund G. C. (2010), "Towards a Prehistory of the Gothic Mode in Nineteenth-Century New Zealand Writing," *Journal of New Zealand Literature* 28, Part 2, Special Issue: Cultures of Print in Colonial New Zealand: 35–57.

Krueger, Kate (2014), *British Women Writers and the Short Story, 1850–1930: Reclaiming Social Space*, Basingstoke: Palgrave Macmillan.

Majumbar, Saikat (2013), *Prose of the World: Modernism and the Banality of Empire*, New York: Columbia University Press.

Mansfield, Katherine (1954 [1927]), *Journal of Katherine Mansfield*, John Middleton Murry (ed.), London: Constable.

——— (1984–1996), *The Collected Letters of Katherine Mansfield*, 5 vols., Vincent O'Sullivan and Margaret Scott (eds.), Oxford: Clarendon.

——— (2012a [1912]), "The House," in Gerri Kimber and Vincent O'Sullivan (eds.), *The Collected Fiction of Katherine Mansfield, 1898–1915*, Edinburgh: Edinburgh University Press, pp. 304–311.

——— (2012b [1912]), "The Woman at the Store," in Gerri Kimber and Vincent O'Sullivan (eds.), *The Collected Fiction of Katherine Mansfield, 1898–1915*, Edinburgh: Edinburgh University Press, pp. 268–277.

——— (2012c [1913]), "Millie," in Gerri Kimber and Vincent O'Sullivan (eds.), *The Collected Fiction of Katherine Mansfield, 1898–1915*, Edinburgh: Edinburgh University Press, pp. 326–330.

——— (2012d [1913]), "Old Tar," in Gerri Kimber and Vincent O'Sullivan (eds.), *The Collected Fiction of Katherine Mansfield, 1898–1915*, Edinburgh: Edinburgh University Press, pp. 340–344.

Mercer, Erin (2014), "'Manuka Bushes Covered with Thick Spider Webs': Katherine Mansfield and the Colonial Gothic Tradition," *Journal of New Zealand Literature* 32, Part 2, Special Issue: Katherine Mansfield Masked and Unmasked: 85–105.

Rudd, Alison (2010), *Postcolonial Gothic Fictions from the Caribbean, Canada, Australia, and New Zealand*, Cardiff: University of Wales Press.

Snaith, Anna (2014), *Modernist Voyages: Colonial Women Writers in London, 1890–1945*, Cambridge: Cambridge University Press.

Stafford, Jane, and Mark Williams (2006), *Maoriland: New Zealand Literature, 1872–1914*, Wellington: Victoria University Press.

Stead, C. K. (1981), *In the Glass Case: Essays on New Zealand Literature*, Auckland: Auckland University Press.
Tomalin, Claire (1988), *Katherine Mansfield: A Secret Life*, New York: Alfred A. Knopf.
Wevers, Lydia (1993), "How Kathleen Beauchamp Was Kidnapped," in Rhoda B. Nathan (ed.), *Critical Essays on Katherine Mansfield*, New York: G. K. Hall, pp. 37–47.
——— (2004), "The Politics of Culture," in Mark Williams (ed.), *Writing at the Edge of the Universe*, Christchurch: Canterbury University Press, pp. 109-122.
Williams, Mark (2000), "Mansfield in Maoriland: Biculturalism, Agency and Misreading," in Howard J. Booth and Nigel Rigby (eds.), *Modernism and Empire*, Manchester: Manchester University Press, pp. 249–274.
Wilson, Janet (2013), "Mansfield as (Post)colonial-Modernist: Rewriting the Contract with Death," in Janet Wilson, Gerri Kimber, and Delia da Sousa Correa (eds.), *Katherine Mansfield and the (Post)colonial*, Edinburgh: Edinburgh University Press, pp. 29–44.
——— (2014), "Veiling and Unveiling: Mansfield's Modernist Aesthetics," *Journal of New Zealand Literature* 32, Part 2, Special Issue: Katherine Mansfield Masked and Unmasked: 203–225.
Wisker, Gina (2012), "Katherine Mansfield's Suburban Fairy Tale Gothic," *Katherine Mansfield Studies* 4.1 (August): 20–32.

CHAPTER 12

Conclusion: "Cicatrice of an Old Wound"

Katharine Susannah Prichard's "The Curse" describes an abandoned Australian hut that is slowly being overtaken by Patterson's Curse, an invasive native flowering vine. The descriptions of the vine are themselves intertwined with segments of short dialogue that tell the fate of the previous owner of the hut, Alf, who is in prison for theft. As two travelers pass by the old hut and see the vine overtaking the dwelling, readers hear more of Alf's story. He "liked reading" and hunting kangaroo, but never tried to keep the "curse" from taking over his house (Prichard 1994 [1932], p. 263). Soon, he resorted to stealing to get by, leaving his loyal but now starving dog behind, awaiting his return.

There are other hints of colonialism in this brief, fragmented story. The white trooper who found Alf is accompanied by an Aborigine "black tracker" (p. 261). The Patterson's Curse is described as a "sea" of blue and magenta, like the "sari of a Tamil dancing girl" (p. 263). The hut itself represents a failed colonial enterprise, with a rusty "old plough," "bush timber falling to pieces," and an old "cart wheel under the fig-trees" (p. 264). The vine competes for dominance with the narrative of Alf's sad life. As the travelers pass the hut, the scene contains both failure and growth:

> Laughter of leaves, inhuman, immortal. From time immemorial into eternity, leaves laughing; innumerable small green tongues clacking, their dry murmur falling away with the wind.

© The Author(s) 2018
M. Edmundson, *Women's Colonial Gothic Writing, 1850–1930*,
Palgrave Gothic, https://doi.org/10.1007/978-3-319-76917-2_12

> Dark in the forest, under the red gums and jarrah. The wood-carter's track, cicatrice of an old wound through the bush; but the leaves still chattering, lisping and muttering endlessly of Alf and the fawn-coloured bitch straining over her puppies down there in the sunshine. Gone from backsliding eyes the sun-steeped valley between folding hills, and hut, dim, ghostly, in calm seas, fading tetratheca and turquoise; birds flying across with jargon of wild cries. (p. 264)

The beauty of the passage is unmistakable, but this beauty is also laced with more ominous notes. Amongst the flowering vine, the gentle wind, and birds flying overhead, there is something unnatural. The path to the hut is a scar upon the land that tells of aborted journeys—an "old wound"—and the dog and her brood struggle to survive in an unfamiliar area where they have been brought and abandoned. Even the hut is "ghostly" as it seemingly floats in the sea of native vine.

There are more than two curses in the story, and the narrative of a plant that covers and thus reclaims its native environment speaks to a greater theme of covering and uncovering, hiding and revealing that has been the focus of this book. Prichard herself is a fitting example of a cosmopolitan woman writer who saw the effects of empire from many different geographical angles. She was born in Fiji and later moved to Melbourne. Her career mirrors the increased opportunities available to women by the early twentieth century. She attended South Melbourne College and then worked for a time as a governess before beginning her career as a journalist in London. After her marriage, Prichard moved to Perth and wrote novels and autobiographical works. "The Curse," published in her collection *Kiss on the Lips and Other Stories* (1932), is a short but memorable glimpse into the aftereffects of empire in a remote area and relies on a sense of fragmentation and unease to describe the failed dreams of one colonial.

Yet, Prichard's story, and her fictional uncovering of the hut and the unsuccessful life of Alf, speak to a greater literary tradition that has been covered and neglected—that is, women's involvement with the debates surrounding colonialism and how it negatively affected those who took part in British expansion throughout the second half of the nineteenth century and into the first decades of the twentieth. In women's stories, we see many more abandoned huts and people like Alf; on the other hand, there are far fewer conquering white heroes and grand buildings that proclaim Britain's dominance over the "dark" places of the world. We also see women take their place within empire in these female-authored narratives. These women are often scared and alone in isolated frontier areas, whether it is Susanna Moodie struggling to make a new home in the backwoods of British Canada, or Isabella Valancy Crawford's Canadian frontier women who must toughen themselves against hostile environments and potentially dangerous people who threaten their families. Like spirits, these anxieties travel, transferring themselves across the world to equally remote and sometimes hostile places such as Australia and New Zealand. Writers like Mary Fortune, Barbara Baynton, and Katherine Mansfield show us examples of a survival-of-the-fittest existence in the back country, where women seemingly have but two choices: become victims to male violence, or become othered versions of themselves in order to fight against their victimization. Though the areas are different, the internal conflicts these women face are largely the same.

Other writers were even more direct in their critique of empire through a Gothic lens. Mary Kingsley and Margery Lawrence use ghosts and ghost stories as a vehicle for questioning British interference in colonial Africa. In writing that spans the continent, from West Africa to Egypt and Rhodesia, both authors show the power of African spiritual belief and how that belief is fundamental to the cultural survival of the African people. For Kingsley and Lawrence, British colonials are the more dangerous force in the land because of their failure to understand—and, perhaps even more importantly, to appreciate—indigenous belief. A similar critique lies at the heart of the Anglo-Indian short stories of Bithia Mary Croker and Alice Perrin. Both authors used their firsthand knowledge of Indian life and customs to present their British reading audience with a very different version of empire than the one most people found on the front pages of their newspapers and in Anglo-Indian adventure and romance novels of the time. In their stories, the British in India, just as in Africa, are often seen as cultural intruders, people who either disrespect local customs or who attempt to force India into a British mold, with fatal consequences.

In his study of the modern ghost story, Simon Hay has suggested:

> As a genre, modern ghost stories are concerned with historical trauma, its remembrance and its lingering consequences. In these stories, the ghost is something that returns from the past, something that irrupts into the present, disrupting both the present's presumed separateness from the past, as

well as its stable inheritance of that past. There are two paradigmatic historical traumas that the modern ghost story responds to. The first is the transition from feudalism to capitalism, and the consequent shift in power from the aristocracy to the bourgeoisie. And the second is in effect a repetition of the first, as under imperialism different parts of the world experience the violent transition to modernity. (2011, p. 227)

I would like to expand this important idea and situate it beyond actual ghosts in order to consider the socio-cultural influence of women's Colonial Gothic writing as a genre. Through narratives with traditional ghosts, as well as through stories that rely on more abstract representations of being haunted, these women challenged contemporary assumptions that held imperialism up as a grand civilizing mission, an opportunity for the British to bring enlightenment and trade to perceived "lesser" peoples. The British public never completely saw nor understood the brutality and suffering that was allowed to occur in order for this "civilizing" to happen. By utilizing the Colonial Gothic, women writers who lived in Britain and in colonial regions call into focus some of these darker motives behind British expansion while, at the same time, blurring this popular vision of empire. And they still have something to tell us.

When we read colonial fiction only through the viewpoint of white male authors—men who were usually imperial apologists—we are only seeing part of the story. We are reading from the center rather than the periphery. In her discussion of Barbara Baynton's short fiction, Lucy Frost has noted that narratives of the colonial frontier have tended to come from this one source, that of the white heterosexual male. She states, "All elements are placed in relation to him and to his aspirations." In order to find the "dissidents," Frost claims, we must look to "those who are not positioned as white or heterosexual or male" (1994, p. 15). In other words, we must look to those in British and colonial culture who were themselves Other in some way, writers who were not at the center of power within the imperialist system. In recent years, several non-white voices have emerged to reclaim and lay bare the devastating consequences of colonialism on indigenous peoples. As postcolonial viewpoints of those who for centuries have been silenced and forcibly removed from the land of their birth or enslaved on that very land, these narratives give us alternative ways of reading the history of empire.

Many of the women writers included in this book were ambivalent about race, or in some ways mirrored many of the prejudiced beliefs of their time, although I would argue that their writing is not as blatantly racialist as many male-authored texts. In much of their writing, these women are guiltier of omitting the indigenous experience from their works. The reasons behind this omission are not always clear. Did these women simply not know enough about the lives of indigenous people? Did they not care about indigenous people? These questions remain. When they did have intimate knowledge of people in colonial regions, their views still varied. Mary Kingsley studied the culture of West Africans and used African customs as the basis of much of her travel writing and works on folkloric belief. Yet, Bithia Mary Croker and Alice Perrin, both of whom spent decades in India, are at times sympathetic toward Indians and their treatment by the British, while at other times these authors revert to racist stereotypes and one-dimensional Indian characters. Florence Marryat also spent time in India, but her views on race, again, often reflect racist assumptions about non-white people. Even her sympathetic reading of Harriet Brandt is infected by an underlying sense that racial intermixture is a bad idea.

Yet, these works remain important because they provide a middle ground from which to view British colonial literature, as well as an expanded understanding of women's involvement with the Gothic and supernatural genres. Like the colonial characters they write about, these authors are themselves in-between. They are between the white, male-authored imperial Gothic texts of the nineteenth and twentieth centuries and the more inclusive postcolonial Gothic of the later twentieth and twenty-first centuries. As women writers, they are the neglected voices that have long been overshadowed by the likes of Rudyard Kipling, H. Rider Haggard, Richard Marsh, and Joseph Conrad. In limiting our reading to these authors, we are also limiting our understanding of British attitudes about imperialism during the high point of the British Empire. By including a greater range of voices, we give ourselves a more complete picture of how the British saw themselves and their place in the world. Often, women's narratives were culturally "inconvenient" because their treatment of the Colonial Gothic disrupted the narrative that maintained the need for British dominance and expansion. If the British felt they were bringing civilized "light" to the "dark" regions of the colonial world, then women's writing often shed light on what, to pro-imperialists, might be considered the wrong subjects. By calling attention to tragedy, violence, and literal and metaphorical haunting in colonial regions, women refused the male-authored narrative of conquest and power over both women and indigenous people. Yet, the very power structures these women were fighting against gave them the impetus to imagine such negative repercussions of the masculinist imperial mindset. Instead of boldly conquering foreign lands, their women characters struggle to survive alone in the backwoods. Instead of braving the attacks of "savages," they suffer sexual and verbal abuse at the hands of British colonial men. Rather than venturing into unknown lands for gold and diamonds, these characters battle against unseen supernatural forces that violently resist efforts to colonize. No riches come from these lands, only trauma, suffering, and death. Likewise, the spiritual forces in many of these narratives—be they West African fetish figures, Afro-Caribbean soucouyants, Indian reincarnations, or Egyptian spirits of the desert—call into question issues of power and influence. These ancient forces symbolize cultures which have existed long before white settlement and which will continue to exist long after colonialism is over. This writing, in turn, haunts the imperial enterprise, forever troubling the narrative of British imperial dominance and its grand civilizing mission.

Bibliography

Frost, Lucy (1994), "A Shape to Suit Desire: Re(reading) Nineteenth-Century Australia," *Critical Survey* 6.1: 14–19.

Hay, Simon (2011), *A History of the Modern British Ghost Story*, Basingstoke: Palgrave Macmillan.

Prichard, Katharine Susannah (1994 [1932]), "The Curse," in Ken Gelder (ed.), *The Oxford Book of Australian Ghost Stories*, Melbourne and Oxford: Oxford University Press, pp. 261–264.

Index

A
abandonment, 206–212, 230–231
Adams, Evelyn, 214n8
  "Cruel Fate," 211–212
Africa
  afterlife beliefs, 103–104
  British anxieties of, 81
  Congo; *Heart of Darkness*, 128–130
  cultural beliefs of the supernatural, 81–82
  effects of missionary involvement in, 131–134
  Egypt, 116; "The Curse of the Stillborn," 15–16, 130–134; feminism in, 136n11
  ghosts, explanations for, 105
  ghosts as metaphor for imperialism, 118–122
  Pemba Island; "The Dogs of Pemba," 15, 116, 122–130
  Rhodesia; "Death Valley," 15, 116, 118–122
  spectral classifications in, 100–107; bibendi, 107; bush soul, 100–101; carrion soul, 102; dream soul, 101; improperly buried souls, 102–103; male versus female, 103; overgod of gods, 105; Sasahbomsum and Shramantin, 103, 106; the shadow on the path, 102
  West Africa; "Black Ghosts," 15, 97, 99–105; fetishism, 105, 107–110; "The Forms of Apparitions in West Africa," 15, 97, 105–110; *Travels in West Africa*, 15, 97, 98, 102
  white ghosts versus black, 120–121
Aitken, Edward Hamilton
  The Tribes on My Frontier, 174n6
Allen, Judith, 214n6
American Gothic, 23
Anatol, Giselle Liza, 80–81
Anglo-Indian Gothic
  "The Biscobra," 17, 168–172
  "Caulfield's Crime," 16–17, 158, 159–165
  culture of silence, 152
  female personification of India, 147
  ghosts/haunting; bungalows, 169–172; palaces, 142–148
  goddesses, 148

246 INDEX

humans taking on animal qualities, 147
"If You See Her Face," 16, 140–147, 152
"A Man's Theory," 165–168
nautch girls/Bayadère/devadasis/dancing girls, 140–148, 154n3, 155n6
objectification of women, 140–142
racial prejudice, 243
"The Red Bungalow," 16, 150–153
reincarnation, 164–165, 168–172, 173n4
sati, 154n5
social status of women, 140, 154n3
tiger symbolism, 147–148, 155n8
Anglo-Indian women
social status of, 140, 154n3
Animal Gothic, 157–175
animal/human characteristic interchangeability, 160, 173n4
"The Biscobra" (Perrin), 158, 168–172
"Caulfield's Crime" (Perrin), 158, 159–165
cultural humanity toward animals, 174n7
dogs, 161
human-to-animal transforming curses, 125–127
hunting stories, 159–160
jackals, 160–161, 165
lizards, 170–172, 174n6
"A Man's Theory" (Perrin), 158, 165–168
rabies in, 162, 172n2, 173n3
and racial otherness, 160
rats, 167, 168, 173n5
reincarnation, 164–165, 168–172
anxiety, 1, 3. *See also* fear
gender-related, 52, 75, 191
reflected in ghosts, 153

reverse colonization, 81
of women's sexuality, 147
Aoraki (Mount Cook), 232
Archibald, J.F., 208
Ascari, Maurizio, 184, 192n4
Atwood, Margaret, 31, 40n3
Australian Gothic, 11, 177–191
Bush Studies (Baynton); "Billy Skywonkie," 209; "The Chosen Vessel," 17–18, 197, 200–201, 202, 206–211, 212; "A Dreamer," 17–18, 197, 200–206, 209, 212
crime and social anxieties, 185–186
"The Curse" (Prichard), 239–240
fear of criminals in, 206–208, 211–212
Gothic aspects of landscape, 203–204
"The Illumined Grave" (Fortune), 17, 181–185
and imperialism, 179, 206
individual selfhood in, 189–190
"Mystery and Murder" (Fortune), 17, 178, 179–181
"The Old Shaft" (Fortune), 17, 186–188
the outback, 197–214
portrayal of Aboriginal people, 214n10
portrayal of villains in, 184–185
secrets uncovered, 179
autonomy of women, 124–128, 130, 190, 212

B
Ballstadt, Carol, 33, 40n4, 41n5
Barry, John Arthur
"'Missing': A Story of the South Pacific," 111n5
Bavin-Mizzi, Jill, 214n6

Baynton, Barbara, 3, 197–214,
    221–222, 241, 242
  Bush Studies, 235n1; "Billy
    Skywonkie," 209; "The
    Chosen Vessel," 17–18, 197,
    200–201, 202, 206–211, 212;
    "A Dreamer," 17–18, 197,
    200–206, 209, 212
  career challenges, as author,
    199–200
  Cobbers; "Toohey's Party," 213n1;
    "Trooper Jim Tasman," 213n1
  critic reviews of work, 200–202
  feminist views, 201
  "Indignity of Domestic Service,"
    213n2
  personal background, 198
  "The Tramp," 213n5
  "Wet Paint," 213n1
Bell, Hesketh
  Obeah: Witchcraft in the West Indies,
    81
Bennett, Edward Turner
  The Tower Menagerie, 161
Bentley, D. M. R., 29
Besson, Gérard
  *Folklore and Legends of Trinidad and
    Tobago*, 81
Bhabha, Homi K., 170
biracial women, 73–91
  portrayal as having animal traits, 79,
    86, 88
  prejudice against, 87–88, 243
Birkett, Dea, 99, 111n4, 111n7
Birkhead, Edith, 47, 49
Blunt, Alison, 110n1, 110n3
body-horror, 188
Boehmer, Elleke, 221
Bongie, Chris, 129
Borlase, James Skipp, 185, 192n6
Bowen, Elizabeth, 220, 235
Braddon, Mary Elizabeth

"The Ghost's Name," 112n11
  Good Lady Ducayne, 73
Brantlinger, Patrick, 5, 96, 117, 121,
  129, 133, 136n5
Brisson, Ulrike, 108, 110n3
Brontë, Charlotte, 49, 75, 84, 91
Brontë, Emily, 46, 75
Brown, Megan, 178, 179, 190–191,
  191n2
Bulfin, Ailise, 131
Burchell, William John
  *Travels in the Interior of Southern
    Africa*, 161
Burne-Jones, Philip
  "The Vampire" (painting), 83
Burpee, Lawrence J., 45
Burton, Richard
  The Lake Regions of Central Africa,
    107–108
Busia, Abena P. A., 129–130
Buss, Helen M., 27

C
Campbell, Sandra, 66
Canadian Gothic, 12–13, 23–39,
  40n3, 45–66, 66n1, 66–67n2,
  67n5, 69n12, 241
  "In the Breast of a Maple"
    (Crawford), 50, 62–65
  distortion of self in, 25
  and Duncan, Sara Jeannette, 50
  "Extradited" (Crawford), 50, 58–62
  frontier life experience, 10–11,
    26–32, 58–62
  mental illness in, 54–58
  "The Perfect Number Seven"
    (Crawford), 50–54
  and portrayal of heroines, 49–50
  romance in, 62–65
  Roughing It in the Bush (Moodie),
    12–13, 26–32

"Sèvres Fulkes" (Crawford), 50, 54–58
short fiction; vampirism in, 53
short stories as "national genre," 45
and social order, 23–24
"The Well in the Wilderness; A Tale of the Prairie—Founded Upon Facts," 13, 35–36, 39
"The Witch of East Cliff," 34
The World Before Them, 34–35
cannibalism, 85, 88, 121
Capes, Bernard
"The Moon-Stricken," 111n5
Caribbean Gothic
belief in the supernatural, 81
biracial women, 73–91
The Blood of the Vampire (Marryat), 14, 73–84, 87–91
A Daughter of the Tropics (Marryat), 84–87, 90
Carpenter, Lynette, 4
castles
and "indoor travel," 48
Chaudhuri, Nupur, 10
Christianity, 108
Clark, Timothy, 163
Clarke, Marcus, 185, 203
closure, narrative, 9
Clouston, Thomas Smith
Clinical Lectures on Mental Diseases, 69n10
Colonial Gothic, 32, 177, 191, 222, 235n2
colonial otherness, 8
colonization, reverse, 81
comedy
and romance, 53–54, 62–65
Compton, Herbert
Indian Life in Town and Country, 149
Conrad, Joseph, 7, 15, 75, 127, 128, 243

Heart of Darkness, 15, 128–130
"The Lagoon," 111n5
Cook, James, 232
Cowell, Pattie, 23, 24
Crawford, Isabella Valancy, 3, 12, 13–14, 45–72, 241
"In the Breast of a Maple," 13–14, 50, 62–65
career challenges, as author, 46, 58
challenging of gender codes, 49
Collected Stories, 46
"Dreams and Manifestations," 68n8
early reputation as writer, 45–46
emigrant life experiences of, 62, 66
"Extradited," 14, 50, 58–62, 69n11, 69n12
"Glass delusion," 68n10
interest in the supernatural, 47
"Mrs. Hay's Ghost," 68n8
Old Spookes' Pass, Malcolm's Katie and Other Poems, 13
"The Perfect Number Seven," 50–54, 65
poetry of, 66n2
political engagement of, 66n1
portrayal of heroines, 48
and publishing industry, 67n5, 69n13
"Sèvres Fulkes," 50, 54–58, 65
Winona; or, the Foster Sisters, 13, 68n9
crime fiction. *See* Fortune, Mary
crisis apparition, 183
Croker, Bithia Mary, 3, 16, 139–155, 241, 243
"The Dâk Bungalow at Dakor," 150
"If You See Her Face," 16, 140–148, 152
"To Let," 150
other works by, 154n2
"The Red Bungalow," 16, 140, 150–153

INDEX 249

sympathy toward Indian women, 140
Crowe, Catherine
    Ghosts and Family Legends, 47, 135n1
curses, 125–127
Curthoys, Ann, 11

D
Dalby, Richard, 115
Dale, Leigh, 202, 209
Dance, Charles
    Chapters from a Guianese Log-Book, 82
Darwin, Charles
    The Descent of Man, 161
Davies, Lawrence, 111n5
Davies, Susanne, 214n6
Davis, Octavia, 87, 90
Davison, Carol Margaret, 7
D'Cruz, Doreen, 230, 234
Defoe, Daniel
    "The Apparition of Mrs. Veal," 47
degeneration, 7, 77, 92n2, 126, 127, 163, 231
Dellamora, Richard
    "Isabella Valancy Crawford and an English Canadian Sodom," 69n12
Depledge, Greta, 74, 79
Dickens, Charles, 2
Dijkstra, Bram, 77, 80
disease
    cholera, 28
    ghosts as metaphor for, 107, 112n11
    scarlet fever, 37
dislocation, 6
displacement, 234
Doerksen, Teri Ann, 81, 89–90

domestic abuse, 179, 186–188, 206, 208, 244
domestic Gothic, 223
domestic space
    the "failed home," 178–188, 220
    haunting of. *See* ghosts/haunting
    invasion by natural environment, 168–172
Doyle, Arthur Conan, 127, 128
Dunbar, Pamela, 229–230, 232
Duncan, Sara Jeannette, 50
Durga, 148

E
Early, Len, 46, 49, 51, 52, 56, 58, 62, 65–66, 67n4, 67n5, 68n7
early settler life, 12–13, 26–32, 58–62
Egyptian Gothic, 15–16, 116, 130–134, 136n11
Ellis, Kate Ferguson, 29
emigration
    Great Britain to Canada, 24–31, 36–39, 40n1
ethnographic Gothic, 235n2
evolutionary theory, 163
exile, 13, 26–31, 35–36, 220. *See also* isolation
extrasensory perception, 32, 35

F
Favenc, Ernest, 185
    "Doomed," 192n5
fear, 1, 3. *See also* anxiety
    and Australian outback life, 197–213. *See also* Baynton, Barbara
    and colonial dwellings, 149
    cross-cultural, of ghosts, 102–103, 106–107
    of degeneration, 163
    of disease, 107, 173n2

of invasion, 81, 89, 97, 159, 162
of isolation and vulnerability, 208
of loss of control, 185
racial, 74, 79, 84, 87
of the supernatural, 34–36, 52
of wild animals, 25, 29–30, 167, 168–172
of witchcraft, 107
Female Gothic, 4, 7, 177, 191
The Female Gothic: New Directions (Wallace and Smith), 4
female selfhood, 190–191
female victims
colonial attitudes toward, 208–209
feminism, 136n11, 201
femme fatales, 8, 80, 84, 91, 103, 147
fetishism, 105, 107–110
Fiamengo, Janice, 10–11
Fleming, George
Rabies and Hydrophobia, 172n2
Forbes, James
Oriental Memoirs, 140–141
Fortune, Mary, 3, 17, 177–191, 241
"Clyzia the Dwarf," 191n1
The Detective's Album, 177
emigration to Australia, 193n9
"The Illumined Grave," 178, 181–185
"Mystery and Murder," 178, 179–181, 192n6
"The Old Shaft," 178, 186–188
"Twenty-Six Years Ago; or, The Diggings from '55," 186
Fowler, Marian, 26, 29
Fox, Kate, 33, 41n5
Frank, Katherine, 111n9
Freeman, Mary E. Wilkins
"Luella Miller," 73
Freud, Sigmund, 227
frontier life experience, 10–11, 26–32, 58–62
Frost, Lucy, 202, 242

G
Gadpaille, Michelle, 45–46, 58
Garrett, Eileen, 115
Garrity, Jane, 117
Gelder, Ken, 153, 179, 182, 189–190, 212
gender
challenging of gender codes in Gothic romance, 49
dynamics of in marriage, 124–128, 165–168
and empire, 7
gender anxieties, 52, 75
male-versus-female-authored Gothic fiction, 4–5
A Geography of Victorian Gothic Fiction (Mighall), 2
Gerson, Carole, 24
Gethlin, Jeuan, 112n11
ghosts/haunting, 8, 118–122, 220–231, 241–242. *See also* supernatural beings/elements
African/British cross-cultural fear of, 103
and Anglo-Indian residences, 142–153, 149–153
crisis apparition, 183
denial of proper burial, 183–184, 191
and domestic abuse, 186–188
explanations for seeing, 105
"failed home," 29, 212, 220
ghost stories as critiques of empire, 117–118
ghosts leading people to their murderer, 183–184, 191
Gothic real supplanting Gothic supernatural, 181
haunted homes representative of failed dreams, 223–227
haunted houses as metaphor for the unrest of imperialism, 153

INDEX   251

homesickness and, 223–226
male versus female ghosts, 103
as metaphor for disease, 107, 112n11; as metaphor for imperialism, 118–122; in New Zealand Gothic. *See* Mansfield, Katherine; retributive capabilities of ghosts, 190; returning home, 179–190; revenge of ghosts, 188; and social relationships, 6; spectral doubles, 227; subliminal abilities of ghosts, 189; "unsettlement" of haunted homes, 153; and violent death, 181–185; white devil, 15, 118–122; women achieving autonomy as ghosts, 189
Glickman, Susan, 32
Glover, William J., 149
Gothic
 as critique of colonial enterprise, 192n5
Gothic hybridity, 73–74
Gothic natural history, 169
Gothic otherness, 87
Gothic romance. *See also* Crawford, Isabella Valancy
 and comedy, 53–54, 62–65
 as genre, 47–48
 "new Gothic," 49–50
 portrayal of heroines in, 47–50
 and vampirism, 53
Grant, Colesworthy
 Anglo-Indian Domestic Life, 149
Great Migration, 40n1
Green, Alice Stopford, 98, 111n6

H
Hackforth-Jones, Penne, 198
Hadgraft, Cecil, 192n6, 193n8

Haggard, H. Rider, 7, 75, 136n5, 243
 She, 75
Halttunen, Karen, 182, 188, 189
Hammack, Brenda Mann
 "Florence Marryat's Female Vampire and the Scientizing of Hybridity," 92n2
Hammill, Faye, 27
Hanson, Clare, 5, 225–227
Harding, Bruce, 223, 233, 236n6
Harrington, Ellen Burton, 5
Hatem, Mervat, 137n11
Hathaway, E. J.
 "Isabella Valancy Crawford," 66–67n2
haunting/haunted spaces. *See* ghosts/haunting
Hay, Simon, 6, 62, 118, 241
Heilman, Robert B., 49–50
Hendershot, Cyndy, 127, 129, 133
heroines
 alternative viewpoints from male characters, 124–128
 and autonomy, 190, 212
 of Brontë, Charlotte, 49, 84
 helplessness versus strength of, 56–58
 and marriage dynamics, 124–128
 modernization of, 49–50
 mothers as, 65
 pioneers as, 66
 as progressive literary figures, 47–49
 vulnerability of, 40n2
Hicks, Mary Jane, 208
hidden identities, 54–58
Hockley, William Browne
 The English in India, 141
Hodd, Thomas, 33–34
Hogg, James
 The Private Memoirs and Confessions of a Justified Sinner, 101
Hogg, Robert, 193n7

home, concept of, 190, 218, 220, 226
"failed home," 29, 212, 220
imagined homeland, 234
Hopkins, Elizabeth, 33, 40n4, 41n5
Hopkins, R. Thurston
Ghosts over England, 115
Hughes, William, 6, 7
Hurley, Kelly, 163, 169
hybridity, 91n2
 animal/human, 78, 80, 170–171
 hybrid identities, 234–235
 national/cultural, 220, 225–226, 231–232
 racial, 75–76
Hyde, Robin, 234
Hynes, C. J. Cutcliffe
 "A Lottery Duel," 111n5

I
identity
 hybrid identities, 234–235; animal/human, 78, 80, 170–171; national/cultural, 220, 225–226, 231–232; racial, 75–76
imperialism
 in Australia, 179
 "civilizing missions," 158–159, 163
 in Egypt, 130–134
 female modernist writing and, 116–117
 gender issues in imperial system, 10
 gendered boundaries of, 143
 ghosts as metaphor for, 118–122
 male-authored narratives of, 128–130
 and paternalism, 129
 power structures and, 8
 "predatory hierarchy" of, 164
 social middle ground of women and, 212

 value of alternative viewpoints on, 242
imprisonment, sense of, 59–62
indigenous people
 absence of voice of, 11
 effect of colonial rule on, 95, 116, 127–128, 134
 prejudice against, 243. *See also* race
infidelity, 125–127
isolation, 13, 18, 35–36, 186, 187, 201–209, 230–234. *See also* exile
ivory trade, 15, 116, 118–122

J
Jackson, Rosemary, 4, 5, 7
Jacobs, Jane M., 153, 189–190
Jagadhatri, 148
Jones, Robin D.
 Interiors of Empire, 149
Jones, Timothy, 217

K
Kavka, Misha, 217
Kelly, John, 112n11
Khair, Tabish, 9
Kimber, Gerri, 227
King, Edmund G. C., 217, 235n2
Kingscote, Georgiana
 "The Brâhmin Girl That Married a Tiger," 155n9
Kingsley, Mary, 3, 15, 95–112, 241, 243
 on Africa's natural environment, 98–99
 "Black Ghosts," 15, 97, 99–105
 criticism of British colonial society, 110, 112n15
 explanations for ghost-seeing, 105
 "The Forms of Apparitions in West Africa," 15, 97, 105–110

humor in writings, 111n6
protectiveness of African culture and
  spirituality, 97–98
scientific interests, 111n8
on similarities between European
  and African spiritual beliefs,
  105–106
Travels in West Africa, 15, 97, 98,
  102
views on British rule in West Africa,
  95–96
"West Africa, from an Ethnologist's
  Point of View," 98
West African Studies, 97, 98
Kipling, John Lockwood
Beast and Man in India, 161, 164,
  165, 174n6
Kipling, Rudyard, 2, 7, 136n5, 243
"The Mark of the Beast," 162, 164
Plain Tales, 157
"The Vampire" (poem), 83
Knight, Stephen, 185, 190, 192n4
Kolmar, Wendy K., 4
Krimmer, Sally, 210, 213n1, 214n5
Krueger, Kate, 221–222, 231
Kulperger, Shelley, 6

L
Lake, Marilyn, 214n6
Lamond, Julieanne, 210
Lane, Christopher, 99
Lang, Andrew
  "The Black Dogs and the
    Thumbless Hand," 111n5
  Cock Lane and Common-Sense, 47
  "Ghosts and Right Reason," 111n5
Langbauer, Laurie, 48–49
Lawn, Jennifer, 6
Lawrence, Margery, 3, 15, 115–137,
  241
  Bohemian Glass, 116

"The Curse of the Stillborn,"
  15–16, 116, 130–134
"Death Valley," 15, 116, 118–122,
  134
"The Dogs of Pemba," 15, 116,
  122–130
early travel escapades and war work,
  135n3
The Floating Café, 115
"Floris and the Soldan's Daughter,"
  135n4
"The House of the Dancing Feet,"
  18, 135n4
"I Don't Want to Be A Mother,"
  115
interest in the supernatural, 115
"The Mask of Sacrifice," 135n4
Miss Brandt, Adventuress, 115
Nights of the Roundtable, 115
other works by, 135n2, 135n4
premonitions experienced by,
  136n10
"The Professor's Ring," 136n4
progressive principles of, 115–116
"The Soldier's Story," 118
The Terraces of Night, 115
"Tinpot Landing," 135n4
"The Traveller's Tale," 122
Lawson, Alan, 210, 213n1, 214n5
Lawson, Henry, 200, 207
  "The Drover's Wife," 221
Lawson, Louisa
  "The Australian Bush-Woman," 186
Le Fanu, Sheridan
  Carmilla, 73, 78, 83
Lecky, William Edward
  History of European Morals, 174n7
Leland, Charles G.
  *The Algonquin Legends of New
    England*, 69–70n14
Leslie, Frank, 46, 68n6
Liggins, Emma, 7–8

Lilley, Norman, 199, 213n4
Linton, Eliza Lynn
 "The Girl of the Period," 50
live burial, 54
loss, 6–7
lost inheritance, 64
loup-garou (loogaroo), 81–82
Lucas, Alec, 24, 29
Luckhurst, Roger, 8, 109, 110n3, 112n12, 130–131, 137n10
Lynch, Gerald, 58

M
MacLeod, Alexander, 45
Majumbar, Saikat, 220
Malchow, H. L., 75, 77, 90
Mangum, Teresa, 158–159, 164
Mansfield, Katherine, 3, 217–236, 241
 "At the Bay," 223
 conflicting cultural identities of, 225–226
 emigration from New Zealand, 219–220
 "The House," 18, 218, 220, 222, 223–227
 "Millie," 18, 218, 220, 222–223, 231–234, 235n3
 "Old Tar," 235n4
 "Ole Underwood," 223
 use of Gothic mode, 223
 "The Woman at the Store," 18, 218, 220, 222–223, 227–231
Māori, 228–229, 232, 235n2, 235n4
Marcus, Sharon, 112n11
marital Gothic, 60
marriage, 58–62, 124–128, 165–168, 231–232
Marryat, Florence, 3, 243
 The Blood of the Vampire, 14, 73–84, 87–91
 A Daughter of the Tropics, 84–87, 90

Gup: Sketches of Anglo-Indian Life and Character, 74
 "Little White Souls," 18
 reviews of work, 74–75
 There is No Death, 91n1
Marsh, Richard, 243
Massé, Michelle A., 60
Matthews, Steven, 221
Maunder, Andrew, 7–8
Maxwell, Anne, 185
McClintock, Anne, 7
McEwan, Cheryl, 99
McKechnie, Claire Charlotte, 126, 162, 173n2, 173n3
McKellar, Campbell, 185
McMahon, Elisabeth, 136n8
McMullen, Lorraine, 66
mental illness, 54–58, 69n10, 101, 170–171
Mercer, Erin, 217, 223, 228
Michelis, Angelica, 78
Middleton, Dorothy, 110n2, 111n9
Mighall, Robert, 2
Miller, John
 Empire and the Animal Body, 160, 162
Millin, Sarah Gertrude, 217
Mills, Sara, 10
mirror symbolism, 225
missionaries, 131–134
Modernism, 220, 221, 222
Moers, Ellen, 4
 and heroinism, 47–48
Moodie, Susanna, 3, 23–39, 40n1, 40n3, 40n4, 41n5, 41n8, 41n9, 66, 193n9, 241
 belief in the supernatural, 32–36
 on drawing fiction from real life, 41n7
 Life in the Clearings Versus the Bush, 68n9

INDEX   255

Mildred Rosier, A Tale of the Ruined City, 33
Monica, 33
Roughing It in the Bush, 12–13, 34, 36
  and the Spiritualist Movement, 33, 34, 40n4
Victoria Magazine, 36, 41n8
"The Well in the Wilderness; A Tale of the Prairie—Founded Upon Facts," 13, 35–36, 39
"The Witch of East Cliff," 34
Witchcraft, 33
"A Word for the Novel Writers," 41n7
The World Before Them, 34–35
writings for *La Belle Assemblée*, 33, 36
Moody, Nickianne, 5
moral choice, 62
Morey, Peter, 162, 164, 172
murder victims
  corpse description significance, 181, 182, 187–188
Murry, John Middleton, 218, 226
Myers, Frederic, 183, 189, 190

N
narrational silence, 163–164
narrative closure, 9
natural environment, 235n5
  harshness of, 234
  invasion of interior domestic space, 168–172
  as predator, 38, 51, 203–205
New Zealand Gothic, 217–236
"At the Bay," 223
"The House," 18, 218, 220, 222, 223–227
and limited history, 217

"Millie," 18, 218, 220, 222–223, 231–234, 235n3
"Old Tar," 235n4
"Ole Underwood," 223
and transference/transformation, 6
"The Woman at the Store," 18, 218, 220, 222–223, 227–231
Ng, Andrew Hock-soon, 6–7
Nischik, Reingard M., 45
North American frontier Gothic, 23
Northey, Margot, 25

O
objectification of women, 140–142
occultism, 117
O'Hagan, Thomas, 67n2
Oyeyemi, Helen
  White is for Witching, 92n4

P
Palmer, Nettie, 200
Palmer, Vance, 200, 213n3
Parthasarathy, Shri A.
  The Symbolism of Hindu Gods and Rituals, 148
paternalism of new imperialism, 129
Paxton, Nancy L., 143
Perrin, Alice, 3, 157–175, 241, 243
  East of Suez, 157–172; "The Biscobra," 17, 168–172; "Caulfield's Crime," 16–17, 158, 159–165; "A Man's Theory," 165–168; reviews of *East of Suez*, 157–158; short fiction compared to work by Rudyard Kipling, 157; time spent in India, 157
Peterman, Michael, 24, 27, 33, 40n4, 41n5, 46, 49, 51–52, 56, 65–66

Petrone, Penny, 46, 61, 64, 67n3, 69n11
Philadelphoff-Puren, Nina, 208
Philips, David, 214n6
Phillips, A. A., 201–203
Phillpotts, Eden
  In Sugar-Cane Land, 81–82
Pietz, William, 109
Pratt, Mary Louise, 10
predators, 51
  disease as, 28, 30, 37
  natural environment as, 38, 51, 203–205
Prichard, Katharine Susannah, 240
  "The Curse," 239–240
Procter, James, 2, 96
publishing industry, 46, 67n5, 68n6

R
race
  racial otherness, 1, 8, 9, 160
  racial prejudice, 243; about biracial women, 73–91; attitudes of women settlers, 10–11; and vampirism, 14, 73–84, 87–91
Radcliffe, Ann, 24, 26, 47–48
rape, 208–211, 214n6
realism, 25, 62
Reeve, Clara, 24
reincarnation, 164–165, 168–172, 173n4
Reiss, Timothy J., 57
repression, 189, 234
retribution, 190
reverse colonization, 81
Rhys, Jean
  "The Day They Burned the Books," 92n4
  Wide Sargasso Sea, 92n4
Rigby, Nigel, 116–117
Ritvo, Harriet, 159

Robbeson, Angela Arnold, 58
Robbins, Ruth, 7–8
Robins, Gertrude Minnie
  The Relations and What They Related, 135n1
Rodwell, James
  The Rat: Its History and Destructive Character, 173n5
Ross, John C., 230, 234
Rudd, Alison, 7, 231
Russell, Penny, 186, 212, 214n9

S
Sástri, Pandit Natêsá
  "The Brâhmin Girl That Married a Tiger," 155n9
Satchell, William, 235n3
Saunders, Kay, 193n7
Schaffer, Kay, 201
Sedgwick, Eve, 54
selfhood, female, 190–191
Sen, Indrani, 74–75, 147, 155n8
Senf, Carol, 83
settler Gothic, 235n2
sexual deviancy, 206, 231
sexuality
  colonial anxiety over, 155n8
  of female spirits, 82
  use by women to control men, 147
  of vampires, 78, 81–82, 83
short stories, 5, 45, 47, 58, 65
Shortt, John
  "The Bayadère; or, Dancing Girls of Southern India," 142, 146, 147
Signorotti, Elizabeth, 84
silence, enforced, 1, 132, 163, 187
silence, narrational, 163–164
Sinnett, Frederick
  "The Fiction Fields of Australia," 178–179, 203
slavery, 76–81, 85, 88, 89

Smith, Andrew, 4, 6, 7, 189
Smith, Angela, 2, 96
Snaith, Anna, 11, 220, 221
Society for Psychical Research, 97, 105
Solomon, Edward
  The Nautch Girl, or, The Rajah of Chutneypore, 154n4
soucouyants, 14, 80–83, 91n4
Spiritualist movement, 33, 34, 40n4
Stafford, Jane, 235n1, 235n3
Stead, C. K., 222
Stephens, A. G., 213n5, 214n5
Stevenson, Robert Louis
  Strange Case of Dr. Jekyll and Mr. Hyde, 101
Stoker, Bram
  Dracula, 73, 83
  The Jewel of Seven Stars, 130
  The Lair of the White Worm, 75
Stott, Rebecca, 8
Strobel, Margaret, 10, 100
Sugars, Cynthia, 39
suicide, 87, 89, 91
supernatural beings/elements, 15–16, 116, 130–134
  Cabresses, 82
  intervention of, 171–172
  Jumby, 81
  Long Bubbies, 82
  loup-garou (loogaroo), 81–82
  Mu-se-gisk, 63, 69n14
  Shramantin, 103
  soucouyants, 14, 80–83, 91n4
  and subversive roles, 82
  Tando the Hater, 107
  vampires. *See* vampires
  Water Mamma, 82
Sussex, Lucy, 178, 187, 191, 191n2, 192n6
Sutherland, Katherine, 66n1
symbolism of dark and light, 123

T
Thomas, Christa Zeller, 28, 40n2
Thomas, Clara, 46
Thurston, John, 24–25, 32, 39
Todorov, Tzvetan, 171
Tomalin, Claire, 222
Traill, Catharine Parr, 26, 33
transgression, 6–7
Tregear, Edward, 235n3
Tresidder, Jack, 155n10
Turcotte, Gerry, 6, 7, 12, 39, 179, 213, 214n10
Turner, Lynette, 111n3
Tylor, E. B., 104

U
Uglow, Jennifer, 7
the uncanny, 149, 164, 171, 218, 222, 228, 231, 232
unheimlich, 226
unsettlement, 153, 190, 204, 212, 220
the unspeakable, 54

V
vampires, 53
  and biracial women, 75–76
  The Blood of the Vampire, 73–84, 87–91
  British fears of, 81
  A Daughter of the Tropics, 84–87
  infants and children as victims of, 82, 88
  loup-garou (loogaroo), 81–82
  and the maternal, 78
  Sasahbomsum, 103, 106
  and sexuality, 78, 81–82, 83
  soucouyants, 14, 80–83, 91n4
veil symbolism, 224
Vidler, Anthony, 149

violence against women, 186–188, 190, 209. See also domestic abuse
voiceless women, 209
Vrettos, Athena, 76

W
Walker, E. D.
 Reincarnation: A Study of Forgotten Truth, 173n4
Wallace, Diana, 4
Walpole, Horace, 24
 The Castle of Otranto, 47
Weaver, Rachael, 179, 212
Webb, W. Trego
 "The Nautch Girl," 141–142
Wells, H. G., 127, 128
Wevers, Lydia, 217, 231
Williams, Mark, 220, 235n1, 235n3
Williamson, John

Medical and Miscellaneous Observations Relative to the West India Islands, 79
Wilson, Janet, 223, 224, 225, 226
Wisker, Gina, 2, 217, 223
 "Celebrating Difference and Community: The Vampire in African-American and Caribbean Women's Writing," 92n3
witchcraft, 34, 107, 136n8
Wright, David McKee, 200

Y
Young, Robert J. C., 75–76

Z
Zieger, Susan, 89

CPSIA information can be obtained
at www.ICGtesting.com
Printed in the USA
LVHW07*2157240518
578385LV00004B/4/P